# Dying & Death in
# Law & Medicine

# Dying & Death in Law & Medicine

## A FORENSIC PRIMER FOR HEALTH AND LEGAL PROFESSIONALS

*Arthur S. Berger*

Medical Foreword by
David V. Schapira, M.B., Ch.B., F.R.C.P.(C)

Legal Foreword by
Judge Raphael Steinhardt

PRAEGER

Westport, Connecticut
London

344.73
849d

**Library of Congress Cataloging-in-Publication Data**

Berger, Arthur S.
  Dying and death in law and medicine : a forensic primer for health
and legal professionals / Arthur S. Berger : medical foreword by
David V. Schapira, M.B., Ch.B., F.R.C.P.(C) ; legal foreword
by Judge Raphael Steinhardt.
      p.    cm.
  Includes bibliographical references and index.
  ISBN 0–275–93928–6 (alk. paper)
    1. Terminally ill—Legal status, laws, etc.—United States.
  2. Right to die—Law and legislation—United States.   I. Title.
KF3823.B47   1993
344.73′04197—dc20
[347.3044197]        92–18875

British Library Cataloguing in Publication Data is available.

Library of Congress Catalog Card Number: 92–18875
ISBN: 0–275–93928–6

First published in 1993

Praeger Publishers, 88 Post Road West, Westport, CT 06881
An imprint of Greenwood Publishing Group, Inc.

Printed in the United States of America

∞

The paper used in this book complies with the
Permanent Paper Standard issued by the National
Information Standards Organization (Z39.48–1984).

10 9 8 7 6 5 4 3 2 1

# Contents

# Medical Foreword

The practice of medicine has become more sophisticated in the past three decades. Coinciding with, and as a result of, advanced technology, issues relating to informed consent, competence, the right to die, and specific advance directives have arisen. These issues, and the recently emerging importance of cost-effectiveness in medicine and the economic burden that is put on the patient and the family, are not addressed in medical schools. Arthur Berger's book on *Dying and Death in Law and Medicine* contains essential information that should be read by both medical students and physicians.

This book is essential reading for several reasons. The important topics discussed here are not consistently taught in medical schools, and therefore most practicing physicians are not familiar with or comfortable addressing these issues, which present themselves frequently in clinical practice. As physicians, we can no longer ignore the economic burden that results from the style of medicine we practice. We have to take into account that the majority of health-care spending occurs in the last few months of most patients' lives. We must learn to be comfortable addressing the medical and legal issues regarding the right to die and advance directives. We must also become comfortable allowing the patient to die with dignity and avoid heroic measures that often do not prolong survival or improve quality of life.

We must guide patients without being paternalistic or authoritarian, yet still allow the patient to participate in decision making relating to treatment and their feelings regarding death and dying. We have to be comfortable with issues relating to death and dying in order to communicate clearly and compassionately with patients when discussing their death. We must also be aware that patients will deny and rationalize, and we have to be sensitive to how much information each particular patient wishes to receive.

The medical and legal issues that are addressed in this book cover all the ground I have described and more. Having been interested for many years in issues of informed consent, the right to die, cost-effectiveness in medicine, and patient and medical undergraduate and postgraduate education, I highly recommend that individuals entering or already practicing medicine read this book. It addresses a gamut of issues not normally discussed in one book, representing the issues every physician comes in contact with on a daily basis. If as physicians we can become informed and comfortable with the issues described in this book, we will practice medicine with greater sensitivity and compassion.

David V. Schapira, M.B., Ch.B., F.R.C.P. (C)

Chief, Cancer Prevention Program

H. Lee Moffitt Cancer Center and Research Institute

Professor of Medicine

University of South Florida College of Medicine

# Legal Foreword

My interest was piqued when I was asked to write a foreword to *Dying and Death in Law and Medicine* by Arthur S. Berger, from the standpoint of a jurist.

Mr. Berger has indeed opened the subject of dying and death to full view by laymen as well as the legal profession. True, those practitioners involved in this comparatively new field of endeavor have at their disposal information and guidelines above and beyond the sphere of what is outlined in this book. Nevertheless, it is a major reference source and a valuable contribution to all, and will assist immeasurably in coming to grips with this complex subject of dying and death.

What should be a simple natural act of dying is really not so simple. As a matter of fact, dying is very complex when one considers what is entailed. For one, do we have the right to a natural death, a death not fraught with life-sustaining systems that foster vegetation with no prospect of recovery? Do we owe protection under the law to health-care providers who aid in natural death when all avenues have been closed and peace should be brought to bear? How do we protect the rights of the patient? Additionally, Mr. Berger has addressed miscellaneous groupings of civil law, criminal law, statutes, case law, and all matters relevant to this subject matter.

Dying and death is the one common denominator. We are destined to follow this path with no deviation, for to live is to eventually die. But with guidelines as to how and when we die set within the framework of the legal system, one need not fear that one's expressed final wishes will not be followed. Nor does one have to fear termination of life will occur without proper oversight by the legal and medical professions. True, no system on earth is perfect—perfection is a utopian ideal that seldom reaches fruition—but, with knowledge of all options available, reasonableness can be achieved.

Mr. Berger is to be commended. He has put the spotlight on a subject shrouded in darkness.

Judge Raphael Steinhardt
State of Florida
Eleventh Judicial Circuit
County Court of Dade County

# Preface

Why this book? In the wake of advances in medical technology, the bright glare of publicity on right-to-die court decisions, the enactment of "natural death" and brain-death statutes, the emphasis on living wills, and the development of the organ transplantation program, there has ensued widespread public and professional concern over the legal and ethical issues raging around these subjects. This book meets the need for effective treatment of these subjects; its text and case studies will sensitize health-care professionals to the problems. The book aims to help the medical community understand the issues and increase its ability to deliver more appropriate patient care.

I came to write this book wearing several badges not normally associated with writers of medicolegal books. I serve on the ethics committee of a 750-bed county hospital. I am a lawyer who hopes to keep health-care professionals out of court and not in it. I also am a thanatologist. Thanatology approaches dying and death from a variety of avenues and includes everyone—physicians, nurses, psychologists, psychiatrists, sociologists, clergy, and philosophers—whose training or specialties lead them to examine or deal with these subjects. This book takes a new approach. It looks at dying and death through the eyes of the law; brings together unrelated case and statutory laws applicable to dying patients, the right to die, advance directives, brain death, and organ transplantation; and formulates them into a "law of dying and death."

Every utopia has been conceived without courts and lawyers. Since our society is very much the opposite of a utopia, it is slave to them. So we find that the most popular programs on television have been "Perry Mason" and "L.A. Law" and other "lawyer" shows. Their immense popularity has gone far to stimulate our interest in and even make us more cognizant of the law. But although knowledge of the workings and tools of the legal system are important and can be useful to us, we remain relatively unsophisticated. I, therefore, have written this book for a second purpose: to help health professionals understand the legal system better and to learn the research tools they can use, if they wish, to examine pertinent case law and statutes. In this respect, this book differs from other medicolegal books as well.

This book also offers professional legal counsel subject matter of growing concern to the law. Medical decisions and issues pertaining to dying and death that once were the sole province of doctors, hospitals, patients, and families have become matters for increasing judicial and legislative attention. Since the Karen Ann Quinlan case in 1976, state supreme courts have intervened in such matters and in 1990, with the Nancy Cruzan case, the U.S. Supreme Court intervened. By 1991, more than forty states had enacted legislation dealing with advance directives; in that same year, the first federal statute to focus on these directives and the rights of adults to refuse life-sustaining treatment became effective.

This book should be useful to lawyers as a primer, also, because the "law of dying and death," like patent law, is generally absent from a law school curriculum except possibly as an aspect of constitutional law. My hope is that, since lawyers have received no formal education on this kind of law, those just becoming interested in these problems will find this book a valuable reference, giving them access to a considerable range of subjects and citations to authority beyond their limited areas of specialization.

Although this book is addressed to members of the medical and legal professions in their capacities as professionals, it is also addressed to them as people with private lives and private concerns. For in the drama of dying and death, the roles of physician, nurse, hospital administrator, or lawyer are only temporary. At any moment, a player can be asked to play a different role—the physician can become a patient, a lawyer can become a family member. Since we are all potential patients and family members, what this book has to say is of concern to us all.

# I

## Death: Issues and the Law

# 1

## Death Comes Alive

### THE SHAPING OF HISTORY

What is history? For some, such as Ralph Waldo Emerson, history is humanity and the emphasis is on dominant personalities on whom events centered and by whom they were shaped. As Emerson said: "There is properly no History; only Biography" (1933:181).

Everywhere I look Emerson's view of history is borne out. When I examined world history, I found a Napoleon or Hitler shaping its eras of war and destruction, and when I took a glance at American history, there were Columbus, Ponce de Leon, Balboa, and Henry Hudson shaping its era of discovery; Alexander Hamilton, George Washington, and Thomas Jefferson its revolutionary and constitutional eras; Lincoln, Wilson, and Theodore and Franklin Roosevelt its political and economic eras. The history of literature in English centers on Chaucer, Shakespeare, Milton, Thoreau, Melville, Whitman, and Emerson himself; of philosophy on the speculative thought of Plato, Aristotle, Epicurus, Descartes, Spinoza, Leibniz, Locke, Kant, and Schopenhauer; of art, on Leonardo da Vinci, Michelangelo, Rubens, Rembrandt, Goya, Turner, and Holbein; of science, on Copernicus, Newton, and Einstein. The evidential corroboration for Emerson's belief is so persuasive that it led me to write a history of parapsychology in America centered on its dominant personalities, such as Joseph B. Rhine (Berger, 1988).

But Emerson's theory does not seem to apply to that era of recent history when America changed its attitude toward death. This achievement was not the work of any extraordinary individual or commanding figure but of two inconspicuous women. They would have lived and died in obscurity but for tragic accidents that made them personifications of the miracles of medical technology. These miracles gave physicians the power to sustain life in situations where two decades earlier a patient would have died naturally. The life sustained, however, is in a senseless state and in a form few would consider worth living.

One of these women was twenty-two-year-old Karen Ann Quinlan who passed into a persistent vegetative state in 1976 after ingesting drugs and alcohol. The other was thirty-three-year-old Nancy Cruzan, whose only claim to fame was that she tried to help handicapped children before her auto accident in 1983, which left her in a persistent vegetative state. Their conditions were the same and their cases were identical: The parents of both women tried in vain to get their hospitals and physicians to terminate their child's life support. But there the similarity ends. A court in Karen's case authorized her parents to remove her respirator and allow her to die while the U.S. Supreme Court affirmed a state court's decision to refuse the removal of Nancy's tubal feeding and thus forced her to live.

## THE KEY ISSUE

Until these cases made headlines, death—like AIDS, VD, and other social diseases—was a pornographic subject not discussed in polite Western society. Gorer observed that, whereas sex and copulation have become more and more mentionable, death has always remained unmentionable (Gorer, 1965). Kalish calls this silence the "horse on the dining room table syndrome" (Kalish, 1977:226). It seems that a group of friends were having an amiable dinner party when a horse walked in and sat on the center of the dining room table. But everyone went on talking as if the horse weren't there. Neither the host nor the guests mentioned the horse for fear of embarrassing each other. So, although the horse, like death, is always uppermost in everyone's mind, it is never talked about.

In Eastern religions—Buddhism, for example—one must be aware of death and meditate upon it in order to appreciate the impermanence of life. Avoidance and aversion were, however, Western attitudes—specifically, American attitudes. As Herman Feifel wrote, we see death "as the destroyer of the American vision—the right to life, liberty and the pursuit of happiness. Hence, death and dying invite our hostility and repudiation" (Feifel, 1977:5).

"The idea of death," said Ernest Becker, "the fear of it, haunts the human animal like nothing else; it is a mainspring of human activity" (Becker, 1973:ix). And society obliges us by affording us a large variety of social activities into which we can and do plunge frenetically in order to avoid thinking about death. Hospitals and medical technology have facilitated the avoidance of death in other ways, too, by saving and extending lives and by postponing death for longer than ever before. Avoidance has also been made easier because few of us ever see death outside our television screens and the movies. Real death is concealed from us. Our family members no longer die at home but in health-care facilities. The care of the dying and the burial of the dead are given over to professionals. We have wanted to know nothing about these matters.

The beginning of a change in these negative attitudes was made with the publication of two important books: Herman Feifel's *The Meaning of Death* (1959) and Elisabeth Kübler-Ross's *On Death and Dying* (1969) in which the "death and dying lady" dealt with dying patients and their care. But the cases of *Quinlan* and *Cruzan* created a tidal wave of controversy over the "right to die" and brought public, scholarly, philosophical, medical, and legal concern to a peak. With general recognition by the American legal system of the "right to die" and "death with dignity," euthanasia and an acceptance of death seemed to be condoned by the courts. They brought home to many that, because of medical technology and unwanted medical treatment, life was more to be feared than death. They forced people to reconsider their concepts of death; people now had to distinguish between death as they had always known it and that strange form of death that comes when life is sustained in the physical body but does not exist in the brain.

The *Quinlan* and *Cruzan* cases compelled society to turn its face thoughtfully in the direction of death. They got many of us over the "horse on the dining room table syndrome" and induced an increasing number of us to think and talk about death. In this sense, death has come alive. We all—lay persons, educators, scholars, psychologists, health-care professionals, lawyers, clergy, social workers, funeral directors and more—have come to realize that dying and death are crucial problems we must face. We have come at last to the conviction that, in the final analysis, the problem of death is, as Feifel writes, "the key issue of life" (1977:xiii).

But there is, in fact, no one "key issue"; there are several distinct ones. Because these matters have been played up in the media, filled the pages of medical and legal journals, and occupied philosophers and ethicists in consequence of the *Quinlan* and *Cruzan* cases and others similar to them, death is able to penetrate the armor that American thought had worn to protect itself from the subject. Leaving some of these issues for treatment in Chapter 5, here we can identify the end of life, time of death and postdeath issues that have and continue to produce conflicts among health-care providers, patients, members of a patient's family, lawyers, clergy, and ethicists over what is "right," "wrong," or "legal."

## END OF LIFE ISSUES

The dying process is related to but is distinguishable from death. We cannot experience death, but we can experience the dying process. Must that process be hard and bitter? Should patients be told that they are dying? How do we address deathbed fears? Should medical technology prolong lives even though patients have descended into the depths of helplessness and uselessness or have no cognitive functions? If competent patients do not want their lives prolonged, can medical treatment without which death will result be withdrawn or withheld upon request? Is artifical feeding without which a person will starve medical treatment that can be refused? What ethical issues are raised by a refusal of life-sustaining treatment? What are the concerns of health-care providers? Is a court the right forum for making decisions whether or not to terminate such treatment? How can litigation be avoided? If such medical treatment can be stopped, what are the legal bases for doing so? If such bases exist, is the legal entitlement to stop treatment an unfettered right? Does stoppage violate the sanctity of life and amount to murder? Or does it make one who withdraws treatment rejected by a patient and without which the patient will surely die guilty of aiding a suicide? What is the prospect of civil or criminal liability for physicians who withhold or withdraw life-sustaining treatment? If the patient is incompetent, who decides to stop life-sustaining treatment? If a third party can decide, what are the guidelines and criteria for deciding? To prevent suffering should a dying person be put to death by a doctor or family? Who has the right to decide? What are living wills and are they a satisfactory solution?

## TIME-OF-DEATH ISSUES

Medical technology and the subject of death raise the question of when death occurs. What is the importance of a determination of death? What are the medical and legal definitions of death? What is "brain death"? What are the merits—and demerits—of the brain-death criterion?

## POSTDEATH ISSUES

What developments have taken place in the program for transplantation of cadaveric organs? What are the functions of the United Network for Organ Sharing? What laws have been enacted in response to the organ transplantation program? What are the ethical problems with the program and what is their importance?

## DEATH AND THE LAW

In 1905, a dead body was the subject of an appeal heard by the Georgia Supreme Court. Justice Joseph Lumpkin, writing the opinion of the court, said:

Death is unique. It is unlike aught else in its certainty and its incidents. A corpse in some respects is the strangest thing on earth. A man who but yesterday breathed and thought and walked among us has passed away. Something has gone. The body is left still and cold, and is all that is visible to the mortal eye of the man we knew. Around it cling love and memory. Beyond it may reach hope. It must be laid away. And the law—that rule of action which touches all human things— must touch also this thing of death. [1]

This eloquent language, quoted with favor by many courts since, acknowledges the mystery of death but also suggests that the "horse on the dining room table syndrome" has never plagued the law. Although right-to-die cases and medical technology have revived death for the rest of us recently, the topic has always been a source of interest and concern for the law. This concern is reflected in hundreds of legislative enactments and judicial decisions. For the benefit of legal counsel, thanatologists, and others who may wish to pursue this interesting subject, Appendix A, Death-Related Statutes and Common Law Doctrines, presents a summary of some of the many subjects from "Abatement" to "Wrongful Death," in which dying or death are implicated directly or indirectly.

## LAW OF DYING AND DEATH

Although all the common-law doctrines and statutes presented in Appendix A deal with dying and death, for purposes of this medicolegal book they are not part of what I call the "law of dying and death" because they do not relate to the difficult end of life, time of death, and postdeath issues.

The "law of dying and death" addresses these issues, and so can be distinguished from a loose collection of dying and death laws that do not. "The law of dying and death," of course, is not any special statutory enactment or some recognized classification of the law. In a sense, it is only a legal pigeonhole for certain legislation and judicial decisions. In it fit the following fifteen forms of legislation that have a direct bearing on end of life, time of death, or postdeath issues. Parenthetical references to chapters at the end of a paragraph indicate where further mention or discussion of the subject can be found.

1. *Assisting Suicide.* Virtually every jurisdiction has a statute that condemns either as murder or as manslaughter in the first or second degree actually aiding or abetting another person to take his or her own life. Under the common law, it was required that the person committing suicide be convicted prior to charging the abettor. Since the suicide was deceased and could not be convicted, neither could the abettor be.[2] Under modern statutes, however, abettors may be convicted of the crime of aiding and abetting suicide. The question would arise in any jurisdiction where a patient's rejection of life-sustaining treatment is considered suicidal and health professionals participate in the rejection (Chapters 4 and 5).

2. *Homicide.* The state protects human life and prohibits the taking of human life; homicide is the unlawful killing of a "person" or "human being." Such homicide is murder, usually punishable by death or life imprisonment, if there is malice aforethought; if there is not, it is manslaughter, either voluntary or involuntary. Since a "person" or "human being" does not exist under the law prior to birth, the abortion of a seven-month fetus was held not to be murder, even without the mother's consent.[3] Under the common law and penal statutes, euthanasia (mercy killing) is a crime, whether treated as murder or as aiding and abetting a suicide. It becomes an issue because medical technology has provided physicians with the ability to sustain and extend life. Euthanasia may surface as an issue in a medical context when a competent patient who is suffering begs a physician for relief from pain, and the physician obliges by assisting the patient to terminate his or her life; or others acting for incompetent patients make the same request of physicians because they believe that to allow the patient's life to continue would be a wrong more serious than to allow the hopelessly ill patient to die naturally. In such cases if a physician terminates the life of a patient who is hopelessly ill and suffering, as by affirmatively acting to poison that person by injecting large doses of morphine, injecting intravenously large doses of air, or withholding or withdrawing life support, and even does so out of great love and kindness, the physician may be charged with murder in the first degree. Conservative legal advice

brings this possibility to the attention of physicians considering helping patients to end their lives humanely, swiftly, and painlessly and giving "aid-in-dying" (Chapter 5).

3. *Inheritance*. Laws have been enacted uniformly to   prescribe rules for the inheritance of property of an owner who dies without disposing of property by will. Laws of descent govern the passage of real property to heirs, and laws of distribution govern personal property that is distributed by order of a probate court among individuals enumerated by statute to take the property. There are also inheritance tax laws that are not the same as estate tax laws. Inheritance taxes are levied on the person to whom the state has given the privilege of receiving property from a person who has died (Chapter 3).

4. *Wills*. A will is an instrument by which a person disposes of property. But there is no inherent right to do so and it is not an inherited or property right. It is a privilege that is created and controlled by legislatures. The privilege is exercised and implemented only at death when the disposition of property becomes effective provided the will has been probated—that is, declared valid by a court. It is valid if the person making the will has testamentary capacity and if the will has met several standards laid down by the state in connection with its execution. Since the power of the state over property passing by will is plenary, there must be compliance with all the statutory requirements. The statutes governing wills are those of the state in which real property disposed of by a will is located and, in the case of personal property, of the state where the person making the will is domiciled (Chapter 3).

5. *Living Wills*. So-called death-with-dignity statutes began to be enacted in 1976. They are also called living-will, natural-death, and right-to-die statutes. These statutes are in effect in forty-five states and in the District of Columbia. In 1990 Congress enacted a Patient Self-Determination Act as part of the Omnibus Budget Reconciliation Act (Chapters 5 and 8).

6. *Durable Power of Attorney*. There are durable power of attorney statutes in every state and the District of Columbia (Chapter 8).

7. *Organ Donation*. The National Conference of Commissioners on Uniform State Laws also drafted a Uniform Anatomical Gift Act in 1968. Unlike the Uniform Rights of the Terminally Ill Act, this

one has influenced the passage of identical statutes in all states. Today all fifty states and the District of Columbia have enacted the Uniform Anatomical Gift Act. Increasing public interest and concern with organ donation and transplantation led Congress to enact the National Organ Transplant Act of 1984 (Chapter 10).

8. *Corneas.* Several types of legislation, described in this and the next four paragraphs, have been enacted further to implement organ and tissue donation. One type of statute provides that a medical examiner investigating a death may remove the corneas of the corpse and give them to an eye bank. The medical examiner and eye bank are protected from liability (Chapter 10).

9. *Eye Banks.* Statutes of many states have authorized private hospitals to set up eye banks (Chapter 10).

10. *Enucleation.* By statutory authority funeral directors may enucleate eyes (Chapter 10).

11. *Routine Inquiry or Required Request.* Sixteen states have passed statutes that require hospitals to offer the family of a potential donor the option to donate or not to donate the organs of the body of a patient. Twenty-two states have statutes that make it obligatory for a hospital administrator or agent, when a person has died or is near death, to request of a person's family or guardian consent to a donation of all or part of the person's body (Chapter 10).

12. *Motor Vehicle Department Programs.* Forty-nine states authorize their motor vehicle departments to develop programs to encourage people to donate organs as part of the process of issuing and renewing drivers' licenses. In Florida, for example, a pamphlet entitled "A Gift of Life" is available at all drivers license bureaus. They contain a registration form that, when completed, authorizes the words "Organ Donor" to be inserted on the license (Chapter 10).

13. *Priority of Death.* To cover situations in which two people have died in a common accident or disaster, and the descent of property depends on the priority of death, in all states simultaneous death acts have been passed. They provide that where, in a common disaster, the evidence is not sufficient to show that the individuals died otherwise than simultaneously, it is considered that they died at the same time so that the property of each is disposed of as if each had survived the other. But if there is

evidence that one person survived the other, even by one second, the presumption that death was simultaneous does not apply (Chapter 9).

14. *Brain Death.* In 1980, the National Conference of Commissioners on Uniform State Laws drafted a Uniform Determination of Death Act based on brain death. This Act has been adopted by some twenty-eight states (Chapter 9).

15. *Dead Bodies.* The interests of the next of kin in a corpse will be protected by the courts. If a body is not claimed, legislation governs its disposition (Chapter 11).

The "law of dying and death" is also a legal pigeonhole for judicial decisions in cases in which end of life, time of death, or postdeath issues may be raised. Into it fit several established classifications of law applied by the courts but which are not necessarily concerned with medical matters, such as constitutional law and the laws governing inheritance, wills, contracts, and guardianship.

But in another important sense, the "law of dying and death" is more than a pigeonhole. It recognizes and deals with civil rights and wrongs in the medical field not recognized by the older classifications of law. These new rights and wrongs have been created by advances in medical technology that far outdistance the established classifications and what they cover. The new areas include the right to refuse life-sustaining medical treatment, surrogate decision making, and advance directives. Thus, the "law of dying and death" casts a net for issues not caught by other laws.

The "law of dying and death" affects the rights and status of three different classes of individuals. One category is composed of people who are competent, another of those who are not, the third with people who are dead. The first two categories are involved in different medical contexts and generally in what are known as right-to-die cases. The "law of dying and death" is of overriding importance because every year more than 1.25 million people die in hospitals, and of these 70 percent are right-to-die cases (Lipton, 1986).

## AIMS OF, NEED FOR, AND METHOD OF THE BOOK

Whatever its other ailments, the law never has been troubled by the "horse on the dining room table syndrome." Dying and death have been continuing sources of concern and interest. Its importance in life-death matters for health-care professionals and their patients cannot be over-emphasized. Courts and legislatures increasingly have become the ultimate life-death mediators and decision makers in controversies between health professions and patients and their families. Yet, with a thimbleful of exceptions (Myers, 1981; Bernard, 1979; McHugh, 1976), the writers of legal books and medicolegal books have not made the connection between law and dying and death the subject of any thorough study, nor have they examined dying and death from the vantage point of U.S. case and statutory law.

This curious omission can be explained by recalling the words of Samuel Johnson: "The whole of life is but keeping away the thoughts of death"; and although the "horse on the dining room table syndrome" has more or less faded with the advent of right-to-die cases such as *Quinlan* and *Cruzan*, it still affects a large segment of society.

It was William James who expressed the futility of any attempt to avoid thoughts of death: "Let sanguine healthy-mindedness do its best with its strong power of living in the moment and ignoring and forgetting, still the evil background is there to be thought of, and the skull will grin at the banquet" (1958:121). The aim of this book is to grin back at the grinning skull and to make the first effort to present to the medical community a comprehensive and up-to-date exposition of the legal aspects of dying and death.

Thanatology, from Thanatos, Greek god of death, is the study of dying and death. It is a response to a phenomenon that has taken place in the last few years, largely because of medical advances and the *Quinlan* and *Cruzan* cases: a burgeoning interest in dying and death on the part of behavioral and medical scientists and academics of religion, philosophy, and humanistic disciplines. This phenomenon created two needs. The first was to globalize the study of dying and death and to examine the multi-disciplinary, cross-cultural, and cross-legal views on these subjects. Another book co-edited by the author (Berger and Berger, 1990) presented these different perspectives, aimed at making interdisciplinary dialogue possible and at improving understanding and communication between the health-care profession and its patients. The second need was for a medicolegal book that would cover the important connections between American law and dying and death. This book presents the perspectives of American case and statutory law on dying and death.

The book is also written with the conviction that death is the meeting place for several areas of human activity including law, medicine, and thanatology, and that the perplexing questions created by medical technology compel us to reflect on our concepts and deepest feelings about death. One of the book's aims is to show how death is tied directly or indirectly to the topics covered here.

But addressing this book to the health-care profession is more than another academic step in the educational process about dying and death; a further need has been created by the fact that the law applicable to dying and death has been clouded by misunderstanding and misconceptions and needs to be understood better by that profession. There is, for example, the significant finding that two-thirds of the physicians and nurses interviewed about their knowledge and ideas concerning brain death and organ transplantation were unable to identify the legal and medical criteria for determining a patient dead (Youngner, et al., 1989). A further illustration of the lack of understanding and certainty about the law prevalent among people in the health professions is the case that took place in Rush Presbyterian-St. Luke's Hospital in Illinois where Rudy Linares's son, an irreversibly comatose sixteen-month-old infant, was a patient. Physicians, confused about whether the law permitted life-sustaining treatment to be withdrawn from a patient who was not brain dead, rejected Linares's plea to disconnect a respirator from his son and to let the child die. As a result, the desperate father returned to the hospital on April 26, 1989, with a .357 magnum. With tears in his eyes, he held the hospital staff at gunpoint while he unplugged the child's respirator and held his son in his arms until the child died (*New York Times*, 1989).

Health-care professionals must become more knowledgeable about the law and legal issues. As one health-law expert observed: "At least a passing knowledge of the law and medical ethics is important in many specialty areas, and perhaps in no area is this more true than the care of dying patients. The knowledge of many physicians in this regard leaves much to be desired" (Meisel, 1991:1497). We hope in this primer to increase the effectiveness of physicians, nurses, and other health-related professions by providing the basic law on specific subjects in the area of dying and death—the "law of dying and death" that is called into play: when a patient is dying; by withdrawing or withholding life-sustaining treatment; by artificial feeding; by surrogate decision making; by advance directives; by the determination of death; and by organ donation and transplantation.

The order of the words *dying* and *death* is noteworthy. Other books, courses, seminars, and conferences use the expression "death and dying." And when we talk about issues raised by terminal illness or caring for seriously ill patients, we usually refer to death and dying issues. But, of course, dying always comes before death. The logical order, therefore, is followed in the title as well as in the content of this book. The Contents shows topics first coming under the rubric of dying—dying patients, right to die, advance directives by terminally ill patients—and then under that of death-related topics—defining death and anatomical gifts.

The method of presentation adopted here is again to follow the logical order and to divide the law of dying and death into five parts. Parts II to VI each represent a significant subject or factual situation with which health-care providers are very likely to be concerned. The "law of dying and death" called into play by each subject is discussed, sometimes with case studies to sensitize health professionals to ethical or legal problems. These discussions address the end of life, time of death, and postdeath issues mentioned above.

The "law of dying and death" is part of the substantive law, that great body of rules governing the rights and obligations of individuals. Virtually this entire body is intimately tied into adjective law—the rules of procedure dealing with courts and the legal remedies and steps taken to enforce rights and duties and administer justice. Both substantive and adjective rules, in turn, are bound up with knowing where and how to locate and use them.

So the final aim of the last part of the book (Part VII), and also a further departure from books for laypeople on legal matters, is to help health professionals understand the law and the judicial system, to make them familiar with the research tools available, and to supply practical guidance on where and how they can find the statutes and judicial decisions bearing on the law of dying and death. Appendix B contains material relating to this system and to legal research. Part VII is not meant to turn physicians and nurses into lawyers or to eliminate consultation with an attorney to seek legal advice when needed. Rather, its purpose is to help providers become familiar with the structure of the legal system and learn how to find legal materials relevant to dying and death so that, first, they can know whether a situation creates a legal problem that makes consultation with a lawyer necessary and, second, they can if they wish research a personal or professional problem or a question about legal rights and issues that has health care or social significance. Citations to statutes and cases are liberally sprinkled throughout the text. Because statutes and case law are essential parts of the American system of law, it seems reasonable to encourage and guide people to find and examine them, and to have at least a nodding acquaintance with the system.

Apropos of law and lawyers, this book is not meant to provide legal advice. It is meant only to furnish general information concerning the "law of dying and death." For specific factual situations and the legal issues they produce, readers should consult attorneys in the states where they reside or pursue their professions or, alternatively, local statutes and case law should be examined. Readers should also consult attorneys in their states when preparing involved wills, living wills, or durable powers of attorney, or else look into the statutes or case law in their states. While this book is not intended to convert lay readers into lawyers, the chapter on legal research will help all readers find these important legal sources to clarify or answer questions about legal issues, wills, or health-care forms.

## LEGAL CITATIONS

1. Louisville & N.R. Co. v. Wilson, 123 Ga. 62, 51 S.E. 24, 25 (Ga. Sup. Ct. 1905).
2. Commonwealth v. Hicks, 118 Ky. 637, 82 S.W. 265 (1904).
3. Hollis v. Commonwealth, 652 S.W.2d 61 (Ky. Sup. Ct. 1983).

## REFERENCES

Becker, E. 1973. *The Denial of Death*. New York: Free Press.

Berger, A. S. 1988. *Lives and Letters in American Parapsychology: A Biographical History, 1850–1987*. Jefferson, NC and London: McFarland & Co.

Berger, A. S. and Berger, J., eds. 1990. *To Die or Not to Die? Cross Disciplinary, Cultural and Legal Perspectives on the Right to Choose Death*. New York: Praeger.

Bernard, H. Y. 1979. *The Law of Death and Disposal of the Dead*. Dobbs Ferry, NY: Oceana Publications. This small book (97 pages) is rather dated and does not take up the significant developments of the last thirteen years. While it may still be of some use for lawyers, it is not addressed to the health-care professional and is sparsely comprehensive on topics of interest to that profession.

Emerson, R. W. 1933. "Self-Reliance." In T. McDowell, ed., *The Romantic Triumph: American Literature from 1830–1860*. New York: Macmillan.

Feifel, H. 1977. *New Meanings of Death*. New York: McGraw-Hill.

———. 1959. *The Meaning of Death*. New York: McGraw-Hill.

Gorer, G. 1965. *Death, Grief and Mourning*. New York: Doubleday.

James, W. 1958. *The Varieties of Religious Experience*. New York: New American Library (first published London: Longmans, Green, 1902).

Kalish, R. 1977. "Dying and Preparing for Death: A View of Families." In H. Feifel, ed., *New Meanings of Death*. New York: McGraw-Hill, 215–32.

Kübler-Ross, E. 1969. *On Death and Dying*. New York: Macmillan.

Lipton, H. L. 1986. "Do Not Resuscitate Decisions in a Community Hospital: Incidence, Implications and Outcome." *Journal of the American Medical Association* 265:1164.

McHugh, J. T. 1976. *Death, Dying and the Law*. Huntington, IN: Our Sunday Visitor Bishops' Committee for Pro-Life Activities, N.C.C.B. This small book of essays (88 pages) by three theologians and one physician, is obsolete. It is valuable only for those who wish to examine its subject matter in terms of the moral and ethical principles formulated by Catholic theology. Although the book analyzes the laws applicable to organ transplantation, the definition of death and living will statutes, the analyses are not done by lawyers and are useful only for those making a special study of these laws from the perspective of Catholic moral theology.

Meisel, A. 1991. "Legal Myths About Terminating Life Support." *Archives of Internal Medicine* 151:1497–1502.

Myers, D. W. 1981. *Medico-Legal Implications of Death and Dying: A Detailed Discussion of the Medical and Legal Implications Involved in Death and/or Care of the Dying and Terminal Patient*. Rochester, NY: Lawyers Co-Operative Pub. Co. This book deals comprehensively with the legal and medical issues relating to death and the dying patient.

*New York Times*. 1989. "Questions of Law Live On After Father Helps Son Die." May 7:26.

Youngner, S. J., Landefeld, S., Coulton, C. J., Juknialis, B. W., Leary, M. 1989. " 'Brain Death' and Organ Retrieval: A Cross-Sectional Survey of Knowledge and Concepts Among Health Professionals." *Journal of the American Medical Association* 261:2205–10.

# II

## The Dying Patient

# 2

## The Dying Patient:
## Nothing But the Truth

### THE SAM JONES CASE

Sam Jones, an unmarried fifty-seven-year-old schoolteacher, had put off physical checkups but was finally forced to see a physician when he found it painful to urinate and ejaculate. A rectal examination detected a hard area on the prostate gland. A blood test for prostate specific antigen proved to be elevated. A prostate biopsy indicated that Jones had a malignant cancer. Further tests indicated that the cancer had spread to his lymph nodes and other parts of his body and was diagnosed as a Stage D cancer, the most advanced stage of the disease. Only 21 percent of men with Stage D cancer survive for five years.

Dr. Brand, Jones's attending physician, believed that revealing this dismal prognosis to his patient would be cruel, would only depress him, deprive him of hope, and make him unwilling to submit either to surgery, including removal of the testes, or to treatment with radiation or hormone therapy. In addition, Dr. Brand was not comfortable with death and with giving bad news. The physician decided not tell Jones the truth about his condition and instructed Nurse Brown not to tell him either, even if he asked.

There are three issues here:

1. Given the above circumstances, if Jones asked whether he had cancer and was dying, and the physician answered that Jones had nothing to worry about and everything was fine, was Dr. Brand right or wrong in withholding the poor prognosis from his patient?

2. Given the same circumstances, if Jones did not ask Dr. Brand any questions and the doctor gave him no information, did the doctor act properly?

3. Given the same circumstances, if Jones asked Nurse Brown for the truth about his condition after the doctor ordered her not to tell, what should the nurse do?

In the Sam Jones case the cancer was detected too late. For Sam Jones, as for most men, removing his pants for an examination was much more difficult than removing his shirt. Prostate cancer causes more than 28,000 deaths each year and is the third cause of death among men of Sam Jones's age and up to age seventy-four. After age seventy-five it is the second cause of death.

The Sam Jones case presents us with a situation in which fundamental concepts of American jurisprudence regarding informed consent, contract, trust, and privilege are interlocked. Together they create a law of dying and death applicable to the issue of whether people should be given bad news by their doctors. The physician has the constant problem of telling people unpleasant facts about a diagnosis and even more disturbing facts if a prognosis is poor.

## PROS AND CONS

Robert M. Veatch, Director of Death and Dying at the Hastings Center in New York, illustrates the confusion and controversy surrounding the question with the example of a patient who, after surgery, was found to be suffering from Stage 4 cancer of the cervix. A dispute erupted among the hospital staff whether to reveal the bleak prognosis to her. The attending physician was determined not to tell her of the condition because he feared that doing so would create a poor medical outcome. The hospital chaplain insisted that she be told so that, as a Catholic, the patient could prepare herself spiritually. The psychiatrist, on the other hand, urged that the information be withheld because of the fear and depression it would create. The hospital resident could not make up his mind but in the end agreed with the attending physician and psychiatrist (Veatch, 1982).

The final decision to keep "the truth, the whole truth, and nothing but the truth" from the patient is one that most physicians would have made. Veatch reports that an "overwhelming proportion"—nearly 88 percent—are opposed to telling their patients the truth (Veatch, 1982:77). For example, a leading authority on working with terminally ill patients, Elisabeth Kübler-Ross, says "Patients should not be told that their illness is terminal or that they are dying. The patient should be informed that he is seriously ill but that everything will be done to keep him comfortable and to help him" (Kübler-Ross, 1974:136). Dr. Brand of the Sam Jones case evidently belongs to this majority of doctors.

Veatch's example gives us a partial look at the problem. There are other ethical difficulties when it comes to telling patients the truth about their diseases or conditions. Is withholding the truth wrong or right? What are the pros and cons? What bearing have the physician-patient relationship, the physician's argument, and the legal perspective on the problem?

The arguments in favor of telling a patient the truth are:

1. There is a moral obligation to tell the truth and it is wrong to withhold it.

2. There is no difference between lying, telling half-truths, and withholding bad news. In all cases a false impression or belief is created in the minds of patients that they have no fatal disease and will recover.

3. It is wrong to withhold a poor prognosis from patients because it deprives them of the opportunity in their last days to complete unfinished business, make peace with the family, make final arrangements for disposing of property, or—for those interested in experimental thanatology—arrange a posthumous experiment if they believe it is possible to give a sign to loved ones that they have survived death.

4. In Veatch's example, the chaplain was concerned with the wrong being done to a Catholic patient who was being prevented from making religious preparations for death. Since ancient times, and in Tibet and elsewhere, a technique or art of dying has been taught. It is a way to face death calmly and bravely, even joyously, and to try to make death a means of shaping future lives. Buddhists, for example, believe that the next incarnation is determined by the last thought at the moment of death. For patients who subscribe to such beliefs, it is thus wrong to withhold the truth that they are dying because it prevents them from preparing for death and at the same time for their future lives.

The reasons and arguments against informing the patient are:

1. To argue in favor of telling the truth overlooks how difficult it is to define truth, especially in medicine. A condition today that

seems incurable or has a bad prognosis may next month or next year be curable. There may even be a miracle. So to tell patients that there is no hope for their recovery may be a far greater wrong than being evasive or telling untruths.

2. Making a prognosis about the course of a disease or the length of time someone is going to live is like betting on a horserace. Doctors can judge probabilities, but they cannot be sure about a prognosis.

3. There are many definitions of truth. It depends on one's philosophy what truth is. Even if we accept the definition of truth as a statement that conforms to the facts and reality, in medicine more important than truth is being kind to a patient and making the patient as comfortable as possible.

## PHYSICIAN-PATIENT RELATIONSHIP

The physician-patient relationship and the physician's duty arising out of it need to be considered. Once a doctor has undertaken to render services to a patient and the physician-patient relationship has been created, a duty arises on the part of the physician to take the best possible care of the patient and to use due skill in making diagnoses and rendering treatment. And the duty does not end unless there is no longer a need for medical attention, the patient discharges the physician, or the physician gives reasonable notice of an intention to stop treating the patient so that the patient can obtain another doctor.[1] Where a physician fails to render service after agreeing to give treatment and this failure causes an injury, the physician may be liable on the theory of breach of contract to supply care and skill.[2]

A physician-patient relationship, then, is contractual; it is, however, also fiduciary. Patients rely on physicians for information concerning their health and lives. A further duty, therefore, is to impart to the patient all facts known to the physician that, however unfavorable, are relevant to the patient's condition. Said one court: "Where an adverse condition is known to the doctor or is readily available to him through efficient diagnosis, he has a duty to disclose and his failure to do so amounts to a fraudulent withholding of the facts."[3]

If the physician-patient relationship is to be a truly collaborative one in which medical decisions will be made, each party must give information to the other regarding the patient's condition or treatment that should not in any way mislead the other, and all material facts ought to be fully stated.

The relationship is built on trust and confidence. It is bound to be weakened if a patient realizes that a physician has been deceitful.

In question number 1 in the Jones case, Jones wanted the truth about his condition. He represents the great majority of terminally ill patients who want the truth, good or bad. A study made of 315 cancer patients showed that "Over ninety percent of [them] wish to learn all information regarding their disease, irrespective of whether the information was pleasant or unpleasant" (Schapira, 1990). This conclusion is in line with other studies and presents an interesting contrast to the almost 90 percent of physicians who will not tell patients their prognoses.

If we go by their relationship, Dr. Brand was wrong to respond to Sam Jones as he did. The doctor deliberately created a misleading impression in his patient's mind and was derelict in his duty. Other physicians may be more subtle and indirect in their responses and still be guilty of dereliction of duty and of failure to divulge the material facts to their patients. To the terminally ill patient who asks, as did Jones, "Am I going to die?" a physician may answer, "We're all going to die"—an evasion that does not communicate the truth. Veatch mentions another device some physicians may use: "truthful jargon" (Veatch, 1982:83). The woman with Stage 4 cancer might have been told that she had "leiomyo-sarcoma with disseminated metastatic tissue growth." This is truthful jargon, but, as far as the patient is concerned, it communicates nothing.

With question number 2 in the Jones case, a different factual situation arises. Even though Jones requested no information, his silence does not vindicate Dr. Brand. The parties here are not dealing at arm's length. *Caveat emptor* (let the buyer beware) does not apply here; Jones is not a consumer who must ask and investigate at his own risk. Patients, especially those with no education in medicine, may be unsophisticated, frightened, confused, or embarrassed and cannot be expected to ask pertinent questions. It is Dr. Brand's duty to volunteer the requisite information.

Studies of terminally ill patients show that those who do not wish to know the truth about their illnesses are rare. But if patients clearly do not want information about their illnesses, it should not be given to them. For Dr. Brand and other doctors who see death as abhorrent, it may be tempting to interpret a patient's actions or words as a justification for not passing on bad news about death and dying. Dr. Kübler-Ross bears this out when she writes that doctors who see death as horrible and a taboo topic "when asked will tell us that their patients do not want to know the truth, that they never ask for it, and that they believe that all is well" (Kübler-Ross, 1960:32).

Physicians sometimes justify not telling the truth on the ground that it is difficult and complex to make a medical diagnosis, that "we can't be sure." Veatch calls the excuse "self-deception" and "a rationalization for failure to disclose what [the physician] does know—that the prognosis is bleak and the likelihood of long-term survival small" (Veatch, 1982:83).

Physicians also will say that the patient's family has asked them to keep a poor diagnosis from the patient for the patient's good. The family, however, can only have found out about the diagnosis from the physician who, by disclosing it, has violated the relationship of trust with the patient, one of the primary tenets of medicine and law set down by judicial decisions and statutes. These tenets require a physician not to disclose any information obtained while attending a patient unless the privilege has been waived by the patient. A justification based on a breach of confidentiality is questionable.

So far, the conclusion is irresistible that Dr. Brand acted improperly in both scenarios presented by questions 1 and 2 unless this physician can legitimate his action in some other way.

## THERAPEUTIC PRIVILEGE

In defense of his refusal to tell Sam Jones the truth about his dismal prognosis, Dr. Brand maintains that, in his judgment, the truth would cause Jones severe psychological and emotional damage, would deprive him of the hope needed to fight for life, and would interfere with the patient's ability to decide rationally about needed medical treatment. He bases his position on that most famous of medical writings: the Hippocratic Oath. Among its other pledges, such as keeping secret all communications with patients, the physician promises to cause no wrong or hurt to patients. This last pledge—*primum non nocere*—Dr. Brand and other physicians consider superior to any obligation to tell the truth. Said one physician, "Ours is a profession which traditionally has been guided by a precept that transcends the virtue of uttering truth for truth's sake; that is, so far as possible, do not harm" (Meyer, 1968:176).

Almost fifty years ago, the question of a physician's telling or not telling the truth to patients who have a serious or terminal illness was taken up by a pair of physicians. One maintained that "in discussing his patients, the doctor realizes that there are some circumstances when he cannot, for the patient's own good, tell him the 'whole truth' " (Lund, 1946:346). The other wrote that he "strongly believes that the physician should be recognized to have a therapeutic privilege to withold [*sic*] part or all of the facts regarding a dread illness when he has reason to believe that communicating them freely to the patient will involve risks of causing his death or serious impairment of his health without any countervailing gain" (Smith, 1946:351).

These physicians were demonstrating that a consensus of the medical community believes it is all right to play god if a physician thinks it is best for a patient. Medical opinion would be behind Dr. Brand's nondisclosure of facts because he thought imparting them to Sam Jones involved risks.

The legal perspective remains to be considered. When the articles by the two physicians appeared in 1946, the concept of "therapeutic privilege" was unknown to the courts, although a hint of it seems to have been given in an 1853 case in Massachusetts.[4] But since 1946, it has been recognized again and again.[5] It seems generally recognized now that the privilege is an exception to the rule of disclosure and allows doctors to withhold information if they reasonably foresee that disclosure will cause psychological or emotional damage or will unduly complicate a medical regimen. Another exception to the rule is an emergency situation in which a patient is unconscious or unable to consent and where harm will result if treatment is not given. In such a situation, however, a relative should be consulted and consent obtained.

But the privilege is not absolute. In *Canterbury* v. *Spence*, where a physician, before performing a laminectomy (an operation on the spine) failed to tell his patient, a nineteen-year-old clerk, that there was risk of paralysis on the ground that the knowledge might have produced adverse psychological reactions, the court said, "the physician's privilege to withhold information for therapeutic reasons must be carefully circumscribed, however, for otherwise it might devour the disclosure rule itself."[6]

Even circumscribed, the privilege to withhold information from competent patients where there is no emergency seems to fly in the face of what has been called "the free citizen's first and greatest right which underlies all others—the right to the inviolability of his person."[7] The doctrine of informed consent and, in turn, the right to refuse life-sustaining treatment, rest on this right. Before people can decide whether to allow or refuse life support that would violate their bodies, physicians must provide them with enough factual information to make a rational decision. Disclosure by a physician, whether it brings bad news or will create damage or impede treatment in the physician's judgment, seems mandated by the informed consent doctrine and the right to die naturally. Truth may injure in some cases. Within my family circle two relatives who were told they had cancer lost all hope and resigned themselves to death. But a false representation injures all patients by violating their right to a free choice in medical matters without being misled. It is a source of wonder that courts have lent their authority to therapeutic privilege and have recognized nondisclosures that cheat patients of this right. Nevertheless, we must recognize therapeutic privilege as entrenched in the "law of dying and death."

Generally the failure to disclose comes up in the courts in three kinds of medical malpractice cases. One involves the statute of limitations on negligence, the question being whether the patient's claim is made too late because the statute has already run. A second type is the unauthorized treatment case: Treatment is given without a patient's consent because the concealment of medical facts rendered an apparent consent invalid. In a third type of case a physician fails to disclose a malignant condition, thus preventing a patient from avoiding or refusing treatment. In no case, however, will liability for damages be imposed on a physician for a fraudulent withholding of facts alone. A patient must show a causal connection between the failure to reveal and the injury suffered by the patient. The patient first must show nondisclosure and causally related damage. The burden then falls on the physician to show that adequate and justifiable grounds existed for nondisclosure. It becomes an issue of fact.

On the facts given in the Sam Jones case, Jones might be able to show nondisclosure but his injury is difficult to see. Even if he had evidence of suffering an injury, Dr. Brand probably would be able to adduce adequate grounds for his professional judgment and therapeutic privilege. He would probably also be able to provide expert testimony that what he did was in conformity with prevailing and good medical practice and that other competent physicians would have withheld facts in similar conditions. The law as well as most professional opinion would likely hold Dr. Brand's action legitimate and resolve both questions in the Jones case in his favor.

## PHYSICIANS' ORDERS AND THE NURSES' DILEMMA

In many states an RN has the responsibility of counting sponges and instruments before and after surgery. Suppose, for whatever reason, a physician orders a nurse not to do so. If the nurse follows the order and makes no count, the nurse may be exposed to malpractice liability even if the physician is willing to take full responsibility. The nurse has a duty to protect the patient, and failure to do so may make the nurse subject to liability. Nurses are required to question the physician and carry out their responsibility to count sponges and instruments. Any not accounted for should be reported to the doctor. If no corrective action is taken, the nurse's obligation is to report the matter to hospital authorities—a nursing supervisor, for instance.

The Jones case also deals with the responsibility of nurses when a physician gives an order that they believe may conflict with nursing standards of care. In this case a physician has ordered a nurse not to impart unfavorable information to a patient. Peggy Anderson's *Nurse* is an account of the experiences of a twenty-seven-year-old nurse on the medical-surgical floor of a large hospital. An oncologist there refused to tell patients their diagnoses so that when the nurse began taking care of his patients she was forced to lie to those who asked questions (1978:111). Following the oncologist's order and lying to patients may have exposed this nurse to malpractice liability because a nurse's duty to protect the patient is independent of a physician's duty.

As a general rule, therefore, although nurses are acting under a physician's direction, they should give truthful information to inquiring patients. In the Sam Jones case, however, there is a complicating factor because therapeutic privilege may have authorized Dr. Brand to withhold information from Jones. To question number three in this case, the answer probably should be that Nurse Brown should not reveal Jones's prognosis to him unless she has observed facts that throw doubt on the physician's claim that telling Jones the truth would cause psychological and emotional damage. The values and fears of a patient are not medical facts peculiarly within a doctor's domain. Indeed, nurses probably know patients better than physicians and are in a better position to determine whether disclosure would create damage. Their observations and testimony would be pertinent to any question of whether a physician was privileged to withhold information.

Nurse Brown and all nurses would be well advised to make entries in the patient's chart of what they have observed, what occurred, and of reports made to hospital authorities and of any actions taken. These entries are evidence of what was done and not done and will help patients establish any claim they may have in a nondisclosure case. The entries will also help nurses in any claim against them for malpractice by showing that they did all they could to discharge their duties.

It would be wrong not to look at the practical side of any situation in which nurses are faced with the dilemma of whether to follow orders or to defy them if they seem inconsistent with nursing practice. Any nurse who defies a physician must realize that being a patient's advocate and opposing the physician in favor of the patient may be costly. Nurses might first air the problem with the physician and explain their feelings and position, but the physician might then ask the hospital administration to discharge the nurse. If the nurse is forced to resign, the law will probably not give him or her any remedy and will not be able to reinstate the nurse. The nurse might also be prevented from getting an appointment in another facility. So before defying the physician, nurses must consider the risk carefully and think about whether their obligation to count sponges or instruments, to report medical malpractice, to protect the patient, or to tell the patient the truth is greater than the threat of losing their jobs.

## LEGAL CITATIONS

1. Gray v. Davidson, 130 P.2d 341 (Wash. Sup. Ct. 1942).
2. Cartright v. Bartholomew, 83 Ga. App. 503, 64 S.E.2d 323 (Ct. App. Ga. 1951).
3. Nardone v. Reynolds, 333 S. 2d 25, 39 (Fla. Sup. Ct. 1976).
4. Twombly v. Leach, 65 Mass. (Cush.) 397 (1853).
5. Roberts v. Wood, 206 F. Supp. 579 (S.D. Ala. 1962); Nishi v. Hartwell, 473 P. 2d 116 (Hawaii Sup. Ct. 1970); Woods v. Brumlop, 377 P. 2d 520 (N.M. Sup. Ct. 1962); Ball v. Mallenkrodt Chemical Works, 381 S.W.2d 563 (Ct. App. Tenn., Eastern Section, 1964).
6. 464 F.2d 772, 789, *cert. den.* 409 U.S. 1064, 93 S. Ct. 560 (1972).
7. Pratt v. Davis, 118 Ill. App. 161, *aff'd* 224 Ill. 30, 79 N.E. 562 (Ill. Sup. Ct. 1906).

## REFERENCES

Anderson, P. 1978. *Nurse*. New York: St. Martin's.
Kübler-Ross, E. 1974. *Questions and Answers on Death and Dying*. New York: Macmillan.
Lund, C. C. 1946. "The Doctor, the Patient and the Truth." *Tennessee Law Review* 19:344–49.
Meyer, B. C. 1968. "Truth and the Physician." In E. F. Torrey, ed. *Ethical Issues in Medicine*. Boston: Little, Brown.
Schapira, D. V. 1990. "The Right to Die: Perspectives of the Patient, Family and Health Care Provider." In A. S. Berger and J. Berger, eds. *To Die or Not to Die? Cross-Disciplinary, Cultural and Legal Perspectives on the Right to Choose Death*. New York: Praeger.
Smith, H. W. 1946. "Therapeutic Privilege to Withold [*sic*] Specific Diagnosis from Patients Sick with Serious or Fatal Illness." *Tennessee Law Review* 19:349–57.
Veatch, R. M. 1982. "When Should the Patient Know?" In E. A. Doudera and J. D. Peters, eds. *Legal and Ethical Aspects of Treating Critically Ill and Terminally Ill Patients*. Washington, DC: AUPHA Press, 77–89 (Reprinted from *Barrister Magazine* 8(1), 1981).

# 3

## The Dying Patient:
## On the Deathbed

### CARING FOR THE DYING

About 2 million people die annually in the United States (U.S. National Center for Health Statistics, 1989) and a million more are diagnosed as terminally ill. Since 80 percent die in hospitals or nursing homes each year (President's Commission, 1983), caring for the dying in these institutional settings is a major problem.

Health-care providers, of course, are committed to caring for the living and the dying. But their duty to the living is not the same as their duty to the dying. It would be as wrong to treat the sick as though there were no hope of recovery as it would be to treat the dying as though there were. Where the preservation of life is impossible, the efforts of providers are redirected to compassionate care and the alleviation of suffering.

While such care is expected and is generally given, when it is not, especially in the largest medical system in the country, it is shocking. The Veterans Administration, which controls 172 hospitals and nursing homes, was shown in 1990 to have failed to meet this standard. Both from ABC's "Primetime" show and elsewhere (*DAV Magazine*, 1990), it appeared that at four Veterans Administration hospitals patients were not fed, were tied to rails in hallways and received the wrong medications or none at all. Such substandard care, however, is an aberration in the hospital system.

Compassionate care for the dying is an art. Being a source of help for a dying patient is hinged to our understanding of death. But helping the dying seems to have two meanings. There is what we can do on the private subjective level to help ourselves, for inevitably we are required to deal with our own feelings about our own deaths. Then there is what we can do on the public or objective level for the dying and their deaths. Since the two levels interact, it would seem that we are not all suited to care for the dying. Caring for them not only requires compassion, trust, skill, and interest; it also requires a caregiver who is comfortable with dying and with death. In short, caring for the dying is or should be as much a medical specialty as any other.

Nursing goals extend beyond taking a patient's history, making a physical assessment, administering medications or treatments ordered by a physician, and charting and generally protecting a patient. Talking and listening to patients and touching them is a general form of help. Patients appreciate the warm, human touch. Dying patients face fears: "Will I be in pain?" or "Will Medicare or my health insurance take care of my expenses?" These questions should not be ignored, evaded, or treated casually. Pattison (1977:48–55, 318–22) reminds us that dying patients face other fears:

1. Fear of loss of autonomy—a disappearance of self-worth and the power of control over one's life, the elements that allow death with dignity. It is helpful to provide patients with the opportunity of participating in many kinds of decisions, even the most minor, such as what to order for dinner, what to see on television, whether to put on makeup, what to wear. These small decisions will increase the power of control and pave the way for the important decisions concerning what shall be done with their bodies and the remainder of their lives.

2. Fear of loneliness—being isolated and ignored. While we must recognize that a triage situation exists in most hospitals with more sick people than staff, nevertheless this fear calls for being with dying patients as often as possible and for keeping them busy with ongoing tasks and relationships.

3. Fear of separation—the inevitable parting with loved ones. The dying person and family should be helped to understand the real meanings of their relationships before death and assisted to recognize that the problem of separation is different from and precedes the problem of death. Pattison likens this process of anticipatory grief to the Eskimo custom of having a feast in which good-byes are said before the elderly person mounts an ice floe and floats off (1977:51).

4. Fears of what death will signify—family affairs or business matters may cause concern. These concerns can be addressed with

practical steps: estate planning and estate administrators who will wind up things; assurances that projects begun will be completed. This fear may take the form of a concern over death: "Am I going to die?" "Is there a life after death?" Some patients never want to speak of death and what may lie beyond. Their wishes should be respected. If patients want to talk about death, it is important to remember a lesson Kübler-Ross learned from a terminally ill patient. The patient wanted her to sit with him and talk about death. But Elisabeth preferred to come back the next day with her students. The next day, however, when she returned with her students, the patient could barely whisper and he died within the hour. He never spoke the words Kübler-Ross and her students had come to hear (1960:23,24). When patients want to talk about dying and death and to ask their questions and express their anxieties, seize the moment. There may never be another.

## DISPOSITIONS OF PROPERTY

Prudent people generally plan well ahead the ways and means of handling their estates. Insurance policies, joint property and bank accounts, and intervivos and testamentary trusts, for example, can be created as alternatives to will probate and administration. But for some who find themselves facing impending death, it may be too late for involved estate and financial planning, for consulting insurance agents, bankers, attorneys, and accountants, and for drawing up complicated instruments.

Two fears earlier mentioned add to the importance for dying patients to consider simple and quick methods for distributing their assets, managing their affairs, and providing for beneficiaries. The fear of loss of autonomy can be mitigated if patients are helped to realize that they still have the power to make and implement decisions about and maintain control over important family, property, and business matters. These kinds of decisions may strengthen the patient's feeling of autonomy and help later when large life-death decisions need to be made. The fear of what havoc death may wreak in family and business affairs may be reduced by taking steps to see that property is distributed as one intends and by the knowledge that one's affairs will be managed by someone trusted and competent. On the deathbed, of course, options are limited by practical considerations to a will, either new or updated, or to a gift.

After lawyers' offices, the next most frequent place where people focus on the disposition of property and where wills are drawn is the deathbed. While practitioners need not be experts, at least they should be fairly familiar with the types of dispositions of possessions patients can make, or the law will make, if the patient has not done so. Practitioners need also to understand the legal principles governing these dispositions. They are very much an integral part of the "law of dying and death."

## INTESTACY

A person dying without a valid will dies intestate. The plans, expectations, or desires the intestate may have had about who should receive a sum of money, say, or a piece of jewelry count for nothing. A couple the author once represented, in reliance on the promise of a physician to give them his house and property on his death, became his companions and worked for him for ten years. But the promise was not reduced to writing and the doctor made no will. When he died, his daughter, as administrator of his estate, claimed the house and property. In this case the court was persuaded to grant specific performance for the conveyance of the house and property to the couple,[1] a rare result for such a case in a court of law in the absence of a will. A promise to convey real property normally is void and unenforceable under the Statute of Frauds, and the testimony of the promisee against the estate of a dead person is disqualified under many statutes on the theory that the law will mute one party when death has muted the other.

When a person has made no will and dies, the state with its statute governing intestate succession and the descent of real property or distribution of personal property plays god and makes a will for the intestate. Real and personal property are distributed generally according to the class in which relatives fall and according to a certain order: surviving spouse; children; grandchildren; parents; siblings; and other heirs. Generally, a surviving spouse takes a share of the estate if there are surviving children and the remainder goes equally to them or, if they have died before the intestate, to their children *per stirpes*—that is, each child of a deceased child receives a portion of the share the dead child would have received. The laws dealing with intestacy are not uniform and the laws of each state need to be consulted.

## WILLS

A person who has made a will is called a "testator" (male) or "testatrix" (female). A will may contain provisions regarding the executor or administrator of an estate or the appointment of a guardian for minor children if a spouse predeceases the person making the will or dies at the same time.

But primarily a will expresses a person's intention regarding the disposition of assets. Patients who make no wills must realize that their assets will be disposed of under the laws of inheritance, perhaps to people to whom they would otherwise have given nothing. A will may avoid sometimes bitter quarrels among heirs or may avoid court battles over the appointment of an administrator of the assets of an estate.

## TESTAMENTARY CAPACITY

Testamentary capacity is vital to a will's validity. An individual below a certain age cannot make a will. Minimum ages, however, are not uniform among the states. In many, including Alabama, California, Florida, and New York, a person must be at least eighteen years of age to bequeath personal property (generally movable objects such as jewels, money, goods, clothing, securities, or furniture). In Alaska, Indiana, Illinois, and Michigan, and other states, the minimum age for bequeathing personal property is twenty-one. To devise real property (land and houses which are immovable and fixed), in Alabama, New York, Virginia, and elsewhere one must be at least twenty-one years of age, while in California, Florida, Illinois, and some other states one need be only eighteen. In Louisiana, sixteen is the minimum age for bequeathing both personal and real property. There is, however, no age beyond which a person cannot make a will.

In addition, individuals making wills must be of what is called "sound and disposing mind and memory" with the ability to understand the nature of what is being done, to recall their property, and to understand their relationships to those who will be the natural objects of their bounty. Neither the religious beliefs nor physical condition of a patient, nor that he or she is at the brink of death, necessarily deprives an individual of testamentary capacity.

### Nuncupative Wills

Ethel May McClellan, an unmarried woman thirty-three years of age, became ill on February 9, 1935, at her home. On February 12, her physician made a diagnosis of acute hemorrhagic nephritis. On February 22, she was taken to the Southside Hospital in Pittsburgh, where her condition worsened and she developed encephalitis. On February 25, before she became delirious and incoherent, and while Nurse Brinkman was in her room, McClellan began to give instructions for disposing of her ring. She also said there were other things she wanted to dispose of. Nurse Brinkman asked the patient if she wanted to make a will. The patient said that she did. The nurse began to make notes about the ring. An intern, Dr. Stiller, came into the room. The patient then said what she wanted done with her estate and specified beneficiaries. For an hour before the patient became exhausted, fell asleep, and went into a coma, the nurse continued to write down the patient's directions for disposing of her estate. The patient died two days later.

May wills made from a hospital bed be oral? Yes and no. The *McClellan* case is an example of a seriously ill patient trying to make oral disposition of property.[2] The nurse who made a memorandum of her wishes also shows how practitioners can be involved in a will situation. Another example is that of Paul Hargis who, while in a Galveston hospital because of a severe heart attack, called in an attending physician to write down how he wanted his assets distributed.[3]

These cases deal with a type of will known as a nuncupative will, an unwritten will in the form of an oral expression of a person's intentions regarding property. As with any other will, testamentary capacity is essential.

The law, however, does not favor wills of this type because of the possibilities of fraud and perjury. Many states, including Arizona, Colorado, Connecticut, Florida, Maryland, and New Jersey, do not recognize them at all. In some states, statutes that previously recognized nuncupative wills as valid have been repealed. Florida's Section 731.06, for example, was repealed in 1974. In other jurisdictions, such as Wyoming, there are statutes that specify that all wills must be in writing. Obviously, such statutes make nuncupative wills invalid.[4]

In the various jurisdictions in which nuncupative wills are valid, states have set up requirements that must be rigidly observed. Thus, in some jurisdictions, such as New York, a nuncupative will is valid only if made by soldiers and sailors in actual military or naval service or by mariners at sea. And the will becomes invalid one year after the soldier or sailor has been discharged from the service unless the person no longer has testamentary capacity. Under the statutes of other states, a nuncupative will is valid only if a specified number of witnesses hear it and can prove it. So in Texas three witnesses must agree to what a testator said or to the dispositions made.

Under the statutes of Alabama, Georgia, Kansas, Maine, Mississippi, Missouri, and other states, people can make valid nuncupative wills, but it is a basic requirement that they be made during the "last sickness" of a testator or testatrix. Courts, however, have not agreed on the meaning of "last sickness." Most courts tend to the view that the person must be attacked by a sudden and violent sickness and be in such condition that there is no time or opportunity to make a written will. A minority of courts adopt the view that it is enough if the testator or testatrix who is sick and in extremis in fact dies from the sickness.

Ethel May McClellan, who dictated her directions during a rational period, must be assumed to have had testamentary capacity. But because the case dealt with an oral will more was required. The court, which followed the majority view concerning "last sickness," held that her expressions concerning the disposition of her property could not be considered a valid nuncupative will. She had not been overtaken by any sudden illness that prevented her from making a written will. For eighteen days between the time she first became ill on February 9 until her hospitalization, she was not so incapacitated that she could not make a will. Even on February 25, when she gave oral directions concerning her property and the nurse prepared a memorandum, a written will could have been made, either by the patient or by someone writing down her directions and by her signing what had been written. A similar result has been reached in other cases where patients who were physically able and mentally competent to make or sign wills during the hours or days before they died did not do so and instead made oral wills.[5]

Nuncupative wills provide too many opportunities for fraud. They are also unreliable because they depend on the memory, intelligence, and attentiveness of people, including health-care professionals, who are with a dying patient. Nuncupative wills are bound to lead to challenges and court contests. And because they are frowned on by the law, courts will reject them even in jurisdictions where they are recognized if they fail to observe statutory requirements. Patients and those practitioners attempting to help them would act wisely or give wise counsel to avoid oral declarations disposing of property and instead use whatever time and opportunity are available to make a written will.

## Holographic Wills

David L. Harrison entered a hospital in Memphis for tests. The following day he asked his wife, Madge M. Harrison, to bring him a yellow scratch pad so that he could write down some matters relating to his farm that he wanted her to manage. The day before he went into surgery, he made a note on the pad. A week later he died in the hospital. A search was made for any will he might have made but none was found except that on one of the sheets of the yellow pad, Harrison had written:

Madge Do what should be done to complete my work. I will all to you.

David Harrison

This type of will is a holographic will—one written in the testator's own hand. The handwriting of the testator gives an assurance of genuineness that does not exist with nuncupative wills. In the *Harrison* case,[6] Harrison's written wishes were held to be a valid will. A similar case was that of Annie M. Kauffman who died of pneumonia. Three days before she died, suffering from bronchitis and not feeling well, she wrote in pencil on a piece of paper:

dear bill
I want you to have farm
Annie Kauffman

This signed writing was held to be a valid holographic will.[7] A letter, too, can function as a holographic will. Jacob Krupp wrote a letter that read: "Since during the last few months I was twice in a critical condition with my health I wish to state here that in case of my sudden death all my property excepting my books and manuscripts should go to my sisters and brother." The court accepted this letter as a valid holographic will.[8]

Not all holographic wills are made by sick or dying people. When James Kidd was in good health, this uneducated miner moistened his pencil with his tongue and scrawled his on a piece of paper, sealed it in an envelope, and placed it in a safe deposit box. Then, apparently while prospecting in the Arizona hills, he disappeared and was presumed dead. His will provided: "sell all my property which is all in cash and stocks with E. F. Hutton Co Phoenix some in safety deposit box, and have this balance go in a reserach [*sic*] or some scientific proof of a soul of the human body which leaves at death I think in time their [*sic*] can be a Photograph of soul leaving the human at death." After it came to light that Kidd had left an estate of about $175,000, batteries of lawyers and 103 claimants appeared to lay claim to it under the terms of the will.[9] The trial was called the "great soul trial" (Fuller, 1969), was the subject of coverage in *Life* and *Reader's Digest*, and made Kidd's the most famous holographic will ever scribbled.

In those jurisdictions where a holographic will is recognized, such as Alaska, Arizona, North Carolina, California, and Texas, such a will is valid if written, dated, and signed in the hand of the testator or testatrix. It need not be subscribed by attesting witnesses. Even in these jurisdictions, however, if the will contains nonholographic matter, such as typed or printed words or words in someone else's handwriting, its validity may be questioned. The question generally arises whether the language used shows testamentary intent—a desire to dispose of property—or whether the writer merely intended the writing to be a letter or an informal expression or vague statement of something that might be done in the future and did not intend to make a disposition of property.

In the construction of wills, there is a rule that a person is presumed not to intend to die intestate but rather to dispose of property. The mere fact that the writing is in the form of a letter or is otherwise informal does not prevent its operation as a will if it declares the intention of the writer to be carried out after death and if it is in the writing of and is signed by the person. Since Harrison, Kauffman, Krupp, and Kidd took the trouble to prepare their writings, the inference can be made that they wanted to avoid dying intestate.

In many states, however, holographic wills are not recognized while in others, such as Florida and Mississippi, such a will is valid only if the requirements of execution and witnesses for a more formal will are observed. Krupp's will met these requirements.

### Formal Wills

While living-will statutes provide sample forms of declarations that may be followed, statutes governing testamentary wills mandate no special form.

An estate may be complicated and may create estate tax and other problems. A testator or testatrix may want to provide for various legacies, general or specific, to be paid out of the estate; to provide against legacies lapsing in case a legatee predeceases the maker of the will; to make different devises of real property in several locations, some with vested estates, some contingent, some life; to disinherit a child or a spouse because of abandonment or a separation agreement or divorce; to set up trusts against estate taxes or to prevent a spouse or children from an imprudent wasting of assets. Wills with various clauses to meet such involved needs should be drawn by a lawyer after consultation with the client.

In most other cases, however, formal wills can be simple—as short as one page and drawn by people themselves without a lawyer. In its simplest form, a will should contain clauses that: (1) identify the testator or testatrix making the will; (2) revoke any prior will to avoid any inconsistency with the present will; (3) give described real property or items of personal property to specific people with an alternate gift if the person dies before the maker of the will; (4) dispose of the remainder of any property not included in the other gifts; (5) designate someone to administer the estate—an executor or personal representative who will probate the will and dispose of property in accordance with the will; (6) designate a guardian for any minor children.

The validity of a will also depends on its meeting other statutory requirements besides testamentary capacity. The requirements concerning execution are strict. Generally, a will must: (1) be in writing; (2) be subscribed at the end by the person making it or the name of the testator or testatrix must be subscribed in his or her presence by someone at his or her direction; (3) be signed or acknowledged in the presence of at least two witnesses in most states, three in others; and (4) be signed by the witnesses who have been asked by the testator or testatrix to do so and who sign in the presence of one another and in the presence of the testator or testatrix. Following the clauses mentioned above for a simple will, therefore, will be the signature of the maker of the will and signatures of witnesses who have signed and subscribed the will as required by pertinent statutes.

Practitioners are not attorneys and should not practice law unlawfully, any more than attorneys should practice medicine unlawfully. Doctors and nurses should not, therefore, undertake the drafting of wills for patients. However, especially when requested by patients, they may help and encourage those who want to make wills. One concrete form of help is to suggest to patients that they collect the information that must be considered when a will is drafted. An inventory of assets and other matters can be prepared by the patient or dictated by the patient to a nurse. This inventory will be useful in the preparation of the will and will prove valuable after the will is probated and the estate is being administered.

Even when their help is not requested by patients, practitioners may be asked to be witnesses to the execution of the wills. In the role of witness, the practitioner may be called upon to testify, if the will's probate is contested, as to the acts of patients and whether they were rational or irrational and of sound or unsound mind. The practitioner may also be asked about the circumstances surrounding the execution of the will in cases where undue influence is claimed or interpretation of ambiguous language of a will is required. For these reasons, practitioners ought to record in the patient's medical record the circumstances and the patient's acts and state of mind when the will was executed. The notation should be made at the time of execution or within a short time later.

## GIFTS *CAUSA MORTIS*

Another disposition of assets patients may make is simply to give away their personal property. In the *McClellan* case, for example, the patient could have given her ring to the object of her bounty. Or, where a patient has money or valuables in a safe, he or she could disclose the combination to a donee or could deliver a key to a locked drawer or room.

The law recognizes two kinds of gifts: gifts *inter vivos*—between the living—and gifts *causa mortis*—deathbed gifts or those made in contemplation of death. The latter is the type of gift in which practitioners are most likely to be interested and form part of "the law of dying and death." In the gift *inter vivos* there must be an intention that the gift be immediate, an unconditional transfer of possession of the item given and a divestiture of control over it and the power to revoke it, and there must be an acceptance by the donee. In the gift *causa mortis*, however, which is limited to personal property, while there must be a transfer of possession and acceptance by the donee, the intention is not to make an immediate gift. The gift is to become effective only if the donor dies. If the donor recovers, the gift is void and can be revoked.

In order to make the gift effective, the patient must believe that death is impending, and, further, the patient must die as a result of the disease from which he or she is suffering. Any notations made by a practitioner when such gifts are made would be valuable in establishing whether the patient was competent to make them at the time and was free of constraint. The notations might also record the patient's words of gift and the general circumstances regarding delivery. Such notations would be highly pertinent in cases in which the question was raised whether a valid gift *causa mortis* was made to a donee or whether the property claimed as a gift remains part of the dead patient's estate.

## ADVANCE DIRECTIVES

When dealing with patients who are conscious and alert yet dying as the result of a progressive disease—cancer, for instance—practitioners should encourage those who have not drawn up advance directives to do so. Forms, such as those for living wills, are generally readily obtainable at no charge from the Concern for Dying/Society for the Right to Die (which changed its name in 1991 to Choice in Dying) and may be available in most large hospitals. These directives permit patients to make known their wishes concerning, and to exercise control over, their medical care should they become critically ill and not able to express their wishes. The subject of advance directives is considered in Part IV.

## DYING DECLARATIONS

During the trial of a case, one of the most frequently heard objections made to the evidence is that testimony is hearsay—that is, it is based on what some other person said and not on what the witness testifying saw, heard, or knew—and so should not be admitted. But there are recognized exceptions to the hearsay rule. A dying declaration concerning facts and circumstances of a homicide is admissible in cases where the death of the person making the declaration is the basis of the charge.

A dying declaration is another aspect of the "law of dying and death" that practitioners attending the deathbeds of murdered patients may encounter. It is a statement made by a victim who is in desperate circumstances and at the very point of death, who is aware that death is very close and has abandoned any hope of recovery. A patient's statement, for example, that "I have no hope of recovery, am going to die and want to make this statement," would suggest consciousness of impending death and that the patient had given up hope.[10] Statements made in response to questions, even leading ones, such as "Do you believe that you are about to die?" also may indicate consciousness of impending death.

The dying declaration may be oral or written or may even be made by signs. A practitioner who is a witness to such a statement should ask the patient to sign it if possible, and the practitioner and others should witness it. If the statement is oral, the practitioner should record it as accurately as possible at the time it is made or within a reasonably short time thereafter. The statement so recorded should be repeated to the patient for verification. The statement should also be reduced to writing and, if possible, signed and witnessed. But even without a written statement, the testimony of the practitioner probably would be admissible evidence of the oral declaration.[11]

## CONFESSIONS

Besides dying declarations made by victims of homicides, practitioners may also be witnesses to confessions by dying criminals. A confession is a voluntary statement that directly acknowledges guilt in a criminal case. If made voluntarily by someone charged with a crime who is in full possession of his or her faculties, it is considered the strongest form of evidence. A confession can be in any form—a formal written statement or an acknowledgment in the form of conversation with one or more people. If it is oral, a practitioner can testify to the whole of what the person said. It would be advisable for the practitioner to record the confession and the circumstances under which it was made promptly on hearing it or very soon after. The circumstances may have an important bearing on the validity and admissibility of the confession as evidence.

## LEGAL CITATIONS

1. Strandberg v. Lawrence, 216 N.Y.S.2d 973 (Sup. Ct., Suffolk Co. N.Y. 1961).
2. McClellan's Estate, 325 Pa. 257, 139 A. 3145 (Pa. Sup. Ct. 1937).
3. Hargis v. Nance, 317 S.W.2d 9922 (Tx. Sup. Ct. 1958).
4. In the Matter of the Estate of William B. Boyd, 366 P.2d 336 (Wy. Sup. Ct. 1961).
5. In re Rutt's Estate, 200 Pa. 549, 50 A. 171 (Pa. Sup. Ct. 1901); In re Shover's Estate, 258 Pa. 70, 101 A. 862 (Pa. Sup. Ct. 1917).
6. Fair v. Harrison, 248 S.2d 798 (Miss. Sup. Ct. 1971).
7. In re Kauffman's Estate, 365 Pa. 555, 76 A. 2d 414 (Pa. Sup. Ct. 1950).
8. In re Krupp's Will, 173 Misc. 632, 18 N.Y.S.2d 813 (Sur. Ct. Kings Co. N.Y. 1940).
9. In the Matter of the Estate of James Kidd, 106 Ariz. 554, 479 P.2d 697 (Ariz. Sup. Ct. 1978).
10. People v. Chase, 79 Hun. 296, 29 N.Y.S. 376, *aff'd* 143 N.Y. 669, 39 N.E. 21 (1894).
11. People v. Apicello, 275 N.Y. 222, 228, 9 N.E.2d 844 (1937).

## REFERENCES

*DAV Magazine*. "Poor Quality Care Charged at Four VA Medical Centers," Nov. 1990, p. 7.
Fuller, J. 1969. *The Great Soul Trial*. New York: Macmillan.
Kübler-Ross, E. 1960. *On Death and Dying*. New York: Macmillan.
Pattison, E. M. 1977. *The Experience of Dying*. Englewood Cliffs, NJ: Prentice-Hall, 48–55, 318–22.
President's Commission for the Study of Ethical Problems in Medicine and Biomedical and Behavioral Research. 1983. *Deciding to Forgo Life-Sustaining Treatment*. Washington, DC: Government Printing Office.
U. S. National Center for Health Statistics. 1989. Monthly Vital Statistics 37:6.

# III

## Right to Die

# 4

## Right to Die:
## Meanings and Strategy

### EMILY BAUER'S STORY

Under the rules of poker, players who don't like the cards they are dealt or who don't want to match a bet can drop out. But in the game of life, even if fate has dealt a terrible hand to someone who wants to drop out, astonishing advances in medical technology have changed the rules. People are now kept alive who would have died and dropped out of the game a few decades ago.

*This Far and No More* (Malcolm, 1987) is the true story of Emily Bauer, a university instructor in her forties, active and happily married with three small children, who developed amyotrophic lateral sclerosis (ALS), popularly known as Lou Gehrig's disease. When Emily Bauer asked her doctor, as had Sam Jones, "Am I going to die?" the physician replied evasively, as had Sam Jones's doctor, "We're all going to die" (Malcolm, 1987:30). He did not tell her that the disease is a fatal condition, but it is.

Emily Bauer fought the disease and even tried alternative healing. But soon she was forced into a wheelchair, then into bed, had trouble breathing, and eventually was confined to a hospital. Unable to swallow, she was fed artificially through a nasogastric tube. She could not breathe without a mechanical respirator attached to her trachea. She could not speak or write. Her body shrank. One day, one of her little daughters who came to visit her in her hospital bed asked, "Is Mommy in there?" (Malcolm, 1987:152). But Mrs. Bauer was still mentally alert and tried to communicate by moving her lips, by trying to talk with an electronic larynx, and by blinking her eyes to answer questions, one blink for "yes," two blinks for "no." Eventually by working a switch beneath her head, she could make a printing machine's cursor stop at a letter and could print her messages out on a monitor screen. One day, as a result of her profound frustration, helplessness, anxiety, and discomfort and the loss of her rich and varied life, she printed out, "I WANT TO DIE." A movie called *The Right to Die* with Raquel Welch was based on Malcolm's book. It was shown on NBC television on October 12, 1987, and 24 million people saw it.

## LIFE-SUSTAINING TREATMENT

The book and movie dramatized several critical medicolegal matters included in the "law of dying and death." The first is that the use of the feeding tube and mechanical respirator are forms of treatment many courts and some legislatures describe as "life-sustaining" treatment,[1] the term we use here. But other legislatures use terms such as "life-saving"[2] and "life-prolonging."[3] There are simply too many confusing terms. Is there any real difference if death is put off for a year or for three months? Has a life been "sustained" or has it been "saved" or "prolonged"? "Life-sustaining" treatment signifies any "treatment, the withdrawing or withholding of which, would, within reasonable medical certainty, be a substantial contributing cause of the patient's death within a relatively short time."[4] "Life-sustaining" seems a better term than "life-saving" or "life-prolonging" because it is not as emotional or as inflammatory.

## RIGHT TO DIE

The title of the movie, *The Right to Die*, is provocative. A famous society in New York was called the Society for the Right to Die (originally the Euthanasia Society of America). The *right to die* is a phrase used by many courts[5] and is also the banner under which patients' rights advocates assemble. In addition, 80 to 90 percent of the people polled on the question are in favor of the "right to die." But few realize that this phrase is only a "shorthand expression"[6] that does not effectively communicate matters of fundamental importance with which it is interlaced. It is, therefore, not surprising that the Society for the Right to Die should have, in 1991, renamed itself Choice in Dying.

The right to die can be reduced to five primary elements, both practical and legal. Three arise out of the physician-patient relationship: the right to know the truth from the physician, already covered in the discussion of the Sam Jones case; the overlapping right under the doctrine of informed consent, to which reference is made in Chapters 6 and 7, to receive full medical information from a physician regarding a diagnosis and recommended procedure or treatment prior to consenting; and the right to hire and fire physicians, to be covered later in Part III. The other two elements come from the law: rights given by the U.S. Constitution and the common law to refuse medical treatment and the right conferred by state statutes to make advance directives expressing our wishes regarding medical care, also covered in Part III.

The expression *right to die* does not convey or express the nature of other problems that cover a wide spectrum ranging from by whom and the forum where life and death decisions are to be made—covered in Chapter 5—to the significance of the term and how the right can be implemented. These latter matters are our immediate concern.

## NATURAL DEATH

With dramatic technological progress in medicine and increasing control over life and the end of life, the power has been given to physicians on the one hand to cure or prevent disease and to put off death as never before. But on the other hand, their power has converted hospitals from places once feared as the loci of death into places now feared as those where dying is prolonged. This is exactly the point that produces the entire right-to-die issue. Medical technology can and does maintain "life" for very long periods of time—say, fifteen to thirty years with artificial feeding, for example. But it is in many cases only a semblance of life limited to its biological aspects. Many patients are kept alive when they have no cognitive functions, no self-awareness, no ability to interact with their environment. Most of them do not or would not want their dying process to be prolonged in this way. Even when patients retain their cognitive functions, few want their dying process prolonged, either, because their lives are dehumanized, mechanized, barren, helpless, useless, and devoid of hope or enjoyment.

Emily Bauer was a member of the latter class, and she opted to die naturally. To some people this is what the right to die means: a natural death. Many living-will statutes that give people the right to choose to refuse unwanted medical procedures, for example, affirm that their aim is to enable people to "die naturally." Indeed, they are called natural-death statutes. The Oklahoma "Natural Death Act,"[7] the Tennessee "Right to Natural Death Act,"[8] and the Texas "Natural Death Act"[9] are examples. Obviously, the right to die is tied in with natural death. If the real import of "right to die" is to be understood, the meaning of natural death must be clarified.

Natural death, as distinguished from death by accident, suicide, or homicide, denotes death by natural causes. But it also has a philosophical and poetic ring to it. Some conceive of death as a phenomenon of nature, part of the grand and overriding evolutionary process. We are all part of the ebb and flow of nature in whose workings birth and death are as natural and inevitable as the coming and going of the seasons. With this romanticization of death, natural death is an ideal death often pictured as the conscious, painless, dignified, and peaceful lapsing into permanent sleep after bidding sweet and brave last good-byes to loved ones. But there are all kinds of natural death. Depending on the type, it may be accompanied by fever, delirium, nausea, vomiting, convulsions, foul smells, gasping, dehydration, pain, and sedation. Not one of these natural deaths is as advertised.

People should be sharply aware, before they refuse treatment, of what kind of natural death may really await them. They should understand that the underlying purpose behind the natural-death statutes and judicial decisions in right-to-die cases is to allow individuals to make decisions relating to their medical care. One of these decisions may be to take no medical steps, to avoid having life extended artificially, to let nature take its course and to die sooner rather than to exist as an object of medical technology. Natural-death and right-to-die legislation and court decisions should be limited to guaranteeing us the opportunity to make this decision. They do not warrant the course nature will take if the opportunity is grasped. Statutes and court decisions may refer to natural-death, but they are careful never to define what is meant by the term and they grant us no right to expect a death that is the good, peaceful, and dignified event we may expect it to be.

## AID-IN-DYING

Choosing to die naturally is one thing. Asking the assistance of others to terminate a life is quite another. But many people would include this additional meaning in the right to die. Possibly encouraged by the successful Dutch experiment with voluntary active euthanasia, they interpret the right to die as entitling patients not merely to the right to refuse life-sustaining treatment and to die; they also believe patients should have the power to enlist the help of others, particularly physicians, to aid them to die or even to kill them if the burdens of a prolonged dying process and the high cost of continuing care outweigh the benefits of the dying process. Doctors' assistance could be prescribing sedatives or drugs and the advice to patients of which dosages are lethal, actual administering of a series of lethal drug injections, or providing the methods of self-destruction as did the "suicide doctor," Dr. Jack Kevorkian, who, in highly publicized cases since 1990, used a "suicide machine" or other methods to help four women die in Michigan (Kevorkian, 1991). As of this writing, murder charges against him have been dismissed in that state.

Several groups are working to implement this interpretation of the right to die and to give assistance to patients wanting to die. Among them are some physicians (Kevorkian, 1991; Goldberg, 1968) and organizations that advocate allowing the terminally ill the option of active voluntary euthanasia, such as the British Voluntary Euthanasia Society (formerly called Exit) and the Hemlock Society in the United States. The British society distributes a "self-deliverance" booklet that describes which and how many sedatives, antidepressants, analgesics, and other substances those desiring to have their lives terminated are to take or be given (Guide, 1981). Derek Humphry, the principal founder of the Hemlock Society, who told of how he had lovingly "delivered" his first wife (Humphry, 1978), also published a best-seller in which he provided do-it-yourself or have-it-done-to-yourself instructions for others contemplating the termination of their lives (Humphry, 1991).

Is aid-in-dying a logical extension of the right to die? There is no legal justification for it either in existing legislation or in court decisions. An affirmative act carried out to terminate a human life continues to be murder. If the means of termination are provided, it also constitutes a felony under the laws of almost every jurisdiction, even if suicide itself is not a criminal offense.

A second objection is that aid-in-dying changes the physician-patient relationship from one in which the physician cures into one in which the physician kills. Physicians become veterinarians "putting their patients to sleep."

The administration of aid-in-dying should be a caring act, prompted by kindness, compassion, and a desire to help someone who is sick, dying, and suffering. It should not serve economic interests. A third objection, therefore, is that physician aid-in-dying may be abused and converted into a vehicle for the private gain of physicians. No agency to regulate and strictly limit the fees for their services exists to prevent this abuse.

Assisted dying is also dangerous. It offers splendid opportunities for greedy relatives to rid themselves of rich family members and for grasping medical doctors to become veterinarians. In England in 1953, for example, a physician was charged with muder after he "eased the passing" of some wealthy ladies who were his patients. It was suggested that he had been motivated by the prospect of generous bequests in their wills (Barrington, 1990). The chapters of history reveal more familiar dangers:

We have witnessed too much history to disregard how easily a society may disvalue the lives of the "unproductive." The "angel of mercy" can become the fanatic, bringing the "comfort" of death to some who do not clearly want it, then to others who "would really be better off dead" and finally, to classes of "undesirable persons", who might include the terminally ill, the permanently unconscious, the severely senile, the pleasantly senile, the retarded, the incurably or chronically ill, and, perhaps, the aged. . . . In the current environment, and it may well prove convenient—and all too easy—to move from recognition of an individual's "right to die" . . . to a climate enforcing a "duty to die" (Siegler and Weisbard, 1985:130–31).

Advocates of voluntary euthanasia and aid-in-dying would give no weight to these objections. They propose legislation under which terminally ill people would be granted the right to ask for and receive from a willing physician aid-in-dying—that is, any medical procedure that would terminate life painlessly and quickly. Thus, in 1991 in Washington State, which has a reputation for its support of individual rights, a group known as the Washington Citizens for Death with Dignity placed on the ballot Initiative 119, which would legalize aid-in-dying. In what was perhaps the most significant right-to-die event of 1991, the voters in Washington rejected Initiative 119 (*USA Today*, 1991). For them objections such as those given have considerable merit. They felt that the legislation proposed to avoid penal statutes makes an unwarranted exception and unacceptable special privilege for physicians requested to administer aid-in-dying.

## NATURAL DEATH STRATEGY

It would nevertheless be callous not to recognize that patients who want to exercise their right to decline life-sustaining treatment and their corollary right to die feel that their existence is or will be burdensome and that medical or surgical procedures will be of no benefit. They are pleading for understanding and compassion. The wise and compassionate physician may perceive another strategy for assisting patients toward a "natural death." This strategy would be an alternative to aid-in-dying or actively euthanizing a patient and would be as well a tactic that would fit neatly into the legal meaning of the right to die: the patient's right to choose to undergo some procedures and to refuse others calculated to extend life artificially.

Physicians know that patients can die from secondary conditions. For instance, instead of dying from emphysema, a patient may succumb to an untreated pulmonary infection. Or a patient with terminal cancer may die from dehydration. By giving the patient information about the types of death that may come naturally and with less pain and discomfort than can be expected from the primary condition, patients are able to make decisions about their care and refuse that treatment without which a death more tolerable and acceptable and less fearful to them probably will result. The role of the physician in this situation is that of "strategist of natural death," whose purpose makes this kind of death the "least worst death" (Battin, 1983).

## LEGAL CITATIONS

1. See Iowa Life-Sustaining Procedures Act [1985] Iowa Code Ann. Secs. 144A. 1 to 144A.11; Louisiana Life-Sustaining Procedures Act [1985] La. Rev. Statutes, Secs. 40:1299.58.1 to 58.11; Maryland Life-Sustaining Act [1985] Maryland Health-General Code Ann. Secs. 5–601 to 5–614.

2. See Mississippi Withdrawal of Life-Saving Mechanisms Act [1984] Secs. 41–41–101 to 41–41–121.

3. See Florida Life-Prolonging Procedure Act [1984] Secs. 765.01 to 765.15; Indiana Living Wills and Life-Prolonging Procedures Act [1985] Secs. 16–8–11–1 to 16–8–11–17.

4. In re Guardianship of Estelle M. Browning, 543 S.2d 258, *aff'd* 568 S.2d 4 (Fla. Sup. Ct. 1990).

5. Brophy v. New England Sinai Hospital, 398 Mass. 417, 497 N.E.2d 626, 642 (Mass. Sup. Jud. Ct. 1986); In re Jobes, 108 N.J. 394, 529 A.2d 434, 452 (N.J. Sup. Ct.); Delio v. Westchester County Medical Center, 129 A.D.2d 1, 516 N.Y.S.2d 677 (N.Y. App. Div., 2d Dep't 1987).

6. Gray v. Romeo, 697 F. Supp. 580, 584 (U.S. Dist. Ct. D. R.I. 1988).

7. Oklahoma Statutes [1985] Secs. 3101–3111.

8. Tennessee Code Ann. [1985] Secs. 32–11–101 to 32–11–110.

9. Texas Rev. Statutes [1977] [1979] [1983] [1985] Article 459h.

## REFERENCES

"A Guide to Self-Deliverance." 1981. London: Executive Committee of Exit.

Barrington, M. R. 1990. "Euthanasia: An English Perspective." In A. S. Berger and J. Berger, eds. *To Die or Not to Die? Cross-Disciplinary, Cultural and Legal Perspectives on the Right to Die*. New York: Praeger, 85–102.

Battin, M. P. 1983. "Least Worst Death." *Hastings Center Report*. April, 13–16.

Goldberg, J. H. 1968. "The Dying Patient: Tackling the New Ethical and Legal Question." *Hospital Physician* 4:33.

Humphry, D. 1991. *Final Exit: The Practicalities of Self-Deliverance and Assistance for the Dying*. Eugene, OR: Hemlock Society.

———. 1978. *Jean's Way*. London and New York: Quartet Books.

Kevorkian, J. 1991. *Prescription: Medicide*. New York: Prometheus.

Malcolm, A. H. 1987. *This Far and No More*. New York: Times Books.
Siegler, M., and Weisbard, A. T. 1985. "Against the Emerging Stream: Should Fluids and
      Nutritional Support Be Discontinued?" *Archives of Internal Medicine* 145:129.
*USA Today*. 1991. "Election '91." November 7: 3A.

# 5

## Playing God: The Issues

"[F]or the first time in history, physicians have the ability, know-how and sophisticated technology to sustain the physical life of patients beyond any reasonable quality of life they might want to endure. What does that mean?" (Scully & Scully, 1987:16).

First, it means that advances in medical technology raise numerous issues relating to life-sustaining treatment. We have noted end of life, time of death, and postdeath issues. But there are others on which this chapter focuses: the religious and value issues; the ethical issues and patient's practical issues; and economic issues that arise in part at the bedside but mainly on the highest level of government and other policymakers.

In addition, the legal issue of whether to stop life-sustaining treatment is addressed on the judicial level. But even before this issue is brought to court, two preliminary but important questions must be answered: Is a court a proper forum for deciding this issue? And how do we prevent the disagreements among patients, families, physicians, and health-care facilities from growing into contested lawsuits? This chapter, therefore, also deals with these preliminary issues. Later chapters deal with the legal issues addressed by courts, the working of the legal system, and the stages of the litigation process.

### RELIGIOUS ISSUE

Religious teachings about right and wrong influence our way of thinking, living, and dying. But is religious conviction an issue in patient care? For patients, religious beliefs can be very important because they may determine the kind of life-sustaining medical treatment a patient will accept or decline. In the *Brophy* case,[1] Patricia Brophy prayed for a miracle for her unconscious husband, forty-nine-year-old Paul Brophy, but when God did not change the situation, she talked with her pastor. Only after she was persuaded that her religion did not prevent her from asking that artificial feeding be withdrawn from her husband did she do so. In the *Quinlan* case,[2] the family decided to ask that the respirator be disconnected from their twenty-one-year-old daughter only after discussing the situation with their parish priest and finding that the Vatican did not see it as a moral sin to stop extraordinary treatment.

The right to die has been prominent and controversial in the Catholic and Jewish religions. Both traditions oppose euthanasia. But there are differences in their other perspectives (McCartney, 1990). The Catholic tradition affirms a right to be let alone—that is, individuals may legitimately decide to refuse medical treatment initially or decide that it be withdrawn after it has proved too expensive or burdensome for them to endure, even if the possibility of success is fairly well assured, and they may ask that their agony not be continued. The Church accepts decisions made in this context as morally persuasive and believes that it is the obligation of health-care professionals to follow the patient's wishes in this respect. On the other hand, the Jewish tradition believes that where there is life there is hope and generally tends to be more insistent than Catholics that life-sustaining treatment be continued. Jews are morally entitled to refuse such treatment if they think it useless for restoring health but, once this treatment is started, Jewish tradition looks on asking for the withdrawal of life-sustaining treatment as morally equivalent to suicide and on acceding to such a request as mercy killing. While life supports may be withdrawn to shorten the dying process for patients who are incurably ill, they may not be if doing so will interrupt life. Yet "who can make the fine distinction between prolonging life and prolonging the act of dying?" asks Judaism (Rosner, 1986:30).

For Jehovah's Witnesses, there is no question in their minds that their religious beliefs force them to decline one form of life-sustaining treatment. Since frequently they are patients at many hospitals, the medical profession should know something about these people who, even if it means increased risk of death, refuse blood transfusions providers think they should have.

Jehovah's Witnesses' beliefs are based on the word of God as stated in the Bible. One of these is that people must not eat the blood of any sort of flesh. Jehovah's Witnesses believe that the blood of a creature represents its life or soul. They must abstain from blood, and this abstinence requires them to refuse taking blood into their bodies in any form, including transfusions. This is a moral imperative, not just a dietary rule. They believe that if they do not obey this scriptural and divine directive, they will be cut off from eternal life through resurrection. So they feel that if life is extended by a blood transfusion, it will mean nothing because eternal life is impossible. Therefore, they are willing to accept greater risks to their health in surgical procedures including blood loss.

The refusal of blood transfusions involves refusal of transfusions of whole blood, packed blood cells, white blood cells, platelets, and fresh or frozen plasma. It also involves the refusal to bank one's own blood because Witnesses believe that blood must be discarded after it has left the body. These are clear areas of refusal. But then there are gray areas, such as hemodialysis (where the patient's blood flows in a continuous circuit), organ transplantation, and heart-lung bypasses. These procedures are not clearly forbidden by scripture and are left to the individual to decide.

Normally, a patient's religious beliefs are of no consequence to health-care providers and have no effect on patient care. If these beliefs impel patients with decision-making capacity to refuse treatment, hospital policies that recognize patient autonomy will govern such situations. In every case, as where a Jehovah's Witness refuses a blood transfusion, a written informed consent should be completed to protect the hospital and health-care provider from charges of neglect. Jehovah's Witnesses will generally sign blood-refusal forms when admitted to the hospital. This refusal should also be noted in the patient's chart.

But the existence of such a policy or the documentation of a refusal does not eliminate the confrontation between Jehovah's Witnesses and the medical staff, or the destructive effect the refusal has on them. A case in point took place in 1991 at the medical center on whose ethics committee I serve. A young male Jehovah's Witness with a serious work-related injury was admitted to the hospital. Because of his convictions, he refused the blood transfusions needed to save his life. He went into a coma and died. A nurse who was on the scene said that his death "was real tough on everyone in that room." Everyone on the medical staff providing care to the patient was emotionally devastated.

To avoid tragic and traumatic situations such as this, health-care providers should be aware that Jehovah's Witnesses provide a hotline (800–255–0666) to enable the local medical staff to consult by telephone with colleagues who may suggest a modification of blood therapy treatment at no increased risk to the patient. The headquarters of Jehovah's Witnesses also has compiled a list of medical doctors who use medical alternatives to blood transfusions and to whom a patient can be transferred. There was, for example, the 1989 case of a Jehovah's Witness who had a large tumor on his spleen. Local physicians reluctantly removed it without the use of blood. But while the patient was recovering, his blood pressure fell and blood count dropped. After a second operation, he lost much blood and his hemoglobin fell well below normal. His doctors told him that he would die without a blood transfusion. But he refused. At this point, as a result of cooperation between the doctors and a committee of elders organized by the Witnesses, the patient was flown to a large medical facility where attending physicians stabilized the patient's hemoglobin, caused his blood count to improve, and released him from the hospital two weeks following the operation there (*Watchtower*, 1991).

## VALUES ISSUES

Some of the issues are: (1) Is it ethical to force an individual to live and tolerate pain, indignity, and helplessness when there is no reasonable prospect of recovery? (2) Is it permissible to allow someone to die to stop needless suffering? (3) What are the values involved in right-to-die cases?

Some arguments against the right to die are:

1.  The greatest value involved in the right-to-die issue is the sanctity of life. This is a religious teaching, yes, but it is as well the basis of our society and laws. The Fifth Amendment of the U.S. Constitution, for example, says that no person shall be deprived of life. The main reason for not allowing a person to choose death is that it violates the fundamental interest of society and the fundamental basis of our laws, which is the sanctity and preservation of life. To allow someone to die violates the principle of sanctity of life; to prevent someone from choosing death is to strengthen the regard for life and increase the value of life.

2.  The refusal of life-sustaining treatment amounts to suicide because it is a decision to do something the individual knows will result in death. In our Judeo-Christian culture, suicide is forbidden and must be prevented. It is not only a crime against God; it is a crime against nature. In many places it is a felony to commit or attempt to commit suicide. It is also morally reprehensible because it is contemptuous of life and society.

3.  Society has a legitmate interest in preserving itself, and its preservation depends on maintaining an active and productive level of population. To permit people to refuse to live involves a danger to the very existence of society by depriving it of its people.

4. When a patient is incompetent and the patient's right of refusal of life-sustaining treatment is exercised by a surrogate, there is the danger that the patient will be allowed to die even though the patient wants and fights to live. In other words, the right to die can be used as a license to murder if a surrogate or others think it is time for the patient to die.

Some of the arguments in favor of the right to die are:

1. If the right to live is protected as a fundamental human right, so should the right to die be recognized. There is no reason for seeing the right to live as forcing anyone to live.
2. One of the values society has is that cruelty should be prevented. It is cruel to force someone to suffer pain, indignity, and depression and to refuse that individual's request to die when life no longer seems worth living. To force a patient to suffer amounts to physical torture. Thus in two Florida cases—one of a dying woman whose veins were being repeatedly cut to permit continuous transfusions, the other of a man with amyotrophic lateral sclerosis whose suffering was caused by a mechanical respirator attached to his trachea—the courts said these patients had the right not to be tortured anymore.[3]
3. Another important value any democratic society has is individual freedom. What threat is there to the public safety, health, and welfare to allow people to exercise their individual freedoms and choose to die? To choose to die does not affect anyone except the individual. There is justification for interfering with individual freedom when some danger to the public is clear. It is difficult to see any danger when a person chooses to die.
4. People argue against allowing someone to die because it violates the sanctity of life. But human life is never sacred. Life always can be and is taken in our society. Killing someone in self-defense is allowed. Capital punishment is sanctioned. Killing in war and in law enforcement is accepted in the national or public interest. It is plain hypocrisy to argue that life is sacred.
5. Actual or attempted suicide at one time was a felony in England, but today there as well as in the United States suicide has been decriminalized. Virtually all modern right-to-die cases do not view the rejection of life-sustaining treatment as actual or at-

tempted suicide. Death in such cases does not result from any self-inflicted deadly injury. It results from an underlying disease that is allowed to take its natural course by the patient's decision to forgo treatment. Additionally, if life-sustaining treatment is refused by a living will, the living-will statutes of a majority of the states declare that such refusal is not to be considered a suicide.

## ECONOMIC ISSUES

When economics clash with ethics, a number of issues emerge. At the bedside level of a patient and physician, economic issues may confront patients and force them to choose to forgo life-sustaining treatment in order to spare their families financial bankruptcy caused by escalating medical expenses. But such issues should not be the concern of physicians. The physician must act in the best interest of the patient and not in the role of keeper of the budget.

At the national level, difficult economic issues confront government and health-care policymakers and hard choices must be made. The number-one issue government faces is dissatisfaction with the health-care system, whose costs have doubled in the last decade without providing access to health care for 37 million Americans who are not covered by private health insurance, group insurance, Medicare, or Medicaid and to millions more who have health insurance but not enough to cover medical costs and needs. To address the problems of spiraling health-care costs and lack of access, several proposals are advocated for the reformation of the health-care system. For example, one proposes the creation of a national plan under which employers would supply insurance for employees. A second would have states establish insured programs and risk pools for poor people. A third proposal would replace the existing pluralistic, decentralized system of health care with a universal health insurance plan administered by the federal government. The Canadian health-care system is mentioned as a model for changing the present U.S. health-care system and setting future health-care policy. Advocates of the Canadian model maintain that it offers much cheaper medical care; opponents argue that, while it may reduce the cost of health care, it also reduces access to treatment and creates long waiting lists for many facilities and procedures. Thus far there is no consensus among the rival factions.

Another significant problem for government and other policymakers is posed by the concept of distributive justice. Should the vast amount of money being expended on health care—$600 billion annually—be curbed because it is taking up a disproportionate amount of scarce national resources and preventing money from being spent on other, equally important sectors of the economy?

Within the health-care segment itself, a further problem raised by distributive justice in the context of high-cost technology to sustain lives is the allocation of resources. Policymakers must consider what phase of health care should receive the most dollars: cancer, heart disease, or perhaps preventive medical education in regard to teenage pregnancy, AIDS, drug abuse, and other health matters? Any allocation of health-care dollars makes it impossible to give everyone all the health care that is possible. It needs, therefore, to be rationed, as it is in the United Kingdom (Schwartz and Aaron, 1984). All lives, therefore, are not going to be sustained. Which will be? Should older people get all they need to prolong their lives or should they be given just comfort and pain relief? Is it a better investment for the nation to give expensive life-sustaining health care or allocate scarce resources only to infants and children whose lives are worth more than those of the elderly?

A recent study (Murphy et al., 1989) reported that, of geriatric patients who had chronic or acute diseases or with terminal arrhythmias, few survived to be discharged from hospitals after cardiac arrest and cardiopulmonary resuscitation. This kind of report suggests that cardiopulmonary resuscitation is ineffective for older patients. Many, therefore, ask: "Is it reasonable or fair to use critical-care beds, which are costly and in short supply, to provide intensive care for these patients . . . ? In this cost-conscious environment our resources must be more efficiently allocated to those who are most likely to benefit from them" (Podrid, 1989).

Cost consciousness and the clash of economics with ethics is especially evident in the Patient Self-Determination Act.[4] Various aspects of the act are taken up in Chapter 8. Since the act is part of the Omnibus Budget Reconciliation Act of 1990, one of these is clearly financial and aimed at lessening annual Medicare and Medicaid costs for expensive treatment. Ostensibly, the act motivates patients to execute advance directives. But the underlying purpose seems to be to encourage them, particularly older ones who are recipients of Medicare and Medicaid, to decline costly life-sustaining treatment, reduce provider costs, and achieve cost containment. Some critics of the legislation view the attempt to persuade people to make advance directives for financial reasons as "unethical" and "reprehensible" (La Puma, Orentlicher, and Moss, 1991:404).

## PLAYING GOD: THE FORUM

Technological developments that make artificial life supports possible signify also that we play god when we decide when or whether to use them to sustain a human life. "Playing god" does not attribute to human beings powers that belong to a divinity. Prior to the development of medical technology, we were incapable of halting the termination of life by nature and an underlying fatal condition. But with the advent of new tools, we have been given the ability to step in and block the natural course of events. Normally, this ability would be beneficial to patients. But it loses that quality when it is used to sustain life at a primitive level or used to remove the dying process, which should be an intensely intimate personal experience, from the patient and to place it in the hands of third parties. That constitutes an invasion of the greatest of all privacies.

But who is best qualified to play god? Some argue that it is the judges who should do so (Kindregan, 1977). In *Superintendent of Belchertown State School* v. *Saikewicz*,[5] the Massachusetts Supreme Court made it plain that the right forum for life and death decisions is the courts and nowhere else:

> We take a dim view of any attempt to shift the ultimate decision making responsibility away from the duly established courts of proper jurisdiction to any committee, family or group, *ad hoc* or permanent. Thus, we reject the approach . . . of entrusting the decision whether to continue artificial life supports to the party's guardian, family, attending doctors, or hospital ethics committee.

One justification for bringing life-death decisions into the courts is that such decisions may be more reliable and valid because they are the result of adversarial proceedings in which one side presents evidence in an attempt to prove facts and the other side offers evidence to disprove them. Another justification is that courts can provide a health professional who withholds or withdraws life-sustaining treatment with immunity from criminal or civil liability.

Health-care providers do not believe that judges have any special qualifications as ethicists, psychologists, and certainly not as physicians (Reiman, 1978). They are offended by judicial mistrust of the trustworthiness and ability of physicians to act as advocates in the best interests of their patients. *Saikewicz* involved a mentally retarded, terminally ill man, and the decision relates only to cases of incompetent patients unable to make their own decisions. But this fact does not lessen the impact of the decision as a call for judicial intervention when life-death decisions need to be made.

Some lawyers (Berger, 1990) take anti-lawyer and anti-court positions, also. They subscribe to the belief that life-death decisions are private and ethical, not legal. If at all possible, problems raised should be solved in a collaborative relationship among patients, families, physicians, and health-care institutions. A solution at the source of the problems is generally the most effective way of meeting the needs and wishes of the patient and family that sometimes can be thwarted in courts. When medical treatment issues are forced beyond the grass-roots level and the courts, and into the public eye, they become emotionally draining and make what should be a strictly personal choice on the part of the patient or family into a decision made by the courts and the state.

Medical cases should be solved without expense of time and money and without having to resort to lawyers and courts in costly and prolonged court battles. While courts have the undoubted jurisdiction over these cases, there are compelling reasons why they should not exercise it. One common, almost routine, type of case where jurisdiction should be avoided is that in which a hospital and physicians are in agreement with a competent patient or surrogate acting for an incompetent one that life-support should be stopped. They are in court on the advice of hospital attorneys in order to obtain legal protection from civil or criminal liability for stopping such treatment. Courts have jurisdiction when some individual right is in question, and a judicial decision is needed to resolve matters in controversy between litigants. But courts should not take cognizance of cases that are not genuine controversies so that there is no conflict between the parties. Cases in which health-care providers and patients or family members are in agreement are candidates for resolution in a private forum. When they are brought to court, the conclusion is irresistible that hospitals and physicians are trying to transfer their responsibilities to the courts.

The question of time and its effect on patients is a further problem that suggests avoiding judicial intervention. In the U.S. courtroom, rules and authority must be followed, and the law applicable to the factual situation and issues must be solemnly determined and declared. Pleadings, petitions, and lawyers' briefs must be prepared and filed. Trials or hearings must be held. Judges must listen, read, and deliberate while they search out precedents for their decisions. A case may reach the appellate level where there will be more deliberation. Whether a case takes a week, month, or even years before it is decided, the patient's dying process and suffering are prolonged to that extent. As a result, patients often die still undergoing unwanted treatment before judicial decisions are reached in their cases. Of the many examples of unfortunate cases of this kind are the death of Brother Fox, a Catholic priest, with his respirator connected;[6] Estelle M. Browning, an eighty-nine-year-old nursing-home resident who died while still being fed artificially;[7] Mary O'Connor, also a nursing-home resident who also died with the feeding tube she did not want intact;[8] and Kathleen Farrell who, in her thirties, had Lou Gehrig's disease and died before her unwanted respirator could be disconnected.[9] And in those cases where the legal system attempts to operate rapidly, as when a judge goes to a hospital to question a patient, judicial intervention is suspect because all the things that give the legal system its strength—the eliciting of facts and issues, the adversarial process presenting arguments, evidence, and witnesses in the solemnity of the courtroom with a robed judge presiding, the careful deliberation before a decision—all these aspects are lacking.

Another difficulty with judicial intervention is the unreal and incomplete relationship that exists between the courts and patients. A judge does not know the patient. Families, surrogates, and physicians are able to make life-death decisions for an incompetent patient because they know the patient's current medical condition. But appellate courts—where most major decisions are made in the law of dying and death—do not and cannot know these things about a patient because the U.S. legal system does not allow it. Appellate tribunals can examine only the evidence presented in the trial court. No evidence is admitted that was not produced in the lower court. Since several months may go by between the lower court decision and the appellate court review, it is apparent that a patient's condition may become worse or better. Yet the appellate courts will not be able to base their decisions on current medical input.

Also, when a case comes to court both the basic relationship between the family and incompetent patients and the accepted logical and medical practice of recognizing the family as decision makers for the patient are disregarded. The wishes of the family either may be excluded as having no probative value[10] or a stranger may displace the family as a decision-making surrogate no matter how loving and capable the family. Thus in the case of critically ill two-month-old Rebecca Muller, "from the moment Rebecca's case was brought to court, her parents were legally disqualified as decision makers on her behalf, and an attorney appointed in their place" (Lutz, 1990:32).

While some courts have reconfirmed *Saikewicz*,[11] a number of other courts have begun to recognize that they should not always intervene. In *In re Jobes*[12] where a nursing home rejected a distraught family's request to discontinue the tubal feeding of their thirty-two-year-old daughter who had been in a permanently unconscious state for seven years, the court ordered stoppage of the feeding and said: "Courts are not the proper place to resolve the agonizing personal problems that underlie these cases. Our legal system cannot replace the more intimate struggle that must be borne by the patient, those caring for the patient, and those who care about the patient." In the *Quinlan* case, the New Jersey Supreme Court gave further reasons for keeping life-death decisions out of the courts: "We consider that a practice of applying to a court to confirm said decisions would generally be inappropriate, not only because that would be a gratuitous encroachment upon the medical profession's field of competence, but because it would generally be cumbersome."[13]

Even the important recent decision by the U.S. Supreme Court in *Cruzan* v. *Director, Missouri Department of Health*[14] has not so affected medical practice as to require prior court approval for medical treatment decisions made in a private forum. Yet many physicians believe they need judicial approval before they stop life support to which objections are made by a patient or family because they "are often given very conservative legal advice by the attorney(s) working for their hospitals" (Weir and Gostin, 1990:1846). The duty of the attorneys is to guard the interests of the hospital and, although their advice that only courts can provide protection is correct, it is not altogether forthcoming on how minute the risk of criminal or civil liability is in cases of withholding or withdrawing life supports. As one observer noted, "physicians should know at least enough law to be able to tell when the advice their lawyers are giving them is so incredible that it is most likely to be wrong" (Annas, 1982).

Much can be done by the legal and medical professions to encourage private treatment decisions and reduce resorting to the courts. Attorneys have the opportunity to apprise people of their rights and to urge them to make individual choices about medical treatment in the form of written advance directives or through the selection of a surrogate to make health-care decisions if clients are no longer competent to make them. Physicians have the opportunity to make judicial intervention unnecessary and private decision making more probable by initiating talks with patients about their conditions and the life-sustaining treatments they may need, and then pressing upon them the desirability of making written advance directives on which physicians can rely instead of oral statements by patients simply declining life-supports that some court decisions render of doubtful value.[15] Medical associations, bar associations, and health-care institutions should be urged also to assume a leadership role by establishing programs to educate the general public.

## AVOIDANCE OF LITIGATION: ETHICAL AND LEGAL CONCERNS OF HEALTH-CARE PROVIDERS

Technological advances have changed the thinking and expectations of physicians. There was a time a few decades ago when physicians could do no more than treat symptoms, inject morphine, and give oxygen. They would tell their patients "There is nothing more I or medicine can do for you." But today new devices, machines, and procedures have expanded the therapeutic arsenal. With these weapons, the patients to whom a doctor says, "There is no more I can do" become fewer and fewer. Medical technology prevents a number of physicians from doing nothing for a patient, gives them all sorts of weapons to use to be aggressive in treatment, and makes it difficult to accept a patient's rejection of treatment and easy to play god. Because the duty "to do what is best for the patient can be clouded easily by doing what is 'technically possible' . . . there is a general impression that . . . patients do not die with dignity, having their wishes honored" (Chuang, 1991:11). As dramatized in Malcolm's story of Emily Bauer (Malcolm, 1987) and in the *Right to Die* movie, the attending physician, doing what was "technically possible," refused to honor her wishes and would not disconnect her respirator. Generally, when doctors such as this one play god and refuse to heed their patient's choices, our litigious society knows only one way out of the clash: Go to court.

This unfortunate outcome can be prevented sometimes if, in the event of a conflict between patient and physician, both make an effort to reconcile their differences in consultation with family members or in consultation with the nurses, social workers, and clergy who make up the health-care delivery team. Although hospital ethics committees generally do not make case-by-case decisions, it may be possible to bring the conflict before such a committee for an out-of-court resolution that will avoid litigation.

The following discussion, centered in this section on the perspectives of the medical team and in the next on what we can expect patients to do in the 1990s and beyond, is aimed at making reconciliation possible and recourse to the courts—well-known mousetraps easy to enter but hard to exit—less probable.

When we speak of ethical considerations, we must consider the integrity and values of the medical profession. Health-care providers see their patients' decisions as wrong when they seem to go against the providers' value systems. These systems assume that when health providers give patients the care they think patients should have, they are doing the right thing for patients. What are the concerns and obstacles that providers see when a patient refuses life-sustaining medical treatment or wants it withdrawn?

The doctor who refused to honor Emily Bauer's wishes probably feared civil liability. This fear, generated by the prospect of stopping or not starting life-sustaining treatment, "often interferes with the physician's ability to make the best choice for the patient" (Wanzer et al., 1985:8) and may prevent acceptance of a patient's wishes and force continuation of life-sustaining treatment. Simple procedures, however, may forestall litigation. As David Schapira, chief of a cancer prevention program at a large hospital in Florida, wrote: "If the conversation with and the wishes of the patient and family are documented in the hospital records, it is extremely unlikely that a physician will be sued." In his opinion, "the fear of litigation following the withholding of life support is grossly exaggerated by physicians" (1990:8).

Civil liability is one thing, but criminal prosecution is another. Another obstacle to stopping life-sustaining therapy already started even if refused by a hopelessly ill competent patient or the family of an incompetent one is both the concern and the belief that stopping treatment is a crime—either murder or aiding or abetting a suicide. There is no denying that there was some justification for exaggeration of the medical community's fear of criminal liability for withdrawing life support when, in 1983 in California, murder charges were brought against a surgeon and internist for hastening the death of a patient in a deep coma. The physicians had acted pursuant to a family's written request and removed artificially delivered nutrition and hydration from the patient who died subsequently. However, the charges were dismissed by an appellate court because the facts did not constitute murder. In this first case to deal with homicide charges against doctors for withdrawing life support and with an end of life issue with which the law of dying and death deals, the court sided with the physicians.[16] Other cases as well that have considered the question of civil or criminal liability likewise have stated that there will be none for physicians or hospitals if they act in good faith.[17] Nor does the withdrawal of life-sustaining treatment constitute aiding or abetting a suicide. The great weight of judicial authority holds that the refusal of treatment by patients even when death will ensue without it cannot be denounced as a suicide or attempted suicide. It is generally recognized that patients rejecting treatment may not have a specific intent to die and that they do not set into motion the death producing agent—that is, the underlying disease or condition. They die from their particular underlying disease or other medical problem and not from the act of stopping therapy that simply allows death to occur from whatever dictated the therapy initially. Since there is no suicide or attempted suicide, physicians who act in accordance with the patient's request cannot be guilty of aiding or abetting it. As the realization grows that courts seem ready to protect physicians, more and more doctors are concluding that they "do not need to fear civil or criminal liability for discontinuing life-sustaining treatment" (Weir and Gostin, 1990:1852). As the spectre of legal liability diminishes, litigation arising out of a physician's insistence on going on with unwanted life supports should diminish as well.

But Emily Bauer's physician may also have been concerned with maintaining his ethical duty to do everything to extend human life. A reluctance to withhold or withdraw life-sustaining treatment may be motivated by a medical staff's belief that extension of life is the clear obligation of the medical profession. A devil's advocate, however, would also bring to our attention that continuing to treat patients even against their wills and to use expensive technology are essential to the entire medical economy. It keeps hospital beds filled, nurses and hospital employees at work, medical supply houses operating; it pays for equipment, augments the personal income and wealth of physicians, and so on. But a more serious objection is that the value system that drives the practitioner to extend life does not take the qualitative aspect of life into account. The English legal scholar Glanville Williams (1978:232,233) argues that doctors and nurses see life as a physical phenomenon only; they ought to consider the quality of life as well. For the dying patient, quality of life signifies *real* life—life that is enjoyable, useful, with hope. It does not mean life that is hopeless, painful, and without dignity. If physicians were less interested in the quantitative extension of the life of the patient and more interested in the qualitative life of the patient, their object might be to make the remaining life as rich and comfortable as possible, not to extend it. They might also realize that the best way they can serve their patients is to accept the patient's request for withholding or withdrawing treatment. If they come to this conclusion, withholding or withdrawing life support would be ethically legitimate.

The medical profession has to realize that allowing hopelessly ill patients to die does not threaten medical ethics. These ethics do not force physicians and nurses to prolong life at all costs. There is a distinction between curing the sick and simply comforting and easing the dying. It is legitimate for doctors and nurses to refuse to treat the curable as if they were dying. It is also legitimate that they should refuse to treat the hopeless and dying as if they were curable.

Assuming that all the medical staff's values were valid, there is now the question of whose priorities should govern. In Emily Bauer's case, there was no shared decision making. The hospital and attending physician allowed their own ethical, social, and religious priorities to influence their refusal of her request to disconnect the respirator. But shared medical decisions require that, once patients have been provided with adequate information and have made a rational decision, great weight be given to their hopes and values and their feelings that life is too burdensome for them. Weight must also be given to any perception they may have of themselves as a family burden and to their legitimate concern that the soaring cost of medical technology may crush the resources of the family. Medical decisions are not shaped by what the heath-care delivery team thinks best for the patient or by whether the team believes a patient's point of view wrong. Nor are they shaped by the specter of a malpractice lawsuit that haunts all physicians. They are not even shaped by court opinions about common law or constitutional rights to refuse treatment. They are—and should be—shaped by the patients' freedoms, needs, and judgments. Respecting these freedoms would reduce claims and conflicts with hospitals and physicians and sound the last trumpet for the litigation process. Before making any decision on religious or ethical grounds in the sphere of life-sustaining treatment, one should go to the bedside of the patient concerned and become familiar with the patient's prognosis and general condition. Then the person should ask: "What does the patient want in this situation?" We have the obligation to find out and protect the patient's needs and wishes, and they should be uppermost when making a judgment.

The doctor who refused Emily Bauer may have been confused about the ethics of discontinuing the respirator she did not want. It is common for health-care providers to think that once respirators or other life-sustaining treatments have been initiated, they cannot ethically be stopped. For all physicians committed absolutely to the prolongation of a patient's life and who will not withdraw life-sustaining treatment in defiance of a patient's or surrogate's wishes, the consequence may be a civil suit in damages. For example, the Ohio Court of Appeals sustained a lawsuit against the Akron Medical Center and physicians brought by the estate of a woman who, like Emily Bauer, had amyotrophic lateral sclerosis and had been placed on a respirator against her express wishes. The actions of the hospital and physicians constituted a battery and, since there was no medical emergency, they would be liable to the estate for the pain, suffering, and mental anguish caused to the patient and her family.[18] This case dealt with the refusal to remove an unwanted respirator from a living patient. Although it strains credulity, a refusal to remove a respirator from a brain-dead patient occurred in another case where a hospital and physicians rejected the demand of parents that a respirator be removed from their brain-dead son and that his body be turned over to them. The hospital and physicians were sued for the tort of outrage and held liable for emotional distress damages suffered by the parents.[19]

Besides inviting litigation, a refusal to discontinue life support on the ground of ethics may be misguided if the treatment proves to be an ineffective way to improve a patient's condition. The President's Commission said: "If a trial of a therapy makes clear that it is not helpful to a patient, this is actual evidence (rather than surmise) to support stopping because the therapeutic benefit that earlier was a benefit has been found to be clearly unobtainable" (1983:76). In other words, under such circumstances, withdrawing treatment is ethically justifiable.

There is also a distinction made by some members of the medical community between withholding therapy and withdrawing it and the belief that withdrawing treatment once begun exposes the practitioner to a greater risk of legal liability. But the distinction is groundless. "Nothing in law—certainly not in the context of the doctor-patient relationship—," said the President's Commission, "makes stopping treatment a more serious issue than not starting treatment. In fact, not starting treatment that might be in the patient's best interest is more likely to be held a civil or criminal wrong than stopping treatment which it has proved unavailing" (1983:77). In any case, concern over civil liability or prosecution for a crime should not override the wishes of a patient or family or humane treatment. Schapira's admonition seems well worth following: "In spite of legal uncertainties, appropriate and compassionate care should have priority over undue fear of liability" (1990:8). Nor should concern over the ethics of stopping treatment be permitted to override the wishes of patient or family or stand in the way of such care. It is noteworthy that, in a major opinion, the American Medical Association's Council on Ethical and Judicial Affairs issued a statement on March 15, 1986, to the effect that it is not unethical to discontinue all life-sustaining treatment for patients who are permanently unconscious or dying if discontinuance is what these patients want.

Concerns over their mission or policies on the part of health-care facilities may create another clash with patients. Hospitals or nursing homes may refuse to carry out patients' wishes to decline life-sustaining treatment on the grounds that they contradict the institution's religious or moral convictions.

Since these clashes, similar to the one between Emily Bauer and her physician and hospital, are on an inevitable collision course with the courts, it seems profitable to consider whether they can be reduced or eliminated and litigation prevented. The questions in this context are: (1) Whose interests should prevail? (2) Can recalcitrant health-care providers be required by a court to accede to a patient's wishes? (3) If not, what is the alternative? In *Bartling* v. *Superior Court*,[20] a hospital, described as "Christian, pro-life oriented," refused to disconnect a respirator in spite of the written requests of a seventy-year-old competent patient and his wife and, in fact, placed restraints on his wrists to prevent his attempts at removing the respirator himself. The court decided that "if the right of the patient is to have any meaning at all, it must be paramount to the interests of the patient's hospital and doctors." The patient's right to refuse treatment could not be abridged and transcends the ethical, moral, philosophical, and religious beliefs or objections of a church-operated or private facility.

But it is not the facility that must actually attend and furnish treatment for a patient; it is the physicians and nurses. In most cases, no court should force them to provide treatment that violates their personal beliefs (President's Commission, 1982:48). The patient should be transferred to an alternative facility. But where there can be no transfer, or other doctors could not be found as in Bartling's case, or if a patient feels so close to the "familiar surroundings and the familiar people" in a hospital that she would be devastated by a transfer to different surroundings in another,[21] some state courts will order private hospitals[22] and nursing homes[23] to comply with the patient's wishes and to care for the patient until death. Publicly-owned hospitals, as arms of the federal, state, or municipal governments that operate them, would not appear to be entitled to adopt religious or partisan policies that contravene patients' rights.[24] Adverse state and federal court rulings such as these suggest that private and public health-care institutions should seriously reconsider interfering with patients' rights because of the philosophies and values of the institution.

## AVOIDANCE OF LITIGATION: PRACTICAL STEPS BY PATIENTS

By recognizing that their ethical and legal fears are exaggerated, getting their priorities straight and correcting some fallacious beliefs, practitioners can do much to reduce the likelihood of cases against them coming to court. For their part, potential patients can take a couple of simple but essential practical steps to make medical decision making at the grass-roots and not the judicial level more probable.

On the basis of what has been happening in the 1990s to the growing consumer movement, physicians should be on guard, ready for patients to take these steps. Consumer protection laws have been passed to protect the rights of consumers. Health issues similarly have alerted consumers to the potentially injurious or fatal use of tobacco or devices such as the intrauterine device as well as against incompetent health-care professionals. In September 1988, for example, the U.S. Department of Health established a data bank to include information on physicians, nurses, and dentists against whom disciplinary action had been taken.

As health issues continue to grow, we should not be surprised to find guidelines to protect patients and to help them evaluate and select physicians to whom they entrust their lives and pay the high cost of medical services. Future patients will no longer take the first doctor to come along but will make careful selections based on several criteria. Among these will probably be:

1. *Referrals.* Teaching hospitals or other health care professionals may be consulted for recommended physicians. Most hospitals have referral services. Friends and family may also be valuable referral sources.

2. *Education and specialty.* Inquiries will then be made into the backgrounds and competence of physicians who are recommended. Specialty guides are provided for physicians listed in the yellow pages of telephone directories, but more serious patients will want to refer to other directories, such as the *American Medical Association Directory*, which provides data concerning the medical school from which a physician graduated, the year of licensing, the physician's primary and secondary specialties, type of practice and any recognition awards.

3. *Fees and services.* Questions might include: What are the fees for services? Is the health insurance policy carried by the patient acceptable to the physician? Will the physician accept the amount paid by Medicare or Medicaid as the full amount expected to be paid?

4. *Accessibility.* Is the physician's office located conveniently to the patient's residence? What are the physician's office hours and will the doctor be available after these hours? If the doctor practices alone, is another doctor on call who will cover? If the doctor is in group practice, will backup coverage be provided by the partners?

5. *Hospitals*. If a special full-service hospital is favored by a patient either because it is convenient or is known to the patient, does the physician have admitting privileges there?

Neither the book by Malcolm nor the *Right to Die* movie showed us clearly how Emily Bauer came to choose her doctor. She did not, however, seem to have used the same care in selecting him as she did in selecting a new car. Perhaps she did use these five foregoing criteria to select him, but she apparently omitted a sixth criterion—the one test of selection that, of all, must be applied: Is the physician one with whom a patient can identify and form a close, compassionate, and trusting relationship?

The Emily Bauers of tomorrow will need to apply this last test in order to avoid the traumas caused by the clash with the physician and a refusal to honor patient wishes. After they have consulted professional medical directories concerning a recommended doctor, looked at the licenses, certificates, and diplomas on the physician's wall, checked with the nurses or office receptionist about fees, services, accessibility, and hospitals, on the first visit to the doctor potential patients must also check on a physician's feelings and attitudes as a human being in order to find one who is *simpático*. One should be satisfied to find a doctor with whom one is comfortable and who one is confident will understand and carry out one's wishes concerning medical treatment. During the initial appointment, besides recapitulating one's medical history for the physician, one should question the practitioner. Will the physician be candid and truthful if the patient has a bleak prognosis and if the patient wants to know? If the patient has a specific illness, what courses of action will be followed and what situations can be anticipated? Will the physician comply with the provisions of the patient's living will? Are the provisions clear and definite enough for the physician? Will the physician deal with a surrogate and accept the surrogate's health-care decisions? Will the physician comply with the patient's refusal of artificial feeding or cardiopulmonary resuscitation? With the patient's request for pain control and comfort?

Every patient must give forethought to the possibility of a serious illness and to the fact that a patient's right to die, like an embryo, begins to develop and take form in the union between a patient and physician who are compatible. A sympathetic and understanding physician-patient relationship is a condition precedent to a private decision by patient and family to forgo life support that will be respected by the physician.

The present health-care system, however, has made it difficult to create this kind of relationship. There was a time when the health-care professional was a compassionate, caring, listening, and touching person. There was the familiar bedside manner that may have been a kind of psychotherapy that created a "transference" by which the patient attributed to the physician attributes of protector and healer. With medical progress, this relationship has been altered and the old bedside manner has gone. Now the primary-care physician has become a channel through whom patients are sent to secondary-care physicians—specialists who have no relationship with the patients or awareness of their feelings and hopes as individuals. It is no longer a one-on-one doctor-patient relationship; it is a relationship of one patient to a team of doctors—in reality, no relationship at all.

In spite of these problems, future patients, looking ahead to the time when decisions may have to be made to sustain or terminate their lives, will try to search for that physician willing to restore the old bedside manner to the physician-patient relationship. To have faith in a doctor's ability to cure is not only key to greatly increasing one's chances of survival and recovery; to have faith that a warm and understanding physician will respect one's autonomy is also essential to ensure that the inchoate right to die will be perfected without any need to have recourse to litigation.

Self-interest should also motivate physicians to try to help future patients rediscover the bedside manner. The breakdown in the formerly close physician-patient relation has led to patient dissatisfaction, distrust, and lawsuits for negligence and malpractice. It has also led to patients' difficulty in understanding the values and attitudes of physicians and physicians' difficulty in understanding the feelings and wishes of patients whether to accept or reject treatment. A return to the bedside manner can only improve matters for both patients and their doctors.

The importance of a good relationship between a health-care facility and the patient is no less than that between a physician and patient. So the patient with forethought also will be careful to seek out a health-care facility whose philosophy will not conflict with the patient's wishes. Before entering a hospital or nursing home, therefore, patients will very likely request the institution's policy or mission statements regarding removal of life supports to be sure that they are compatible with the wishes of the patient, should he or she want to refuse life-sustaining treatment.

The Emily Bauer story told in Malcolm's book and the *Right to Die* movie demonstrated what resourceful patients and families can and should do when they want to have their medical decisions respected but discover that their values and interests and those of their physicians diverge and that their decisions are not being honored. They can take a second practical step. They can free themselves by discharging recalcitrant physicians unwilling to honor their wishes and by finding others who are understanding and supportive. If hospitals are uncooperative, patients can move, or the families of incompetent ones can transfer them, to hospitals elsewhere in the state or out of state, where patients' or families' decisions will be respected. It is always surprising that most people don't seem to realize that they have these powers. If patients are competent, they can fire their doctors and find others. In Emily Bauer's story, after the physician and hospital refused to disconnect her respirator, she did exactly that: left the hospital and went home to find the kind of physician she should have chosen in the first place. There her family and friends gave her a going away party and took their tearful leave of her. Her new doctor gave her an injection to make her unconscious, disconnected the respirator, and she died. If a patient is incompetent, the family or legal guardian can seek legal authority to take similar steps. In the case of *In re Quinlan,*[25] after the doctors and hospital also refused to disconnect a woman's respirator, the patient's father, as her guardian, was authorized by the court to find another physician. Just as with hiring the right physician at the start or entering the right hospital, the right to die can depend on firing the wrong doctor or leaving the wrong hospital. Similarly, with the wrong physician no longer in attendance or the patient taken out of the wrong hospital, a patient's decision to be allowed to die will be made at the grass-roots level without vexatious litigation.

## LEGAL CITATIONS

1. Brophy v. New England Sinai Hospital, 398 Mass. 417, 497 N.E. 2d 626 (Mass. Sup. Jud. Ct. 1986).

2. In re Quinlan, 70 N.J. 10, 355 A. 2d 647 (N.J. Sup. Ct.), *cert. den. sub. nom.* In re Garger v. New Jersey, 429 U.S. 922 (1976).

3. Palm Springs General Hospital v. Martinez, No. 71–12687 (Fla. Cir. Ct. July 2, 1971); Satz v. Perlmutter, 362 S.2d 160, *aff'd* 379 S.2d 359 (Fla. Sup. Ct. 1980).

4. Omnibus Reconciliation Act of 1990. Title IV. Public Law 101–508. Section 4206.

5. 373 Mass. 728, 370 N.E.2d 417 (Mass. Sup. Jud. Ct. 1977).

6. Soper v. Storar and Eichner v. Dillon, 52 N.Y.2d 363, 420 N.E.2d 64 (N.Y. Ct. of App. 1981).

7. In re Guardianship of Estelle M. Browning, 543 S.2d 258, *aff'd* 568 S.2d 4 (Fla. Sup. Ct. 1990).

8. In re O'Connor, 72 N.Y.2d 517, 531 N.E.2d 607 (N.Y. Ct. of App. 1988).

9. In re Farrell, 108 N.J. 335, 229 A.2d 1104 (N.J. Sup. Ct. 1987).

10. Cruzan v. Director, Missouri Department of Health, 497 U.S. 261, 111 L.Ed. 2d 224, 110 S.Ct. 841 (1990)

11. In re Spring, 380 Mass. 629, 405 N.E. 2d 115 (Mass. Sup. Jud. Ct. 1980).

12. 529 A.2d 434 (N.J. Sup. Ct. 1987).

13. In re Quinlan, see *supra*, note 2.

14. See *supra*, note 10.

15. In re O'Connor, see *supra*, note 8; Soper v. Storar, see *supra*, note 6; Cruzan v. Director, Missouri Department of Health, see *supra*, note 10.

16. Barber v. Superior Court, 147 Cal. App. 3rd 1006, 195 Cal. Rptr. 484 (Calif. Ct. of App., 2nd Dis., 1983).

17. John F. Kennedy Memorial Hospital v. Bludworth, 452 S.2d 921 (Fla. Sup. Ct. 1984).

18. Leach v. Shapiro, 13 Ohio App. 3d 393, 469 N.E.2d 1047 (Ohio Ct. App. Summit Co. 1984).

19. Strachan v. John F. Kennedy Memorial Hospital, 209 N.J. Super. Ct. 300, 507 A.2d 718, *aff'd* in part, *rev.* in part, 109 N.J. 523, 538 A.2d 346 (N.J. Sup. Ct. 1988).

20. 163 Cal. App. 3rd 186, 209 Cal. Rptr. 220 (Calif. Ct. App. Rptr. 1984).

21. In re Requena, 213 N.J. Super. Ct. 475, 517 A.2d 886, *aff'd* 213 N.J. Super. Ct. 443, 517 A.2d 869 (N.J. Sup. Ct., App. Div., 1986).

22. In re Requena, see *supra*, note 21; Gray v. Romeo, 697 F. Supp. 580 (U.S. Dist. Ct. D. R.I. 1988).

23. In re Jobes, see *supra*, note 12.

24. Hathaway v. Worcester City Hospital, 475 F.2d 701 (First Circuit 1973)

25. See *supra*, note 2.


## REFERENCES

Annas, G. J. 1982. "Reconciling Quinlan and Saikewicz: Decision Making for the Terminally Ill Incompetent." In A. E. Doudera and J. D. Peters, eds. *Legal and Ethical Aspects of Treating Critically and Terminally Ill Patients*. Ann Arbor: AUPHA Press, 28–62.

Berger, A. S. 1990. "Last Rights: The View from a U.S. Courthouse." In A. S. Berger and J. Berger, eds. *To Die or Not to Die?: Cross-Disciplinary, Cultural and Legal Perspectives on the Right to Choose Death*. New York: Praeger, 129–51.

Chuang, M. 1991. "A Nurse's Perspective of Bioethics." *The Record* November 43 (10):11.

Kindregan, C. P. 1977. "The Court as a Forum for Life-Death Decisions: Reflections on Procedures for Substituted Consent." *Suffolk University Law Review* 11 (4): 919–35.

La Puma, J., Orentlicher, D., and Moss, R. J. 1991. "Advance Directives on Admission: Clinical Implications and Analysis of the Patient Self-Determination Act of 1990." *Journal of the American Medical Association* 266:402–405.

Lutz, H. 1990. "Ethical Perspectives on the Right to Die: A Case Study." In A. S. Berger and J. Berger, eds., *op. cit.* 25–39.

Malcolm, A. H. 1987. *This Far and No More*. New York: Times Books.

McCartney, J. J. 1990. "Perspectives from the Catholic and Jewish Traditions." In A. S. Berger and J. Berger, eds., *op. cit.* 13–24.

Murphy, D. J., Murray, A. M., Robinson, B. E., and Campion, E. W. 1989. "Outcomes of Cardiopulmonary Resuscitation in the Elderly." *Annals of Internal Medicine* 111:199–205.

Podrid, P. J. 1989. "Resuscitation in the Elderly: A Blessing or a Curse." *Annals of Internal Medicine* 111:193–95.

President's Commission for the Study of Ethical Problems in Medicine and Biomedicine and Behavioral Research. 1983. *Deciding to Forgo Life-Sustaining Treatment.* Washington, DC: Government Printing Office.

————. 1982. *Making Health Care Decisions: A Report on the Ethical and Legal Implications of Informed Consent in the Patient-Practitioner Relationship.* Washington, DC: Government Printing Office.

Reiman, A. 1978. "The Saikewicz Decision: Judges as Physicians." *New England Journal of Medicine* 298:508.

Rosner, F. 1986. *Modern Medicine and Jewish Ethics.* Hoboken, NJ: KTAV Publishing House and New York: Yeshiva University Press.

Schapira, D. V. 1990. "The Right to Die: Perspectives of the Patient, Family and Health Care Provider." In A. S. Berger and J. Berger, eds., *op. cit.*, 3–11.

Schwartz, W., and Aaron, H. 1984. "Rationing Hospital Care: Lessons from Britain." *New England Journal of Medicine* 310:52–56.

Scully, T., and Scully, C. 1987. *Playing God: The New World of Medical Choices.* New York: Simon and Schuster.

Wanzer, S. H., Adelstein, S. J., Cranford, R. E., Federman, D. D., Hook, E. D., Moertel, C. G., Safar, P., Stone, A., Taussig, H. B., and Van Eys, J. 1985. "The Physician's Responsibility Toward Hopelessly Ill Patients." In *The Physician and the Hopelessly Ill Patient.* New York: Society for the Right to Die.

Weir, R. F., and Gostin, L. 1990. "Decisions to Abate Life-Sustaining Treatment for Nonautonomous Patients: Ethical Standards and Legal Liability for Physicians After *Cruzan.*" *Journal of the American Medical Association* 2264:1846–53.

*Watchtower.* 1991. "Doctor-Patient Communication: A Key to Success." March 8, 12–13.

Williams, G. 1978. "Euthanasia Legislation: A Rejoinder to Nonreligious Objections." In T. Beauchamp and S. Perlin, eds. *Ethical Issues in Death and Dying.* Englewood Cliffs, NJ: Prentice-Hall.

# 6

## The Last Resort

The creation of legal issues has been a product of the ability of medical miracles to maintain life in a twilight zone. Ideally, all settlements of differences in medical situations and medical decisions should be made in a collaborative relationship among patient, family, and physician. As a forum for such decisions, courts are a last resort.

Yet they are the most important. For above and beyond every other in our society, the judicial system has played the supreme role as resolvers of disputes between patients and hospitals or physicians. Judges, not physicians, ethicists, or clergy, are the decision makers. It is their case law, and their explication and application of the law of dying and death to the issues raised by cases, that patients and health professionals depend on for guidance. An understanding of this law may prove helpful to physicians and hospitals and for the seriously ill patients under their care. It also may point up uncertainties in clinical practice. A further understanding of the U.S. legal process is essential, and so Part VII considers the court system, the procedure followed in a civil case, and how to find the law. Here, however, we deal with when courts become the forum and with the case law they have developed in relation to life-sustaining treatment.

### WHEN COURTS DECIDE MEDICAL ISSUES

Basically, six types of situations within the sphere of life-sustaining treatment can be identified as occasions for judicial intervention for the purpose of deciding medical cases:

1. A judicial decision may be needed concerning prospective treatment for an incompetent patient. A court's intervention may be requested by a surrogate who wishes to withhold or withdraw life-sustaining treatment, or it may be sought by a hospital or physicians who challenge the decision of the surrogate.

2. Courts may be called upon to become arbiters in a situation involving a dispute between a hospital or physician and a competent patient over medical treatment. Health-care providers may ask a court to deny the patient's request to terminate life-sustaining treatment because of some state interest, such as the preservation of life or the ethics of the medical profession.

3. Physicians or hospitals may fear legal liability or be unsure of the law if they withhold or withdraw medical treatment from a patient, whether competent or incompetent. They may come to court because they want legal protection or immunity before not starting or stopping treatment.

4. A claim may be made against a physician or hospital for civil liability for damages. The claim may be for a battery—as when a patient is placed or kept on a life-support system against the patient's wishes—or for malpractice because what was done to or not done for a patient did not conform to the degree of care ordinarily exercised by physicians or nurses with similar education and training.

5. The withdrawal or withholding of life-sustaining treatment may involve criminal proceedings in which physicians are prosecuted for homicide or for aiding or abetting a suicide.

6. When a legal guardian must be appointed, the courts give authority to someone to make special treatment decisions for a patient unable to make his or her own.

## RELIGIOUS BELIEFS

Religious beliefs have had an impact upon the courts. Up until 1976, when the *Quinlan* case[1] was decided, there were few right-to-die cases. The pre-1976 cases in which patients refused life-sustaining treatment involved religious beliefs, especially of Jehovah's Witnesses. The legal questions in these cases were: (1) When a Witness on religious grounds refuses a blood transfusion even if it means death, is a court authorized to step in and decide for the Witness? (2) Do people have a right to die for their religious beliefs?

In these cases, the important clause of the U.S. Constitution was the First Amendment that provides that "Congress shall make no law . . . prohibiting the free exercise" of religion. This provision is made applicable to the states by the Fourteenth Amendment. So in the well-known case of *In re Brooks*,[2] where a Jehovah's Witness without minor children refused a blood transfusion although doctors thought it was urgent to allow her to recover from a peptic ulcer, the court decided it could not interfere, notwithstanding its belief that the woman's decision was "foolish and unwise." The First Amendment conferred the right to exercise religious beliefs, and since there was no threat to the morals, welfare, or health of society and no minor children involved, there was no ground for judicial intervention. In these cases of childless adults, the free-exercise clause of the U.S. Constitution is unqualified, admits no exceptions, and is the basis for the right to die. How unqualified is this clause in cases of adults with children?

J. Luther Pierson had a daughter less than two years old who contracted whooping cough in January. By February 20, the cough had developed into pneumonia. The child's symptoms were dangerous, but the father believed in divine healing and, because of his religious faith, believed that the child would get well by prayer. The child died on February 23 and Pierson was prosecuted and charged under the New York Penal Law with willfully omitting to perform a duty imposed by law to furnish medical attendance for his infant child.[3] Pierson claimed his constitutional right to freedom of religion. The prosecution of the father tested the strength of the free-exercise clause and raised the constitutional issue of whether the right to exercise religious beliefs is absolute. If it is, then, in spite of a tragedy such as occurred in the *Pierson* case, a parent can stand on these beliefs and justify preventing medical treatment for a child.

The court in the case held that a parent under the guise of religious beliefs cannot be relieved of the care of children. The holding shows that there are limitations on the right to exercise religious beliefs. It is not absolute when state interests are endangered. Each case must be determined according to whether the exercise of religion threatens these interests. In cases where children are involved, such as when a parent supplies religious literature to a child to sell in violation of a statute[4] or where the religious beliefs of parents prevent a child from receiving medical treatment, as in the *Pierson* case, the interest of society to protect children and the state, as *parens patriae* (i.e., "father of the country"), and legal guardian and protector of children and incompetents, infringes the religious rights of parents.

The *Pierson* case was decided in 1903, yet the issue of whether the state can infringe the religious rights of parents keeps appearing.

Generally it arises today when Christian Science parents who believe, as did Pierson, that prayer can cure sickness, do not get medical treatment for their children who die as a result. In the last ten years, there have been eleven prosecutions for involuntary manslaughter and convictions of parents who relied on spiritual healing instead of medical healing. The lesson of *Pierson* and these other cases is that, while people have a right to die for their religious beliefs, it seems clear that children do not need to die because of their parents' religious beliefs. But may a parent with minor children and also with strong religious beliefs die because of these beliefs?

Jesse F. Jones, a twenty-five-year-old mother of a seven-month-old child, was brought to Georgetown University Hospital by her husband because she had lost two-thirds of her blood from a ruptured ulcer. She and her husband were both Jehovah's Witnesses. Blood transfusions were necessary to save her life, but both the patient and her husband refused because of their religious beliefs. A judge was asked to make a decision in the case. If you were the judge, would you rule:

- For the hospital and force Mrs. Jones to have a transfusion?
- For Mrs. Jones out of respect for her religious beliefs?

In this case, the court ordered the transfusion.[5] The reason was the same as in the *Pierson* case: the state as *parens patriae* would not allow a parent to abandon a minor child. The court would not let the mother die because death was the ultimate abandonment.

It is interesting to compare all these cases. In the case of *In re Brooks*, where a Jehovah's Witness without minor children refused a blood transfusion, the court would not order one and interfere with the decision of an adult. In the *Pierson* and *Jesse F. Jones* cases, however, there were children directly or indirectly involved. But in the *Pierson* case, the state intervened because the health of a child was directly threatened. In the *Jones* case, however, the health of a child was not threatened at all. Apparently the state in the *Jones* case intervened because of a concern about who would care financially and otherwise for the child if the mother died. Should an individual's right based on religious belief be taken away because that person is a parent? If we think that it should because the child needs financial support, what do we do if the parent is penniless, unemployable, or a homeless person? Or if, as in the case of Emily Bauer, she is terminally ill, incapable of earning money, or of caring for a child? It would not make sense to deny the parent's rights in such cases. Once the rule is applied to protect children whose health is not directly threatened, it would seem that we have to look at each case to see what sense it makes to interfere with religious liberty and deny a parent's religious rights.

## LEGAL BASES FOR REFUSAL

The Jehovah's Witness, Christian Science, and other cases in which religious beliefs are implicated continue to appear today. But because of two developments, cases of refusing life-sustaining treatment by people who assert as justification no religious beliefs have multiplied and will continue to do so. One of these developments includes medical technology capable of maintaining a species of life and of forcing unwanted treatment on patients. Between 1976 and 1988, there were over fifty of them reported—with undoubtedly a far greater number of cases in trial courts not reported—that involved, not the free-exercise clause of the U.S. Constitution and religious liberties but other guaranteed individual liberties. A second development is the soaring rate of AIDS victims—over 75,000 died world-wide of the disease in 1987, for example, and the disease is expected to continue to mow down thousands more, up to and beyond the year 2000; by 1993, AIDS is expected to be responsible for one-third of the deaths of men from 25 to 44 years of age and the main killer of women between the ages of 15 and 44 (*Wall Street Journal*, 1991). As AIDS spreads, more and more of its victims may refuse life-sustaining treatment and increasing numbers of cases involving these liberties can be expected to appear.

Typical cases of the kind that involve individual liberties other than religious beliefs would have been that of Emily Bauer and is that of Elizabeth Bouvia.

Elizabeth Bouvia was a patient in her twenties in High Desert Hospital in Los Angeles. She was not terminally ill, was intelligent, and mentally competent, but she had suffered from cerebral palsy since birth, was a quadriplegic, and because of chronic arthritis, was in pain continuously without morphine. She was physically helpless and dependent on others for all her needs, including feeding, washing, turning, and being helped with elimination and other bodily functions. To eat, she had to be spoonfed. Eventually she refused to eat because she could not swallow without nausea and vomiting. Her clear intention was to starve to death. Against her will, the hospital inserted a nasogastric feeding tube. She caused a petition to be filed for a court order to stop the tubal feeding.[6] The medical staff opposed it on the ground that the tube removal would violate medical ethics and that physicians had the right to keep a patient alive in spite of the patient's wishes to the contrary.

The Emily Bauer and Elizabeth Bouvia situations also represent one of
the several categories of patients with whom the law of dying and death
deals: they are competent adults who may or may not be terminally ill or
for whom a semblance of life is being maintained artificially. The first case
in this category to come before the courts was that of Abe Perlmutter,[7] a
seventy-three-year-old man who, like Emily Bauer, had developed Lou
Gehrig's disease. After he was hospitalized and a mechanical respirator
was attached to his trachea, he made known his suffering and his wishes
to have it removed. But the hospital staff would not disconnect the
respirator and even reattached it after Perlmutter tried to disconnect it
himself. His case and those of Emily Bauer and Elizabeth Bouvia have
common threads. One is that, although all three were adults who rejected
life-sustaining treatment with a clear understanding of their physical
conditions and with the ability to reason and make judgments, their wishes
were not respected by medical personnel. Emily Bauer was able to leave
her hospital and find a sympathetic physician who would honor her wishes.
But Perlmutter and Bouvia were forced into litigation in order to implement theirs.

All three cases ask the same question: Does a competent adult who objects
to life-sustaining treatment have the right to refuse it even if that refusal means
death? This brings us to the first nonreligious legal basis for declining such
treatment. There is no constitutional right to die given in so many words in
the U.S. Constitution but does the document grant it anyway? The case of
*Cruzan* v. *Director, Missouri Department of Health*[8] was of great importance
because the U.S. Supreme Court had never directly addressed the constitutional right of a person to refuse life-sustaining treatment. It focused national
attention on the right to die issue. With Justice Rehnquist writing the opinion
and describing the case as entailing the right to die, the majority of the Court
held that under the U.S. Constitution a competent adult has a right to refuse
life-sustaining treatment. The majority analyzed it as a "liberty interest" under
the Fourteenth Amendment that prohibits a state from arbitrarily depriving
an individual of life, liberty, or property without due process of law. In so
doing the High Court carved out of the Constitution a new interest and bent
the document to fit the times and developments in medical technology. The
due process clause becomes the first basis in the law of dying and death for
the right to die.

Physicians and lawyers alike speculate about the significance of the
*Cruzan* decision. Some obervers maintain that the case "does not alter the
laws, ethical standards and clinical practices permitting the forgoing of
life-sustaining treatment that have evolved in the United States" (Annas,
Arnold, and Aroskar, 1990). However, this evaluation seems too narrow

and overlooks the case's many ramifications. While the affirmation of the individual's right to decline medical treatment did not make any substantial alteration in existing law—for, as will be shown presently, state courts had recognized this right—it would appear to have a chilling effect on medical practice and the integrity and interests of the medical profession. The ruling by the highest court in the land that the U.S. Constitution guarantees competent patients the right to refuse life-sustaining treatment makes almost untenable the objections of physicians, hospitals, and nursing homes based on religious, ethical, or moral convictions and policies that prevent them from acceding to patient wishes to discontinue such treatment.

Aside from this affirmation, *Cruzan* was also a *cause célèbre* because a lot more was at stake than the constitutional right to decline medical treatment. Like a nuclear explosion, the case produced its fallout. Chapter 1 mentioned the case as one that removed the "horse on the dining room table syndrome" from the minds of many and brought death to life. But besides this, it forced us to take a long, hard look at whether unwanted treatment will be forced on us and who plays god with the power to decide when and how we die. It impacted upon incompetent patients and the surrogates who act for them. It spurred competent adults to make advance directives. It clarified whether artificial feeding was medical treatment that can be refused by patients. It cast the shadow of doubt over the validity of some living-will statutes. It elevated abstraction over reality and left many physicians and hospitals in doubt as to what to do in clinical situations, for it upheld the standard of "clear and convincing evidence" and undermined the general medical practice of accepting family treatment decisions for incompetent patients. The case also led to the third type of situation described earlier in this chapter, in which hospitals and physicians seek judicial intervention unnecessarily. All these effects coming in the wake of *Cruzan* will be taken up where appropriate.

Prior to the High Court's finding of a new constitutional basis for the right to forgo life-sustaining treatment, state courts had analyzed the right in different terms. They found a second legal basis for it: a "right to privacy," or what is called the right to be let alone, that the U.S. Supreme Court had recognized in 1965 in *Griswold* v. *Connecticut*.[9] Although the Constitution does not expressly confer this right either, the High Court in *Roe* v. *Wade*[10] interpreted the Fourteenth Amendment as creating it and observed that courts or individual justices had also pointed to the First, Fourth, Fifth, and Ninth amendments as its sources. This right has been construed as giving autonomy in many areas. It is really a bundle of rights, such as the right not to be spied on in our bedrooms, not to have our phone conversations listened to (at least not without a court order), or not to have our photographs used in advertising. The right of privacy also gives us the right to make intimate choices. Thus, the U.S. Supreme Court extended it to procreation decisions, such as whether to use contraception, as in *Griswold*, or to have an abortion, as in *Roe* v. *Wade*. But it had never recognized medical decisions or the right to refuse treatment as embodied in the right to privacy, nor had any state court. Therefore when, in the case of *In re Quinlan*,[11] the New Jersey Supreme Court's holding that the right to privacy is also "broad enough to encompass a patient's decision to decline medical treatment," and thereby to end a life that is no longer worth living and that had no prospect of returning to a cognitive state, was a landmark. It was the first authority for the principle in the law of dying and death that, although no right to die is given in the Constitution, it supported treatment refusal. Following *Quinlan*, the privacy right was thereafter used by many state courts as a basis for treatment refusal.

In contrast to the U.S. Constitution, which does not put the right to privacy into words, in some states the right is specifically conferred by their constitutions[12] and is interpreted by the courts of these states as even broader and stronger than the right of privacy in the U.S. Constitution and as allowing the rejection of life-sustaining treatment.[13]

While *Quinlan* influenced much of judicial opinion to base the right to refuse life support on the constitutional right of privacy, it must be noted that not only did the U.S. Supreme Court fail before *Quinlan* to include treatment refusal in the right to privacy but also that, after *Quinlan*, the majority of the U.S. Supreme Court in *Cruzan* continued to decline to extend the privacy right past the begetting of children and to such a refusal. Several state courts also have declined to use this basis. They prefer to base treatment refusal on a right long recognized by the common law: the right to self-determination.[14] An opinion by one of the judges in Elizabeth Bouvia's case describes her right to self-determination:

> Elizabeth apparently has made a conscious and informed choice that she prefers death to continued existence in her helpless and, to her, intolerable condition. I believe she has an absolute right to effectuate that decision. The state and the medical profession, instead of frustrating her desire, should be attempting to relieve her suffering. . . . The right to die is an integral part of our right to control our own destinies so long as the rights of others are not affected.[15]

The right to self-determination can also be described as the freedom each individual has to choose a lifestyle and course of action. Since the declining of life-sustaining medical treatment determines if a patient will die, it obviously "entails significant ramifications for a person's future lifestyle or condition" (Cantor, 1973:241).

Still another common-law principle has been adopted by the courts in order to support treatment refusal. Every competent individual has the right to bodily integrity and to be free from bodily invasions for which no consent has been given. If a person has the right to consent to treatment, the corollary of this doctrine is that an individual has the right not to consent—that is, to refuse medical treatment. Although some courts, such as the Missouri Supreme Court in *Cruzan*[16] and the New York Court of Appeals[17] declined to recognize the constitutional right of privacy as supporting treatment refusal, they were willing to recognize the right to refuse medical treatment under the common-law doctrine of informed consent. For them this doctrine was the exclusive authority for treatment refusal. Other courts, however, were prepared to base the right to refuse treatment on both the right of privacy and the consent doctrine.[18]

## STATE INTERESTS

From the foregoing, it would seem to be the established rule that every competent patient has unfettered constitutional and common law rights to refuse treatment. But the state sometimes will play God and assert one of its overriding interests to force patients against their wills to undergo medical treatment. These interests include preservation of life, prevention of suicide, protection of innocent third parties, and the ethics of the medical profession.[19]

There have been several cases in which courts have intervened on the grounds of the state's interest in the protection of innocent parties. One example was mentioned earlier: the protection of minor children. There are two general types of these cases in this category. One, exemplified by the *Pierson* case, is when a parent asserts a religious belief as a reason for refusing medical treatment for a child. In such a case, the state as *parens patriae* will step in to see that the child receives needed treatment in spite of the parents' religious beliefs. In the *Jones* kind of case, where a parent with a minor child refuses treatment for himself or herself, the state will intervene as well.

The state is not loath, however, to step in and force an adult patient to undergo unwanted medical treatment even when there are no minor children. The most widely cited case in this second category was decided by the New Jersey Supreme Court in *John F. Kennedy Memorial Hospital v. Heston*[20] where a twenty-two year-old unmarried woman refused a blood transfusion because she was a Jehovah's Witness. She was forced to have one anyway because of another of the state's interests: the preservation of life. But this was a 1971 case. In the course of the 1970s and 1980s, there has been great social change. The godlike authority of the state began to be challenged and individual freedom and autonomy have been emphasized. Perhaps because of this phenomenon, the state courts beginning with *Quinlan* in 1976, using one or more combinations of the legal bases described—the rights of privacy, self-determination, and informed consent—upheld the patient's autonomy and refusal of treatment.

For two decades the state was not allowed to intrude on the right to refuse treatment, and it was not forced on unwilling patients. For example, in the case of *Bouvia*, the medical staff refused to remove her feeding tube inserted in violation of her instructions because its removal would hasten her death and violate medical ethics. But this argument was overruled by the court. The ethics and interests of the medical profession would be subordinated to the patient's right of self-determination. In *Quinlan*, a respirator was disconnected as the right of privacy of an incompetent woman was allowed to overcome the state's interest in the conservation of human life. "The interest of the state weakens," said the *Quinlan* court, "and the right of the individual grows as the degree of bodily invasion increases and the prognosis dims."[21] In the New York case of *Brother Fox*, this Catholic priest in a vegetative state made it known before he became incompetent that he would not want to be maintained by a respirator. His right of self-determination was not subordinated to the state's interest in preserving life.[22] Similarly, two other cases prevented the state's intrusion on the right of treatment refusal. In a Florida case where an incompetent woman was maintained by a feeding tube, the court would not use the interest of the state in human life to override her right of self-determination to end the feeding.[23] In another New Jersey case, where the doctrine of informed consent and the right to self-determination of an elderly incompetent patient prevailed over the state's interest and tubal feeding was terminated, the court said: "On balance the right to self-determination ordinarily outweighs any countervailing state interests."[24]

But then came *Cruzan* v. *Director, Missouri Department of Health*. In the case, to be discussed at length in Chapter 7, the parents of Nancy Cruzan, a thirty-three-year-old patient in a persistent vegetative state, requested a court order to stop tube feedings. The Missouri Supreme Court ruled that the interest of the state in preserving life would be used to force the patient to be artificially maintained.[25] In order to assert the state's interest, the Missouri court adopted a "clear and convincing" standard of proof in the proceedings brought by the patient's parents to terminate artificial feeding. This placed the burden of proof on them to show their daughter's intentions regarding stoppage. They could not do so and their request for termination was denied.

On the parents' appeal, the U.S. Supreme Court granted *certiorari* and reviewed the case. Its holdings[26] both elated and discouraged patients'-rights advocates. Elation came when the majority of the court assumed that competent individuals have a constitutionally protected right to refuse life-sustaining treatment. But while competent patients can exercise this right, incompetent patients cannot do so, and for them and surrogates making decisions for them the majority's holding was a disappointment to patients'-rights supporters and a source of satisfaction to their "right to life" rivals. The U.S. Supreme Court had granted *certiorari* to review the case on the issue of whether the Constitution allowed Missouri's actions. This was the heart of the case. The majority found that the Constitution did not prevent Missouri from adopting the standard of "clear and convincing evidence" to advance its interest in preserving life and that this interest was unqualified and absolute. The High Court's holding is narrowly limited to Missouri, but it is alarming to supporters of patients' rights. It opens wide the legal door to any other state wishing to ape Missouri and to assert such an interest to prevent the parents of patients from protecting them and acting on their behalf and to deny patients what appear to be their wishes and rights to refuse treatment. As one respected authority on health law wrote: "The truth is, if the state of Missouri can inflict its will on Cruzan and her family, none of us are safe from states that wish to control our health-care decisions and our death" (Annas, 1990:672).

The holding means that the highest court in the land has given its blessing to the proposition that the state's interest in preserving life is an unchecked power to play god, and to decide whether we die or must undergo unwanted life-sustaining treatment no matter the burden and futility of life.

The Court's affirmation of Missouri's unqualified and absolute interest in protecting and preserving life is also doubly curious. It is curious first because of Missouri's statutes. Missouri statutes impose capital punishment. The state's assertion of an unqualified interest in life seems inconsistent with its invocation of the death penalty. Missouri, as do forty-five other states, also has a living-will statute that permits competent adults who are terminally ill to direct the withholding or withdrawing of life supports and to choose death over life.[27] Thus even in Missouri the interest of the state in preserving life is not unqualified and absolute. This conclusion is reinforced by fiat of the Missouri legislature, which makes the preservation of life a state interest to which the individual's right to refuse treatment is not subordinated. Section 459.055 of the Missouri living-will statute declares that "each person has the primary right to request or refuse medical treatment subject to the state's interest in protecting innocent third parties, preventing homicide and suicide and preserving good ethical standards in the medical profession." The state's interest in the preservation of life is excluded from those other state interests that might override the right of refusal.

The affirmation is also curious because it allowed Missouri simply to assert, without more, its general interest in conserving life. As Justice William Brennan, who wrote the dissent in *Cruzan* argued, the state is obliged to make a greater showing than this since it has no legitimate general interest in an individual's life completely abstracted from the interest of the individual who lives that life. The Court's affirmation seems to overlook that the state's interest is really twofold. One aspect of it is the undifferentiated interest in conserving life, and there is no doubting this aspect. All states and civilized countries demonstrate their general commitment to human life with their laws against homicide and their police forces, and a majority of states have laws against assisting suicide. But when we consider the special life of Mr. Jones or Ms. Smith, we come to another and different side of the state's interest. The question is, why should the state wish to play god in regard to the life of a particular person? Perhaps its interest may be justified and an unwilling patient kept alive if minor children are not to be abandoned, though we have questioned depriving a person of rights because of parenthood. But in the case of Nancy Cruzan, it is impossible to see any benefit or protection for innocent third parties or to society in general for a state to oppose a patient's apparent wish or the family's decision to stop life support and keep alive a childless woman in a permanent vegetative state with no hope of recovery. The *Cruzan* holding seems to suggest that on occasion judges are more concerned with abstract legal principles than with life's realities.

## ARTIFICIAL FEEDING AND THE ETHICAL ISSUES

Nancy Cruzan was maintained by a gastrostomy tube (G-tube) that provided her with nutrition and hydration. Her case gives us a springboard for looking at some of the ethical issues involved in artificial feeding. It is a timely look because, according to the American Medical Association, each day there are 10,000 patients in this country in permanently unconscious or persistent vegetative states who are maintained by artificial feeding. Anyone in the health-care field is bound to encounter these patients. It is, therefore, profitable to think about the basic ethical questions in artificial feeding: whether the family or surrogates are doing something ethical or unethical when they ask that artificial feeding be terminated when a patient is in such a state even though there is reasonable prospect that the patient can be maintained for fifteen to thirty more years.

This issue should be distinguished from the legal issue of whether the right to refuse medical treatment includes the right to refuse artificial feeding.

Various pro and con arguments have been assembled to help us consider the debated ethics of the matter and to sort out our own thoughts.

### Arguments Against Termination

One of the main arguments against termination is that without artificial sustenance a patient will starve to death. Someone starving who becomes emaciated or disfigured and who is suffering does not make a pretty picture. A dissenting opinion in *Brophy* v. *New England Sinai Hospital*,[28] described the effects to be expected of the removal of the G-tube from Paul Brophy and the lack of hydration and nutrition: his mouth would dry out; his lips would become parched and cracked; his tongue would swell; his eyes would recede into their orbits; his cheeks would become hollow; his skin would hang loose; his urine would become highly concentrated leading to burning of the bladder; his brain cells would dry out leading to convulsions; and so on. The judge said this amounts to "a particularly difficult, painful and gruesome death."

We have to assume that incompetent patients, such as Nancy Cruzan, who left no advance directions about medical treatment, want to have foods and fluids as well as beneficial medical treatment. In fact, one state has enacted a statute establishing that there is a legal presumption that incompetent patients have directed health-care professionals to provide sufficient hydration and nutrition to sustain life.[29]

Patients may be in persistent vegetative states or permanently unconscious and incompetent now to express their wishes, but they are still human beings and not "vegetables." When we use the word *vegetable,* we are dehumanizing a person and make that individual into a thing.

If tube feeding were discontinued in the case of incompetents who have left no advance directives, it amounts to killing them when they have not asked to be killed. It is also wrong to kill them and wrong of parents such as the Cruzans to ask that a child be killed because these patients may still have some hope of recovery. Some people have made a recovery from states such as Nancy Cruzan's, although the prognosis was that there was no reasonable prospect of recovery. The gastrostomy tube is effective as a means of keeping someone alive. Nancy Cruzan and others like her should be kept alive because "where there's life there's hope."

We may save medical expenses by allowing patients to die, but we all pay a greater price when we sacrifice our duty to protect life and when we allow people to die who cannot speak for themselves.

### Arguments in Favor of Termination

Some arguments in favor of termination can be divided into lay and medical opinion. A general lay argument is based on the meaning of the persistent vegetative or permanently unconscious state. The patient's body is alive, but the center of life—that which makes a person a human being—is gone. The patient has no consciousness, no capacity for reasoning, no capacity for creative or value decisions. The patient is only a "vegetable," an unconscious body, a living corpse oblivious to everything. We cannot say that the patient is a person at all. A corpse has no present interest in life or any future interests that the family or society should protect.

A second general argument is the terrible financial toll that maintaining a patient will take on the family. It is estimated that artificial feeding can maintain someone for fifteen to thirty years. Nancy Cruzan was not a burden on her family. She was a patient in a state hospital, so that the State of Missouri paid the cost of her care—$130,000 annually or almost $4 million if she had lived another thirty years. But such costs would wreck the family of a patient in a private hospital. If the state and society will not bear the cost, they have no right to dictate that the family should bear it.

Then there is the emotional toll on those who watch—seeing loved ones without the ability to eat or eliminate lose weight until they weigh less than 100 pounds. It is heartbreaking to see someone loved dehumanized in this way.

We should also consider medical opinion based on the physical state of the patient just described. Since the patient exists in that comatose state, the American Academy of Neurology believes that the patient does not experience pain or suffering and, if sustenance is withdrawn or withheld, death will be peaceful with no pain or discomfort. The picture of a painful death by starvation is therefore false. Also, in the vegetative state, the damage to the cerebral hemisphere is such that patients have lost the capacity to interact with their environment. For this reason, many physicians think that artificially supplied nutrition and hydration should be withheld from patients in that state. This is consistent with their belief that it is not appropriate, either, to attempt resuscitation, dialysis, or ventilator support in these cases.

## ARTIFICIAL FEEDING AND THE LEGAL ISSUE

For the medical profession, the artificial delivery of food and water is indistinguishable in a medical or ethical sense from other life-sustaining measures. Thus, the American Academy of Neurology states that the "artificial provision of nutrition and hydration is a form of medical treatment . . . analogous to other forms of life-sustaining treatment, such as the use of the respirator" (Position of the American Academy of Neurology, 1989). A statement of the Council on Ethical and Judicial Affairs of the American Medical Association issued on March 15, 1986 adopted a similar position: "Life-prolonging treatment includes medication and artificially or technologically supplied respiration, nutrition, or hydration." The logic of this position seems hard to assail. Artificial feeding, whether intravenously or by nasogastric tube, is the same as artificial breathing helped by a respirator. In both instances, the body is unable to carry on essential functions and in both medical devices are used to sustain life.

The federal government also looks on artificial feeding as medical treatment. It regulates feeding tubes as medical devices[30] and describes formulas used in enteral feeding as "medical foods."[31]

Likewise in the legal community, state courts generally make no distinction between artificial feeding and other medical treatment. As was said in *Delio* v. *Westchester County Medical Center*, where the wife of a thirty-three-year-old patient in a chronic vegetative state requested discontinuance of feeding tubes:

> In our review of the decisions of other jurisdictions, we have failed to uncover a single case in which a court confronted with an application to discontinue feeding by artificial means has evaluated medical procedures to provide nutrition and hydration differently from other types of life-sustaining procedures.[32]

In the *Cruzan* case, however, the Missouri Supreme Court made this evaluation. It refused to permit the termination of the artificial feeding of Nancy Cruzan because, in the view of the court, tubal feeding was not a medical procedure but a form of sustenance that could not be refused.

It was, therefore, of great interest to see what the U.S. Supreme Court would say on the issue of whether forced nutrition and hydration are different from other life-sustaining procedures and can be refused just as any other form of medical treatment can be. The one issue before it was whether the Constitution prohibited Missouri from insisting on "clear and convincing" evidence of a patient's wishes expressed prior to incompetence before permitting surrogates to exercise the patient's right to decline medical treatment. The Court was not called on to hold squarely on the artificial-feeding issue. Nevertheless, the opinions of various members of the Court dealt with it. The majority opinion, written by Justice Rehnquist, assumed "that the United States Constitution would grant a competent person a constitutionally protected right to refuse lifesaving hydration and nutrition." In her separate concurring opinion, Justice O'Connor stated that artificial feeding could not be distinguished from other forms of medical treatment and that its refusal was encompassed within the Fourteenth Amendment. In their dissents, Justices Brennan, Marshall, and Blackmun similarly affirmed that no material distinction could be drawn between the artificial delivery of nutrition and hydration and any other medical treatment. These expressions of opinion strongly suggest that the artificial-feeding issue is resolved and that the conflict between the Missouri Supreme Court and the majority view has been settled in favor of the majority. In a later chapter, it is suggested that these opinions also make highly suspect all living-will statutes that disallow or restrict the refusal of artificial feeding.

## LEGAL CITATIONS

1. In re Quinlan, 70 N.J. 10, 355 A.2d 647 (N.J. Sup. Ct.), *cert. den. sub. nom.* In re Garger v. New Jersey, 429 U.S. 922 (1976).

2. 32 Ill. 2d 361, 205 N.E.2d 435 (Ill. Sup. Ct. 1965).

3. People v. Pierson, 176 N.Y. 201, 68 N.E. 243 (Ct. App. N.Y. 1903).

4. Prince v. Massachusetts, 321 U.S. 158, 88 L.Ed. 45, 64 S. Ct. 438 (1944).

5. Application of the President and Directors of Georgetown College, 331 F.2d 1000 D.C. Cir. Ct., *cert. den.* 377 U.S. 978 (1964).

6. Bouvia v. Superior Court, 179 Cal. App. 3rd 1127, 225 Cal. Rptr. 297, *rev. den.* (Ct. App. Cal., 2nd App. Dist., Div. 2, 1986, *rev. den.* June 5, 1986).

7. Satz v. Perlmutter, 362 S.2d 160, *aff'd* 379 S.2d 35 (Fla. Sup. Ct. 1980).

8. 497 U.S. 261, 111 L.Ed.2d 224, 110 S.Ct. 841 (1990).

9. 381 U.S. 479 (1965).

10. 410 U.S. 113 (1973).

11. See *supra*, note 1.

12. See, for example, Florida Constitution, Art. 1, Section 23.

13. In re Guardianship of Estelle M. Browning, 543 S.2d 258, *aff'd* 568 S.2d 4 (Fla. Sup. Ct. 1990).

14. Matter of Claire Conroy, 98 N.J. 321, 486 A.2d 1209 (N.J. Sup. Ct. 1985); In re Eichner (Storar), 52 N.Y.2d 363, 420 N.E.2d 64, *cert. den.* 454 U.S. 858 (1981); Satz v. Perlmutter, see *supra*, note 7.

15. Bouvia v. Superior Court, 179 Cal. App. 3rd 1127, 1146–1148, 225 Cal. Rptr. 297 (Ct. App. Cal., 2nd App. Dist., Div. 2), *rev. den.* June 5, 1986.

16. Cruzan v. Harmon, 760 S.W. 2d 408 (Mo. Sup. Ct. 1988).

17. In re Storar, 52 N.Y.2d 363, 420 N.E.2d 64, *cert. den.* 454 U.S. 858 (1981).

18. Superintendent of Belchertown State Hospital v. Saikewicz, 373 Mass. 728, 376 N.E.2d 417 (Mass. Sup. Jud. Ct. 1977).

19. In re Quinlan, see *supra*, note 1.

20. 58 N.J. 576, 279 A.2d 670 (N.J. Sup. Ct. 1971).

21. See *supra*, note 1, 355 A.2d 664.

22. In re Eichner, see *supra*, note 14.

23. In re Guardianship of Estelle M. Browning, see *supra*, note 13.

24. Matter of Claire Conroy, see *supra*, note 14.

25. Cruzan v. Harmon, see *supra*, note 16.

26. Cruzan v. Missouri Department of Health, see *supra*, note 8.

27. Missouri Life Support Declarations Act, 1985, Mo. Ann. Stat. Sections 459.010–459.055 (Vernon Supp. 1987).

28. 398 Mass. 417, 497 N.E. 2d 626, 640, 641 (Mass. Sup. Jud. Ct. 1986).

29. Oklahoma "Hydration and Nutrition for Incompetent Patients Act" 63 Okl. Statutes Ann. Sections 3080.1 et. seq.

30. 21 Code of Federal Regulations Section 876.5980 (1989).

31. 21 U.S. Code Section 360ee.

32. 129 A.D.2d 1, 516 N.Y.S.2d 677, 689 (N.Y. App. Div., 2nd Dept. 1987).

## REFERENCES

Annas, G. J. 1990. "Sounding Board: Nancy Cruzan and the Right to Die." *New England Journal of Medicine* 323:670–73.

Annas, G. J., Arnold, B., Aroskar, M., et al. 1990. "Bioethicists' Statement on the U.S. Supreme Court's Cruzan Decision." *New England Journal of Medicine* 323:686–87.

Cantor, N. L. 1973. "A Patient's Decision to Decline Life-Saving Treatment: Bodily Integrity Versus the Preservation of Life." *Rutgers Law Review* 26:228–64.

"Position of the American Academy of Neurology on Certain Aspects of the Care and Management of the Persistent Vegetative Patient." 1989. *Neurology* 39:125.

*Wall Street Journal.* 1991. "New Cases of AIDS in U.S. and Europe to Taper Off in '95, Says Health Group." June 18:B4.

# 7

## Competence and Incompetence

### INFORMED CONSENT

The doctrine of informed consent is founded on the common law principle of bodily integrity and the rights of individuals to consent before any contact is made with their bodies. This doctrine forces physicians to make disclosures to patients concerning a proposed treatment or procedure in order that any consent will be based on full medical information. Patients are to be informed about their diagnoses, the nature of the proposed treatment or procedure, its benefits and risks, alternative therapies and their benefits and risks, what may happen during the recuperation process after the procedure or treatment, and what may happen if the proposed course of action is not followed.

This doctrine forms one of the bases for the right to refuse life-sustaining treatment. Although the judicial forum should be used only as a last resort, we have noted that courts have played the principal role in settling bioethical controversies. In the key area of treatment refusal and with their development of the informed-consent doctrine, the courts have emerged as the patient's protector. On the other hand, physicians see informed consent as a legal burden imposed on them by hostile lawyers and judges, as irrelevant to the well-being of their patients, and as reducing the physician's status and authority (Schouten, 1989). In spite of the medical profession's resistance to the doctrine, however, and because of the courts' insistence on it, the doctrine of informed consent has become central to the physician-patient relationship and all health care is predicated on it.

Two forms of consent are generally obtained from patients prior to initiating any procedures. The first is a general consent signed when entering a hospital. It relates to routine hospital and nursing services and noninvasive diagnostic procedures. In addition to the admission consent form, hospitals and physicians use a special consent form for invasive diagnostic and surgical procedures.

Generally, apart from the element of disclosure of information by the physician, there are three essential components of informed consent: (1) treatment decisions by patients must be free of coercion and voluntary; (2) patients must have the mental capacity to comprehend the nature of their medical conditions, their prognoses, and the risks of death or serious physical harm as well as the benefits of the proposed course of action and the alternative procedures or treatments possible; and (3) patients must have the mental capacity to make rational judgments (Appelbaum and Grisso, 1988). The last two factors are all-important. In order to accept a patient's choice of death over life, we must be reasonably sure that the patient has the cognitive ability to make it. The right to refuse life-sustaining treatment is interwoven with a patient's competence. If a patient is not competent, other decision makers make life-death determinations for the patient so that competence and incompetence are an integral part of the law of dying and death and form the subject matter of this chapter.

## MEANING OF COMPETENCE

*Competence* is a legal term, but the meanings of *competence* and its judicial tests vary according to the situation. In the context of trials, the common law decreed that witnesses were competent to testify if no privileged communication, such as husband and wife or attorney and client, existed; if they had a religious belief and swore to tell the truth; had the mental capacity to receive, record, and narrate impressions; and had not been convicted of an infamous crime. Modern statutes have changed the common law, notably by eliminating religious belief as a reason for disqualifying a witness. In the context of a will probate, it must be shown that the testator was competent to make the will—competence in this situation meaning that testators had mental capacity to understand the nature of the transaction, to recall their property, to know of what it consisted, and to understand the objects of their bounty. In the context of medical treatment, a patient is competent if he or she has the "mental ability to make a rational decision, which includes the ability to perceive, appreciate relevant facts and to reach a rational judgment upon such facts."[1] It is the test of whether the patient can understand the information given and make a valid choice to give or not give informed consent to a proposed course of action.

The question of a patient's competency has been raised when patients have refused to consent to life-sustaining treatment. The decisions in these cases shed light on what courts consider competence to decide to choose death over life. In all such cases, the law presumes patients to be competent. Those who attempt to subject patients to medical treatment not wanted by them have the burden of proving the patients incompetent. In a Jehovah's Witness case, in which the patient would not accept blood transfusions needed to save her life, her decision was attacked as "foolish or ridiculous." But while the court agreed, it did not look on such a decision as indicating incompetence and would not override her. She and not the court could decide what was best for her.[2] In the amputation case of Rosaria Candura,[3] a seventy-seven-year-old widow stubbornly rejected her physicians' recommendation that her gangrenous right foot and lower leg be amputated immediately. Although she was aware of the situation, her mind wandered and became confused. Her daughter petitioned to have the court rule her mother incompetent and to have herself appointed temporary guardian with authority to consent to the operation. The court, however, ruled Mrs. Candura competent. The case shows that daring to disagree with medical opinion or even making what others consider an unfortunate or irrational decision does not add up to incompetency. Nor does the fact that a patient's train of thought gets sidetracked or memory fails, if these states of mind do not impair the patient's ability to understand the consequences of rejecting life-sustaining treatment. The court said that "whether [Mrs. Candura's] decision was wise or unwise" the law would protect her right to make her own decision to accept or reject treatment. On the other hand, in another amputation case, the court found a seventy-two-year-old woman incompetent to make a rational decision to reject the amputation of her feet that would save her life. While she appeared to be mentally sound and clear, she was also blind to and unaccepting of the one fact that constituted a threat to her life: that her feet were "dead, black, shriveled, rotting and stinking" and that, unless they were amputated, she would die.[4]

## DECISION-MAKING CAPACITY

But competence is only of concern to the courts who make rulings about it and appoint legal guardians for people adjudicated incompetent. In hospitals and with respect to medical care, the real issue is not what is called competence but what is called *decision-making capacity* (President's Commission, 1983). The President's Commission found that the attending physician has the primary responsibility for evaluating decision-making capacity prior to accepting a patient's decision concerning medical treatment. Normally, as part of the physician-patient relationship, a physician can observe a patient and make this evaluation. On what are these evaluations based? The medical literature (Appelbaum and Grisso, 1988) suggests some standards, but no legal standard has been established for physicians to follow. They make a commonsense evaluation of the facts according to the way patients receive and understand what their physicians tell them and are able to appreciate and manipulate the information rationally. A way to test these abilities is to ask patients to paraphrase and express in their own words what they have been told and what they choose to do. Evaluations are also based on observations and information from other members of the health-care team and the family and friends of the patient. Cases in which doctors and other members of the health-care team cannot agree do not arise frequently. But if they do, consultations with a specialist, such as a psychiatrist, may be advisable. Or it may become necessary to ask a court to determine whether a patient is competent and a legal guardian should be appointed to make treatment decisions.

## KAREN ANN QUINLAN AND NANCY CRUZAN CASES

While the law of dying and death is concerned with critically ill competent patients, such as Emily Bauer, Elizabeth Bouvia, Abe Perlmutter, and Rosaria Candura, who are alert and have the mental ability to make rational choices, it is equally directed toward another category of patients: those who are not dead because they do not fit into legal and medical brain-death definitions; they are, however, in permanent comas or persistent vegetative states and nature has deprived them of the mental capacity to grasp information and use any rational decision-making process. The *Quinlan* and *Cruzan* cases illustrate this group.

### Karen Ann Quinlan Case

Karen Ann Quinlan was a twenty-one-year-old woman who, after taking drugs and alcohol in 1975, went into a coma and was rushed to a New Jersey hospital. Doctors agreed that her brain, although functioning, was damaged. Her heart was functioning as well. Her parents asked the physicians and hospital to take their daughter off the mechanical respirator that was artificially maintaining her life. When they refused, the parents filed a complaint in Superior Court, Chancery Division, asking that Karen be declared incompetent and appointing her father legal guardian with power to discontinue all extraordinary means of sustaining his daughter's life. The Superior Court refused the parents' petition because it said that the matter should be left to the medical profession. Karen's father then appealed to the New Jersey Supreme Court, which reversed the lower court in 1976 and granted the petition.[5]

### Nancy Cruzan Case

Nancy Cruzan was twenty-five years old when, on the night of June 11, 1983, she lost control of her car and it overturned. She was found lying face down in a ditch without respiratory or cardiac functions. Paramedics restored her breathing and heartbeat at the accident site. Unconscious and with cerebral contusions and anoxia, she was taken to the Mt. Vernon State Hospital in Missouri. She suffered permanent brain damage and went into a coma and a persistent vegetative state. She was kept alive by nutrition and hydration delivered through a gastrostomy tube implanted by surgeons in her stomach. Although the state was bearing the cost of her care, her parents asked the hospital and physicians to terminate the feeding, but they refused. On the ground that Nancy Cruzan had a right and would have chosen to end the feeding and die, her parents, acting as her guardians, requested authorization from the state trial court in 1987 to discontinue the feeding. Their petition was granted, but the Missouri state attorney general and the guardian ad litem appointed by the court for the patient appealed the trial court's order to the high court of Missouri. By a four-to-three vote in 1988, the Missouri Supreme Court reversed the trial court. In 1989, the U.S. Supreme Court granted *certiorari* to hear arguments in 1989 and in 1990 affirmed the Missouri court's decision.[6]

Both cases are significant for several reasons. Each was a legal first. *Quinlan* was the first state high court decision ever handed down that extended a constitutional right of privacy to a refusal of life-sustaining treatment. Between 1976 when *Quinlan* was decided and 1988, there were fifty-four right-to-die cases decided by state courts, but not one decided by the U.S. Supreme Court. When that Court heard *Cruzan*, it became the first such case considered by the High Court. Its affirmation in 1990 that the due process clause granted a right of liberty to refuse life-sustaining treatment was also the first such interpretation of the U.S. Constitution.

*Quinlan* and *Cruzan* dramatized for the world two pictures. One was the glowing image of the success and benefits of medical technology. Twenty to thirty years ago, the lives of these women would never have been prolonged. Without new medical techniques, the conditions of Karen Ann Quinlan and Nancy Cruzan would have brought on death. The other picture was dark; it showed the dangers of medical technology. After

Quinlan was removed from the respirator in May 1976, she was taken from the hospital to a nursing home in New Jersey. Kept alive there by nasogastric feeding, she lived on in a vegetative state, in a fetal position and weighing less than ninety pounds until her death nine years later. Nancy Cruzan was kept alive by a gastrostomy tube in a persistent vegetative state for eight years—a living, breathing corpse without the power of thought or speech or the ability to recognize her own parents. Had a subsequent court hearing unopposed by the Missouri state attorney general and guardian ad litem not authorized her tubal feeding to be discontinued on the basis of new "clear and convincing" evidence and allowed her to die in December 1990, she would have continued to be maintained by a feeding tube in a vegetative state for another fifteen to thirty years.

Their impact on the judicial trend is another reason why these cases are important. *Quinlan* was a remarkable decision. Before it, lawyers and courts did not touch medical matters. *Quinlan* took matters in the area of terminal care out of the hands of the medical profession and started a judicial trend in this direction. In *Cruzan*, by contrast, the Missouri Supreme Court, ruling against the parents who wished to withdraw tubal feeding,[7] shocked patients'-rights advocates and went against the prevailing judicial trend since *Quinlan* toward supporting treatment decisions by loving families.

The importance of these cases is heightened also by their impact on legislation. *Quinlan* ignited the enactments of living-will statutes by state legislatures while Cruzan stimulated Congress to pass the Patient Self-Determination Act.

## THE RIGHTS OF INCOMPETENT PATIENTS

The importance of *Quinlan* and *Cruzan* also lies in their presentation of the significant issue of whether incompetent patients are denied the right of treatment refusal or have rights that include the right to refuse life-support. Some authorities appear to believe that: "Competent patients have the right to decide whether to accept or reject proposed medical care. Patients thought to be incompetent are denied this right" (Applebaum and Grisso, 1988). Such views are in need of clarification. Under the law of dying and death laid down by *Quinlan* and numerous other cases, the right to accept or reject life-sustaining treatment is not limited to competent patients and is not lost because of mental or physical incapacity. The case of Joseph Saikewicz carried this principle even further. In *Quinlan, Cruzan,* and other cases cited,[8] the patients were in noncognitive states but prior to entering them had been competent and their parents or others had been close to them and could use that relationship to arrive at judgments concerning the needs and wishes of the patients. But Saikewicz was a sixty-seven-year-old man in a state mental institution who had been profoundly mentally retarded all his life and had never made any decisions, so no one could know what he really wanted or needed. Yet the Supreme Judicial Court of Massachusetts ruled that the rights of patients who have always been incompetent are the same with regard to refusing life-sustaining treatment as those of patients who are competent or were competent at one time. "The value of human dignity extends to both" competent and incompetent individuals.[9] And this makes sense. In a country where fundamental rights are supposed to be guaranteed and protected, it is essential to protect them for all, especially for the mentally incompetent who no longer have or never had the ability to assert these rights themselves.

But if physically or mentally incapacitated people leave no advance directives prior to incompetency, and now do not have the ability to make conscious choices and personally and directly to express their choices to refuse life-sustaining treatment, how can they exercise this right? This is the real question. In *Cruzan*, the U.S. Supreme Court said that the issue of whether an incompetent has a right of refusal only begs it.

## SURROGATE DECISION MAKING

The only way to prevent the right of refusal from being lost or destroyed is for surrogate decision makers to act for incompetent patients and to exercise their rights of refusal. Where there is a question about competence, all states have one or another kind of machinery set up for this purpose. There are procedures for judicially declaring incompetence and appointing legal guardians with the authority to exercise patients' rights and make treatment decisions for them. But a surrogate need not necessarily be a legal guardian. Chapter 8 describes how proxies, health-care surrogates, or attorneys-in-fact can be appointed prior to incompetence as individuals who can make these decisions. If such appointments have not been made, some statutes permit certain classes of individuals to make them. For example, one permits a decision maker to be one chosen in the following order of priority: the judicially appointed guardian, the patient's spouse, the patient's adult child, or, if more than one, the majority of adult children of the patient, the patient's parents, the patient's adult sibling, or, if more than one, the majority of the patient's brothers or sisters, or a close adult relative of the patient, or close personal friend of 18 years of age or older.[10] If no person in one class is reasonably available or willing and competent to act, individuals in the next priority class may make decisions. Should those in one class disagree concerning a decision, that of the majority will be given effect unless the surrogates seek and obtain a court order in the matter.

In many states, however, there are no statutes to authorize medical treatment decisions by the family for patients. It is in these states that the U.S. Supreme Court decision in *Cruzan*, if correctly understood, may have a great and disturbing impact, particularly on medical practice. Courts have long recognized as surrogate decision makers close members of the family and have accorded them the right to make treatment decisions for incompetent family members.[11] The assumption is that parents will act in the best interests of their children.[12] The medical community also has traditionally recognized that the family is best qualified to make substituted medical judgment for an incompetent loved one. This recognition is shared by the President's Commission (1983) and the Hastings Center (Guidelines, 1987).

In view of this medical practice and recognition, the Missouri court's decision in *Cruzan*, to which the authority of the U.S. Supreme Court was added, shocked many by rejecting the parents' decision to withdraw artificial hydration and nutrition from their daughter on the ground that "clear and convincing" evidence had not been provided of her wish to refuse life support. Unless states without statutes now enact them to allow medical treatment decisions to be made by a family on behalf of an incompetent patient, *Cruzan* probably will force hospitals and physicians to think twice about whether or when to accept family treatment choices for patients who are not competent and have left no advance directives or other reliable oral or written evidence expressing their wishes.

This doubt, in turn, is likely to beget unfortunate consequences. It may result in continuing unwanted or useless life-sustaining treatment for incompetent patients. It may create administrative problems for health-care institutions. In the normal operations of any hospital, reliance is generally placed on treatment decisions made by surrogates acting on behalf of incompetent patients. But with these decisions now questionable in cases where these patients have given no "clear and convincing" evidence of their wishes, hospitals are virtually compelled to seek prior judicial approval and protection for stopping or not starting life support. In addition, since hospitals may be exposed to legal liability for stopping life support, they may feel forced to oversee physicans and the medical care they provide to incompetent patients.

## ESSENTIAL INFORMATION FOR MAKING
## TREATMENT DECISIONS FOR INCOMPETENT
## PATIENTS

When should the surrogate's decision about medical treatment for the incompetent be made? It should be made as expeditiously as possible and before a patient is forced to continue suffering as an object of unwanted medical technology. What essential information should be obtained and considered by the surrogate in order to make a decision? The decision-making process should include all those individuals whose input and interests should affect the decision—physicians, family, friends. But in the final analysis, the decision is made by the surrogate alone.

The decision maker should have up-to-date information on a variety of matters. One court advised that there should be evidence available on four issues: (1) Is the patient suffering from a medical condition that would permit the patient, if competent, to forgo life-sustaining treatment? Such a condition would include an irreversible coma or permanent vegetative state—conditions which provide no reasonable prospect that the patient will ever regain cognitive brain function and in which the life of the patient is being sustained by artificial life support. (2) Is there any reasonable probability that the patient will regain competency so that the treatment decision can be made by the patient? (3) Where the subjective test for surrogate decision making is used, is the patient's personal decision on this matter sufficiently clear to enable the surrogate to make a substituted judgment? (4) Is the patient's right to forgo treatment outweighed by state interests?[13]

Economics may be a further legitimate and realistic factor entering into a surrogate's decision. The surrogate should receive input concerning the expenses of hospitalization, nursing care, drugs, procedures, operations, and other medical interventions for the maintenance of the patient. These mount quickly and frighteningly. It should be ascertained whether the patient is covered by Medicare, Medicaid, private health insurance, or group insurance. Even if there is coverage, it may not cover all expenses and benefits may stop after a specified period or amount. If there is no insurance coverage or if it stops, costs continued for a prolonged period of time will not only exhaust the resources of the patient but drain those of the family as well and threaten it with bankruptcy. Other indirect economic effects a surrogate should consider include loss of income for relatives who miss work in order to be with the patient as well as travel expenses for those coming from long distances.

Quality of life? There is no judicial unanimity on whether a court can and will apply the quality-of-life criterion in making its decision whether to stop life support for an incompetent patient. Some courts use it, but others will not.[14] Among these is the Missouri Supreme Court, which said in *Cruzan*: "The state's interest is not in the quality of life. . . . Instead, the state's interest is in life; that interest is unqualified."[15] In its affirmance of *Cruzan*, the U.S. Supreme Court said that a state may decline to make a judgment about the quality of life.

Except in states such as Missouri or New York,[16] which look on quality of life as irrelevant, a surrogate's decision whether to forgo life-sustaining treatment seems inevitably to take quality of life into account. But while a term of worldwide currency, it remains vague, a catchall for many social factors such as lifestyle, economic state, social status, and relationships with others as well as psychological factors such as happiness, self-esteem, anxiety, and individual goals. In relation to an incompetent patient on life support, its components probably include the present pain and suffering caused by the treatment and a patient's dissatisfaction with the hopeless, degrading, diminished, twilight-zone existence technological intervention creates.

To enable a surrogate to assess the patient's quality of life or medical condition or both, the surrogate should have current medical input. Rather than oral information from physicians, the surrogate should ask for written medical evidence on which the surrogate can rely. Certificates or sworn statements from physicians should be secured to provide: (1) a summary of the patient's current medical condition, including the level of mental and physical functioning; (2) the degree of pain and discomfort experienced currently by the patient and expected by the physician in the future; (3) the nature of the medical treatment that is to be withheld or withdrawn, including its benefits, risks, invasiveness, painfulness, and side effects; (4) the prognosis of the patient with or without the medical assistance, including life expectancy, suffering, and the possibility of recovery; (5) whether the physician believes it is appropriate within medical ethics to withdraw the treatment.

## CRITERIA FOR MAKING TREATMENT DECISIONS FOR INCOMPETENT PATIENTS

Two kinds of legal criteria have been set up by the courts for decision making by surrogates. The first is the subjective test or "substituted judgment" criterion used by the *Quinlan* court and the majority of other courts.[17] This criterion does not permit the surrogate decision maker to substitute his or her judgment for the patient's. The object is to determine the wants and needs of the patient, and to decide on the course of action the patient would have decided to take if he or she were competent. The decision maker stands in the shoes of the patient and must make the treatment decision the patient would have made even though the decision is different from what the decision maker would have made and even if the decision seems wrong or foolish.

In order for a substituted judgment to be made, it is imperative the surrogate know what a patient's personal decision would have been. In *Cruzan*, where Nancy Cruzan's parents were not allowed to make a treatment decision for her, substituted judgment was not possible because they could not meet Missouri's evidentiary standard and show by "clear and convincing" evidence what their daughter's decision would have been. If a living will has been made, it should be given great weight. If none has been made or has been revoked, the evidence, written or oral, should be reliable and strong enough to produce a firm conviction of what a patient would have decided before becoming incompetent.

The second standard is the objective test or "best interests" criterion. The courts using this test assume that patients will agree to treatment decisions that will serve their best interests.[18] The court in *Matter of Claire Conroy* said that the best-interests criterion should be applied in one of two situations.[19] Where the evidence is not trustworthy or clear enough to allow a subjective judgment to be made but there is some to suggest that the patient would have refused treatment, then a "limited objective" test would be used. Treatment can be withheld or withdrawn if the burdens of the patient's life outweigh its benefits. But where there is no evidence and it cannot be determined what the patient's choice would have been—say, in the case of a newborn infant or a person who had never been competent—there remains the "pure objective" test. Treatment may be withdrawn or withheld if: (1) the benefits derived by the patient from continuing life are clearly outweighed by the net burdens of life with treatment, and (2) it would be inhumane to administer the treatment if the pain of the patient's life with treatment is severe, recurring, and unavoidable.

The "pure objective" test is subject to the criticism that it seems too restrictive because of its emphasis on the severity of pain. It excludes other factors that also might increase the burdens of a life with treatment, such as the patient's noncognitive state, the invasiveness of treatment, the use of mechanical restraints, and the feelings of helplessness, hopelessness, and degradation the patient may experience. A more sweeping criticism of the "best interests" standard is that decisions are based on matters independent of the patient's wants and needs. Some courts, therefore, reject the criterion because "it is not a remedy to fulfill a constitutional right of privacy. It is a test under which the surrogate decision-maker seems to make the decision which a public referendum or benign leader would reach. We cannot afford to confuse the patient's right of privacy with a public opinion poll."[20] Such criticism, however, does not provide a solution in cases where the patient's wishes cannot be ascertained.

## MINORS

Minors, generally someone under the age of eighteen, also have a constitutional and common-law right to refuse life-sustaining treatment that may be exercised by surrogates. The right is not lost by reason of age. The law draws no distinction between minors and incompetent adults who have made no living wills.[21]

Parents have the constitutional right to the care and custody of minor children.[22] There is a legal presumption "that the natural bonds of affection lead parents to act in the best interests of their children"[23] when decisions need to be made concerning withholding or withdrawing life-sustaining treatment. Physicians are urged to cooperate with parents early on in a collaborative decision-making process relating to stopping or withholding such treatment (Ruark, Raffin, and Stanford University, 1988). Generally, in order of priority, parents, the nearest relatives, or a court-appointed legal guardian of a minor can make such decisions. When a guardian makes the decision, a copy of the court order should be placed in the patient's chart. Performing a procedure on a minor without the surrogate's consent, however, is an actionable battery.

A minor may be considered emancipated enough to do without parental consent and to give an informed consent to or refusal of medical treatment. An emancipated minor is someone who is not under the parent's custody— a married minor, one in the armed services, or someone living independently and taking care of his or her own affairs.

## JAMES MCGUIRE CASE

James McGuire was a patient evaluated as lacking full decision-making capacity. He was an elderly widower with no family except for two sisters he had not called on for eight years and a female friend with whom he was close. He was also fond of the gambling casinos in Las Vegas. After he developed renal failure and cardiomyopathy, a dispute developed between the sisters and friend over the question of whether McGuire should be dialyzed. Each side called the other "vultures." The former urged that he should be dialyzed, but the friend told the social worker that dialysis was out of the question because it would "cost too much." She produced for

McQuire's attending physician an advance directive signed by the patient in which she had been designated proxy, empowered to make McGuire's treatment decisions. It was of the "death directive" type that instructed physicians to take no steps to keep him alive. When the document was shown to McGuire, he seemed confused and unable to make a choice that showed that he understood the consequences of refusing or accepting dialysis. But he was able to identify the document and to say that he had signed it. He also admitted that he was afraid of dialysis and uncomfortable about the prospect of it. But he protested that he was willing to undergo the treatment because he wanted to be able to keep returning to Las Vegas. He also said that the female friend had prepared the advance directive and asked to discuss it with her. McGuire added that he had changed his will to leave his friend the lion's share of his $400,000 estate.

The *McGuire* case raises two questions: In the circumstances of the case, what are the legal and ethical duties of the patient's attending physician? Is the physician required to accept the treatment decision by the legally empowered proxy and not proceed with dialysis?

Surrogate decision making for the incompetent patient can create problems for the health-care professional and place the incompetent in danger by preventing life-sustaining treatment. The patient's physician has the legal and ethical duty to do all that is possible to extend the patient's life, to supply the patient with all medical treatment that is necessary to this end, and to go on supplying the patient with the best service the physician can until the patient recovers, dies, or the physician-patient relationship ends by the discharge of the doctor or the physician's withdrawal from the case. A patient's lack of decision-making capacity does not terminate the physician's duties.

But with various procedures for appointing surrogates, the power to stop these duties and service for incompetent patients seems to have been delegated to third parties legally empowered to decide what medical treatment should be stopped or withheld. The fact that patients, prior to incompetency or lack of decision-making capacity, have made advance directives designating surrogates who have been given such legal status, however, does not displace the physician as the patient's protector. Physicians continue to play their original vital role and should be certain that a surrogate decision maker is acting in accordance both with sound medical practice and the interests and wishes of the patient.

That the law has given the surrogate the right to make treatment decisions does not automatically ensure that this third party knows or is following a patient's wishes or values, or is free from conflicts of interest, undue influences, or motives that may compromise a treatment decision.

Therefore, besides the legal test of whether someone fits into the right category of people qualified to act as surrogate, a physician is entitled to administer another test—the "test of moral validity" (ACCP/SCCM Consensus Panel, 1990:952). If the physician is satisfied that the surrogate's treatment decision is in accord with the patient's best interest and with medical practice and ethics, that decision should be accepted. But if, prior to incompetence, a patient has made an advance directive or otherwise clearly manifested wishes concerning life-sustaining treatment, medical ethics continues to protect the patient as does the physician's duty to see that the patient's wishes are honored. Therefore, should the attending physician have reason to doubt that the decision is identical with the patient's known wishes or even suspects the impropriety of the designation of the surrogate, undoubtedly the physician will be placed in "an extremely sensitive position . . . but the physician is also the last safeguard for the patient and must stand against [the] decision" (ACCP/SCCM Consensus Panel, 1990:952). This stand can be taken in court especially if the local statute provides for judicial review of a surrogate's decision.[24]

The factual situation in the *McGuire* case was reported by two physicians (La Puma and Schiedermayer, 1991). Since the female friend seemed motivated by financial benefit and had a clear conflict of interest, the physicians brought an ethics consultant into the case and also felt required to oppose the treatment decision and to proceed with dialysis. After being dialyzed, the patient's condition improved. He was able to return home and presumably now is in a Las Vegas casino betting to his heart's content.

## LEGAL CITATIONS

1. Department of Human Services v. Northern, 563 S.W. 2d 197 (Tenn. Ct. App. 1978).

2. In re Brooks, 32 Ill.2d 361, 205 N.E.2d 435 (Ill. Sup. Ct. 1965).

3. Lane v. Candura, 376 N.E.2d 1232 (Mass. App. Ct. 1978).

4. Department of Human Services v. Northern, see *supra*, note 1.

5. In re Quinlan, 70 N.J. 10, 355 A.2d 647 (N.J. Sup. Ct.), *cert. den. sub. nom.* In re Garger v. New Jersey, 429 U.S. 922 (1976).

6. Cruzan v. Director, Missouri Department of Health, 497 U.S. 261, 111 L. Ed. 2d 224, 110 S.Ct. 841 (1990).

7. Cruzan v. Harmon, 760 S.W.2d 408 (Mo. Sup. Ct. 1988).

8. In re Colyer, 99 Wash. 2d 114, 660 P.2d 738 ( Wash. Sup. Ct. 1988); In re Drabick, 200 Cal. App.3rd 185, 245 Cal. Rptr. 840 (Cal. Ct. App. 1988), *rev. den.* (July 28,1988), *cert.den.*109 S. Ct. 399 (1988); Brophy v. New England Sinai Hospital, 398 Mass. 417, 498 N.E.2d 626 (Mass. Sup. Jud. Ct. 1986); John F. Kennedy Memorial Hospital v. Bludworth, 452 S.2d 921 (Fla. Sup. Ct. 1984); Satz v. Perlmutter, 362 S.2d 160, *aff'd* 379 S.2d 359 (Fla. Sup. Ct. 1980).

9. Superintendent of Belchertown State School v. Saikewicz, 373 Mass. 728, 370 N.E.2d 417 (Mass. Sup. Jud. Ct. 1977).

10. Florida Statutes, Section 765.07.

11. Meyer v. Nebraska, 262 U.S. 390 (1923); Pierce v. Society of Sisters, 268 U.S. 501 (1927); John F. Kennedy Memorial Hospital v. Bludworth, see *supra*, note 8; In re Farrell, 108 N.J. 335, 529 A.2d 404 (N.J. Sup. Ct. 1987).

12. Parham, Commissioner, Department of Human Resources of Georgia v. J.R., 442 U.S. 585 (1925).

13. In re Guardianship of Estelle M. Browning, 543 S.2d 258, *aff'd* 568 S.2d 4 (Fla. Sup. Ct. 1990).

14. Superintendent of Belchertown State School v. Saikewicz, see *supra*, note 9.

15. Cruzan v. Harmon, see *supra*, note 7.

16. In re Westchester County Medical Center, 72 N.Y.2d 517, 534 N.Y.S.2d 886 (N.Y. Ct. App. 1988).

17. Brophy v. New England Sinai Hospital, see *supra*, note 8; In re Colyer, see *supra*, note 8; Superintendent of Belchertown State School, see *supra*, note 9; In re Guardianship of Estelle M. Browning, see *supra*, note 13; In re Spring, 380 Mass. 629, 405 N.E.2d 115 (Mass. Sup. Jud. Ct. 1980).

18. In re Drabick, see *supra*, note 8; In re Guardianship of Hamlin, 102 Wash.2d 810, 689 P.2d 1372 (Wash. Sup. Ct. 1984); Matter of Claire Conroy, 98 N.J. 321,486 A.2d 1209 (N.J.Sup. Ct. 1985); Rasmussen v. Fleming, 154 Ariz. 207, 741 P.2d 674 (Ariz. Sup. Ct. 1987).

19. See *supra*, note 18.

20. See *supra*, note 13.

21. In re L.H.R., 253 Ga. 439, 321 S.E.2d 716 (Ga. Sup. Ct. 1984).

22. Lassiter v. Department of Social Services, 452 U.S. 18 (1981).

23. Parham, Commissioner, Department of Human Resources of Georgia, see *supra*, note 12.

24. Florida Statutes Sec. 765.10.

# REFERENCES

ACCP/SCCM Consensus Panel. 1990. "Ethical and Moral Guidelines for the Initiation, Continuation, and Withdrawal of Intensive Care." *Chest* 97(4):949–58.

Applebaum, P. S., and Grisso, T. 1988. "Assessing Patients' Capacities to Consent to Treatment." *New England Journal of Medicine* 319 (25):1635–38.

*Guidelines on the Termination of Life-Sustaining Treatment and Care of the Dying.* 1987. New York: Hastings Center.

La Puma, J., and Schiedermayer, D. L. 1991. "The Bookie, the Girlfriend and the Vultures." *Annals of Internal Medicine* 114:98.

President's Commission for the Study of Ethical Problems: Medicine and Biomedicine and Behavioral Research. 1983. *Deciding to Forgo Life-Sustaining Treatment.* Washington, DC: Government Printing Office.

Ruark, J. E., Raffin, T. A., and Stanford University Medical Center Committee on Ethics. 1988. "Initiating and Withdrawing Life Support—Principles and Practice in Adult Medicine." *New England Journal of Medicine* 318:25–30.

Schouten, R. 1989. "Informed Consent: Resistance and Reappraisal." *Critical Care Medicine* 17: 1359–61.

# IV

## Advance Directives

# 8

## Advance Directives and Death with Dignity

### CLEAR AND CONVINCING EVIDENCE

In view of the *Cruzan* decision, physicians, surrogates, as well as we who are still competent must be wary about the weight courts in Missouri, Florida, New York, Illinois, and Ohio—as well as future state legislatures and courts in other states—may give to the evidence of a patient's wishes to be allowed to die. In the *Cruzan* case, a year before the automobile accident that precipitated her into a persistent vegetative state, she had a fairly serious conversation with a roommate and said that she "didn't want to live" as a "vegetable" and that if she "couldn't do for herself things even halfway, alone not at all, she would not want to live that way and she hoped that her parents would know that." Her father and mother, knowing "in [their] hearts" that their daughter would not want to live in her present condition tried to exercise their daughter's right to decline life support. They thought they knew what course their daughter would have followed and asked that life support be stopped, but the Missouri Supreme Court discarded Nancy Cruzan's statements made before her incompetence on the ground that they were unreliable. It insisted on "clear and convincing" evidence of her wishes; these statements, it said, were not such evidence. The requirement of "clear and convincing" evidence was a strict standard of persuasion. When *Cruzan* came before the U. S. Supreme Court, the High Court was faced with the issue of whether to require Missouri to give weight to Nancy Cruzan's words that she would rather die than endure a vegetative existence or whether to permit the state to force her to be kept alive because the surrogates had not met its strict evidential standard and produced "clear and convincing" evidence of the patient's previously expressed intentions to stop life support.

The U.S. Supreme Court held that the Constitution does not preclude a state from playing god and adopting this heightened evidential requirement in order to advance its interest in preserving life. The requirement imposed by Missouri is not unusual. Florida, Illinois, New York, and Ohio have also ruled that before life support can be stopped there must be "clear and convincing" proof articulating a patient's wish to terminate treatment.[1]

The "clear and convincing" standard is the highest possible in civil cases. Its adoption stems primarily from the belief that, if the weight of the evidence raises any question about the patient's wishes that life support be terminated, all doubts must be resolved and any decision by the trier of fact made on the side of preserving life. But if the decision in favor of not withdrawing life support is wrong, it wreaks havoc with the patient and family. As was said in Justice Brennan's dissent in *Cruzan*: "an erroneous decision not to terminate life-support robs a patient of the very qualities protected by the right to avoid unwanted medical treatment . . . [a] degraded existence is perpetuated; his family's suffering is protracted; the memory he leaves behind becomes more and more distorted."[2] Normally, all that is required to resolve an issue in a civil case is a "fair preponderance" of the evidence. To invoke and for the U.S. Supreme Court to affirm the strictest standard is to be doctrinaire and to ignore practical matters and the general attitude toward death. This attitude is like Woody Allen's when, on his fortieth birthday, he said: "I shall gain immortality not through my work but by not dying" (Feifel, 1977:4). It is an attitude of aversion and evasion. Most of us ordinarily will not think or speak of our dying and deaths. In those rare moments when we do with someone close, there is never a great deal said and what is said is not spelled out in the form of an insurance policy with terms and conditions when and under which specific kinds of life-sustaining treatment will be stopped. People generally express their wishes about being allowed to die as did Nancy Cruzan, who wanted death in preference to existing as a "vegetable" or as did Paul Brophy, the fireman. Talking about the *Quinlan* case to his wife, he said: "I don't ever want to be on a life-support system. No way do I want to live like that; that is not living."[3] Now to require us—as the "clear and convincing" standard does—to dot every *i* and cross every *t*, to make written statements that are notarized, to speak like lawyers as we express our intentions about life supports, or to gather around us credible witnesses in a kind of press conference in which we make carefully worded statements about our intentions, all in order to convince a court to give weight to the evidence, seems to elevate the abstract over the real and to evade the actual state of things.

It also impinges upon patients, families, and medical practice in several ways. The affirmation that "clear and convincing evidence" of a patient's wishes expressed prior to incompetency must be provided before life support will be discontinued will force patients without living wills to undergo medical treatment that those closest to them such as their spouses, children, parents, or friends, know they would not want. Since only the patient's wishes have probative value, the evidence of those who knew the patient best will not have any value.

Moreover, because of the "clear and convincing" standard, a heavy cloud of uncertainty hovers over clinical practice. Physicians must wonder whether they can rely any longer on oral statements made by a patient before incompetency as "clear and convincing" evidence of the patient's wishes to refuse life-sustaining treatment, and doctors may feel constrained to continue it even though it is ineffective and provides no therapeutic benefit. In addition, as suggested in the dissenting opinion of Justice Brennan in *Cruzan*, the "clear and convincing" standard may result in more deaths of patients because physicians, faced with doubt about not being able to withdraw life-sustaining treatment, may be inclined not even to begin it. More than likely, this doubt will lead physicians and conservative hospital attorneys and administrators straight to the courthouse door to seek judicial protection or immunity prior to removing life-supports.

Although the Constitution does not forbid a strict standard of persuasion, it does not require it either, nor does it prevent states from using a lower standard more in keeping with reality, such as the "fair preponderance" test. Physicians and surrogates will need to determine with which one compliance is necessary.

The fallout from the U.S. Supreme Court's holding in *Cruzan*, of course, does not affect cases of competent patients or those incompetent ones who, prior to incompetency, left clear evidence of their desires. But the holding substantially affects incompetent patients who have given no advance directions and are unable to express their wishes, and it affects decisions by surrogates and their exercise of the incompetents' rights to refuse medical treatment. It also forces us to realize that the *Cruzan* case is not the case of Nancy Cruzan. It is the case of all of us who now or one day will be unable to speak for ourselves and for whom life-death decisions will be made by surrogates; of the 10,000 patients in the United States who every day lie in their beds permanently unconscious; of other patients in states of irreversible coma, severe dementia, mental retardation, Alzheimer's disease or senility; of millions more now and in the future—young and middle-aged adults as well as the elderly ones—who, through neglect or inability to confront their mortality or discuss problematical future medical situations, have given no advance directions. The holding serves notice that the common law and constitutional right to refuse treatment, while granted to all, will be exercisable by surrogates only in the few cases of those willing to think about dying and death who have had the foresight to leave clear and specific directions spelling out their intentions about being allowed to die. It serves notice on everyone that we must anticipate the future and possible mental incapacity to participate in treatment decisions and leave these instructions, or else run the risk of having a state like Missouri impose a strict standard of persuasion concerning our wishes and require clear and convincing evidence of them before stopping life support that sustains us as objects of medical technology. The lesson of *Cruzan* is that we had better become informed about and prepare advance directives if we want to avoid happening to us and our families what happened to Nancy Cruzan and her parents so that treatment decisions can be made intelligently for us and in line with our wishes expressed before incompetency.

But will the lesson be learned? Before *Cruzan*, survey after survey showed that only a small minority of the public executed living wills (Emanuel and Emanuel, 1989; Cassel and Zweibel, 1987). "The horse on the dining room table syndrome" was at work in the minds of the great majority of Americans who associated the living will with dying and death and could not bring themselves to sign and issue their own death warrants. But with *Cruzan*, which focused the public eye on the right to die and encouraged a greater acceptance of dying and death, the "horse on the dining room table syndrome" was so lessened that organizations such as Choice in Dying reported receipt of an overwhelming number of requests for living-will forms and their distribution throughout the country of 250,000 advance directive forms in the six-month period after *Cruzan* (Concern for Dying/Society for the Right to Die, 1990). People began to recognize the need for and to ask questions about living wills. So it seems now to be possible to teach the old dog new tricks.

Another reason to draft living wills is mentioned in connection with some legislation regarding artificial feeding. An *advance directive* may be defined as a written or oral expression of choices and instructions concerning future medical treatment or the appointment of a person to make these decisions if one is not able to do so. It may take the form of a living will, the designation of a health-care surrogate, a durable power of attorney for health care, or a do-not-resuscitate order. Health-care professionals can help their patients and answer their questions by becoming familiar with what these forms are and how they differ from one another.

## LIVING WILLS

The history of the living will can be traced to England. In 1936 and again in 1969, the Voluntary Euthanasia Bill was proposed to the House of Lords to allow people suffering from an irremediable condition to request in advance the administration of euthanasia. Although both bills were defeated, the concept of a living will was born. Its birth as well as a patient's right of self-determination were implemented further by Pope Pius XII's *allocutio*, or address, to anesthesiologists on November 24, 1957. The Pope distinguished between "ordinary" and "extraordinary" medical treatment and said that a request to terminate extraordinary life-sustaining treatment would not involve euthanasia and would be morally acceptable.

The "living will," a term proposed by attorney Luis Kutner in 1969 (Kutner, 1969), is generally a written medical directive executed by competent adults and witnessed like a will. However, the laws of a few states allow the directive to be oral if the directive cannot be signed. The directive permits adults in advance of the time when they cannot take part in medical decisions to accomplish two purposes. The first is to provide a clear expression of the wishes of patients about what medical steps they want or do not want taken in certain foreseeable situations such as cardiac failure or a persistent vegetative state.

The designation of living-will statutes as natural-death legislation created the notion in the public mind that living wills are to be used exclusively to reduce or refuse life-sustaining medical intervention so that one can die naturally and with dignity. The impression is that living wills are "death directives" in which people say, in effect, "when a certain point is reached, I want my physician to take no steps to keep me alive." But since living wills can also be used to insist that physicians provide aggressive support and employ every sophisticated piece of technology to sustain life and stave off death, this notion is clearly erroneous. The living will can be as well a "life directive" that, in substance, states, "it doesn't matter how bad my prognosis is or how sick I am. I want my physician to do everything to keep me alive."

Where living-will statutes authorize it, and not all do, the second purpose of the living will is to designate a surrogate or proxy to make medical decisions in case the declarant is not capable of doing so at the time they have to be made.

But there is a condition attached to the living will. It cannot be given effect and the wishes of these adults cannot be carried out unless they are terminally ill—that is, unless they have a hopeless mental or physical condition that will bring death in a relatively short time.

When they are in writing, these documents are like testamentary wills because they express a person's intentions and instructions, except that testamentary wills become effective only when the people making them die. Medical directives are called living wills because they become effective while adults are alive, even if comatose or incompetent.

With a living will, the family, the physician, and the courts will know how an individual feels. All courts hold that a living will is a valid way to express a patient's wishes concerning medical treatment. When a patient who has become incompetent has made no will and family, physician, and health institution cannot make private decisions, the result is only expensive and dragged out litigation. *Cruzan* is a case in point. Nancy Cruzan, the woman in a vegetative state, had not executed a living will. But if she had expressed her intentions in a living will in which she refused artificial feeding, we are on safe ground to speculate that there would not have been any litigation forced up to the U.S. Supreme Court on whether her feeding should be stopped. The living will should have been "clear and convincing" evidence and should have allowed her parents to exercise her right to refuse artificial feeding without opposition from their daughter's physicians or the State of Missouri.

It can safely be said also that today health-care professionals support living wills (Orentlicher, 1990) because these documents are one method by which physicians can find out what the wishes of a patient are concerning life-sustaining treatment. If drafted with care and clarity, living wills are meant to give them detailed instructions to follow and tell doctors exactly what to do or not to do when attending comatose or incompetent patients or those in a permanently vegetative state who can no longer speak for themselves.

## State Level

On both the federal and state levels legislative action has been taken in regard to living wills. On the state level, legislative activity in this area resembles a bull market in which stocks rise steadily to reach all-time highs. Motivated by the *Quinlan* case, decided in 1976, California passed the first living-will statute, and from that time the numbers of states have followed the same bullish pattern. Within three years, nine states enacted such statutes, and by 1991 thirty-five more and the District of Columbia had followed suit. As of this writing a total of 45 states had passed living-will statutes as had two U.S. territories: Puerto Rico and Guam.[4] Five states had not. It is probable, however, that feverish legislative activity in some of these states will result before long in the passage of such statutes in these states as well. In states where repeated attempts to introduce living-will legislation has met with strong opposition, those objecting to voluntary euthanasia have argued that living wills only give legal sanction to euthanasia and thus violate the sanctity of life. Lawyer objectors have maintained that living-will statutes are unnecessary since many court decisions have repeatedly affirmed the existence of rights to consent to or reject medical treatment. However, the inexorable upward trend of states in the column of those with living-will statutes suggests that the opposition is gradually crumbling.

Should residents of states not on the list of states with living-will statutes make living wills anyway? And if yes, what weight will they receive in these states? Florida's Supreme Court was the first to answer these questions. Before Florida adopted a living-will statute, Francis Landy had made a living will in 1975. Then he became legally incompetent and terminal and was placed on a life-support system. The court held that, even without a living-will statute, a living will should be given "great weight" and should be "persuasive evidence" of Landy's wishes for his guardian.[5] Even in New York, where life-sustaining treatment will be stopped only if there is "clear and convincing" evidence of a patient's wishes that it be terminated,[6] a living will was held to meet this test and to be a "clear and convincing demonstration" of the wishes of a terminally ill patient to stop treatment.[7] In states with no living-will statutes, then, a living will is recognized and enforced as an exercise of one's common law and constitutional right to accept or reject treatment. In any case, it is certainly better to have something in writing to express an individual's wishes than nothing at all.

## State Living-Will Statutes: Key Features

What follows are some key features relating to living-will statutes and references to the states where these features are recognized. This summary is intended to supply general information about significant aspects of the subject only and is not meant to give legal counsel as to what the law presently is in a particular state. The law is a changing thing and states are constantly making significant amendments in their living-will laws. Therefore, readers should consult the statutes of their states for special and specific provisions.

All statutes are founded on the idea that we have the right to control decisions about our health care. They furnish vehicles for the implementation of health-care decisions for people no longer competent to make them, and provide that, before incompetency, competent adults may make declarations and give directions relating to medical care. The rationale of the statutes is that if competent adults can personally accept or refuse medical or surgical treatment, there should be no legal or other reason why they should not be able to accept or refuse it through a directive or even through an agent in advance of incompetency.

In all states, the declaration must be in writing. Some mandate that the execution of the declaration meet the strict requirements for the execution of a testamentary will (Arkansas, Illinois, Nevada, New Mexico). In other states (Florida, Louisiana, Virginia) if the person is not, for physical reasons, able to sign the declaration, an oral one may be made also, but then one of the witnesses must sign the person's name to a written declaration in the person's presence and at the person's direction. The person has the responsibility of notifying the attending physician that a living will has been made. But the declaration does not become effective or controlling until the individual is diagnosed as suffering from a terminal condition (Alabama, Alaska, Arizona, California, Colorado, Connecticut, Delaware, District of Columbia, Florida, Georgia, Hawaii, Idaho, Indiana, Iowa, Kansas, Louisiana, Maine, Maryland, Mississippi, Missouri, Montana, Nevada, New Hampshire, New Mexico, North Carolina, Oklahoma, Oregon, South Carolina, Tennessee, Texas, Vermont, Virginia, Washington, West Virginia, Wisconsin, Wyoming). A "terminal condition" generally means a condition caused by injury, disease, or illness from which there is no recovery and which makes death imminent.

Artificial feeding is not included in the life-sustaining procedure that may be withheld or withdrawn (Arizona, Colorado, Connecticut, Georgia, Hawaii, Illinois, Iowa, Kansas, Maryland, Montana, New Hampshire, Oklahoma, Oregon, South Carolina, Tennessee, Vermont, Wisconsin, Wyoming). In some states artificial feeding is included while in others another statutory provision is added to the effect that artificial feeding can be included as a life-sustaining procedure if a person has expressed in a living will the wish that it be withheld or withdrawn.

All statutes describe the basic living will. Any competent adult may make a declaration that directs physicians what to do or not to do if that person is terminally ill. The intent here is not to require the existence of a terminal condition at the time the declaration is made. The declaration is for people looking ahead and who want to participate in decisions about their treatment in the event they have a terminal condition. Generally, the declaration must be signed by two subscribing witnesses, one of whom is not a spouse or blood relative. Since patients may request a health provider to witness a declaration, it should be noted that, while statutes may preclude a provider or its employees from serving as a health-care surrogate, no statute disqualifies a health professional from being a witness to a declaration.

All state statutes suggest a form of declaration that, with little variation, is also suggested by virtually every other living-will statute. In some states, a declaration must substantially follow the statutory form (Alabama, Arizona, California, Connecticut, District of Columbia, Georgia, Idaho, Illinois, Indiana, Kansas, Maryland, Mississippi, Nevada, New Mexico, Oklahoma, Oregon, South Carolina, Vermont, Washington, West Virginia, Wisconsin, Wyoming). In those states where artificial feeding may be refused in a living will, care should be taken to insert in the living will a clause to express the person's desire to withhold or withdraw it, such as: "I (do) (do not) wish that nutrition and hydration (food and water) be withheld or withdrawn when the application of such procedure would serve only to prolong the process of dying."

Some states (Arkansas, Colorado, Delaware, Florida, Hawaii, Idaho, Indiana, Iowa, Louisiana, Texas, Vermont, Virginia, Wyoming) permit the designation of a proxy to make treatment decisions if the patient cannot participate in a medical decision. Making a designation is optional. Patients should, however, consider filling in the designation clause in the form and authorizing a proxy to make medical decisions for them when they cannot speak for themselves. The proxy can make decisions in medical situations and for medical conditions or medical interventions they could not foresee and can make these decisions in line with what the patients want. The designation of a proxy is a highly practical way people can make sure that their wishes will be honored.

Some statutes provide that if the individual making the declaration is a pregnant female, the living will is not effective during the pregnancy (Alabama, Alaska, Arizona, California, Colorado, Connecticut, Delaware, Georgia, Hawaii, Illinois, Indiana, Iowa, Kansas, Maryland, Missouri, Montana, Nevada, New Hampshire, Oklahoma, South Carolina, Vermont, Washington, West Virginia, Wisconsin, Wyoming). Under these statutes, the life of the pregnant individual will be sustained until the fetus is viable—that is, able to survive outside the womb. Other statutes (Florida) do not permit a proxy to consent to withholding or withdrawing life-sustaining treatment for a pregnant patient prior to viability unless a living will has delegated this authority to the proxy or the proxy has court approval.

The declaration can be revoked at any time either by an oral declaration, by a signed and dated writing, by physically cancelling or destroying the will, or by making a subsequent declaration materially different from the previous one. The cancellation must be communicated to the attending physician, proxy, or health-care facility to be effective (Alabama, Alaska, Arizona, California, Colorado, Delaware, District of Columbia, Florida, Georgia, Hawaii, Idaho, Illinois, Indiana, Iowa, Kansas, Louisiana, Maine, Maryland, Mississippi, Missouri, Montana, Nevada, New Hampshire, New Mexico, North Carolina, Oklahoma, Oregon, South Carolina, Tennessee, Texas, Vermont, Virginia, Washington, West Virginia, Wisconsin, Wyoming). Many who have made a living will to exercise their right to die and in order to be able to die a "natural death" may later discover that the natural dying process is not either dignified or peaceful. If they decide that letting nature take its course has become unbearable, is not what they really wanted, and want now to receive the medical treatment they refused earlier, the directive may be revoked.

In most states, if because of moral or ethical beliefs, an attending physician will not comply with the living will, the physician must make reasonable efforts to transfer the patient to another physician. Statutes also generally contain a guarantee to a health-care facility, physician, or any one under the physician's direction, immunity from criminal prosecution, civil liability, or of being disciplined for unprofessional conduct for carrying out the wishes expressed in a living will by a patient with a terminal condition (Alabama, Alaska, Arizona, Arkansas, California, Colorado, Connecticut, Delaware, District of Columbia, Florida, Georgia, Hawaii, Idaho, Illinois, Indiana, Kansas, Louisiana, Maine, Maryland, Mississippi, Missouri, Montana, Nevada, New Hampshire, New Mexico, North Carolina, Oklahoma, Oregon, South Carolina, Tennessee, Texas, Vermont, Virginia, Washington, West Virginia, Wisconsin, Wyoming). This is a very important provision. Without it, in our litigious society physicians might be afraid to carry out the patient's wishes to stop or withdraw treatment. But with their immunity guaranteed, the provision reinforces the patient's right to refuse medical treatment. Virtually all statutes provide that refusing life-sustaining medical treatment does not constitute a suicide. They also provide that making a living will does not affect life insurance policies. Existing policies will not be invalidated nor can people be turned down by insurance companies because they have made living wills.

Some statutes provide for the recognition of a living will executed in another state if it is validly executed under its laws or the laws of the other state (Alabama, Alaska, Hawaii, Florida, Maine, Maryland, Missouri, Montana, Nevada). However, recognition of an out-of-state will only goes as far as its execution. For example, the force to be given its request for termination of artificial feeding will still depend on the law of the state in which the living will is carried out, not the law of the state in which it was executed. In some states, for instance, the right of a person to reject artificial feeding by a living will is hedged by severe limitations.

### Federal Level: Patient Self-Determination Act

*Cruzan* sent shock waves through Washington, and on the federal level it produced the first congressional legislation to deal with living wills: the Patient Self-Determination Act.[8] The aim of the act was not to create any new rights but merely to educate patients about their existing rights. Nor was the object to force patients to make advance directives but only to motivate them to do so.

To achieve this aim, Congress did in the medical field what the U.S. Supreme Court did in the field of law enforcement. Its decision in *Miranda* v. *Arizona*[9] had forced police to advise suspects of their rights, including the right to remain silent. With the new legislation, Congress required all health-care facilities in receipt of Medicare or Medicaid funds, including hospitals, nursing homes, hospices, home health agencies, and prepaid health maintenance organizations, to "Mirandize" all patients being admitted by providing them with written information explaining their rights to accept or refuse medical or surgical treatment and of the sorts of advance directives they could make. The act imposed four further requirements on provider organizations: (1) documentation in the patient's medical records of whether or not an advance directive had been executed; (2) education for the community and staff on issues concerning advance directives; (3) maintenance of written policies and procedures to implement patients' rights to accept or refuse life-sustaining treatment and execute advance directives; (4) providing patients with written information about such policies.

The act has been hailed by some patients'-rights organizations as promising "a dramatic increase in nationwide awareness of patients' rights" and as "a tremendous gain" (Concern for Dying/Society for the Right to Die, 1991:3). In one respect, this evaluation is justified because another provision of the act requires the U.S. Department of Health and Human Services to promote a national program to apprise the general public and those receiving Social Security benefits of their rights regarding treatment and advance directives and to supply health-care facilities with informative materials to provide to patients. The act is an advance because it mandates the entry of the federal government as a powerful educational force.

But other aspects of the act raise questions about whether it deserves the high marks it has been given. Its encouragement of advance directives that might refuse expensive life-sustaining treatment in order to reduce provider costs and save money for the federal government presents serious ethical issues. In addition, the act does not specify that patients must be made aware of their rights to accept or decline medical treatment as interpreted by the U.S. Supreme Court in *Cruzan* and guaranteed by the Constitution. The act mandates only that patients are to be informed of their "rights under State law (whether statutory or as recognized by the courts of the state)." We noted in Chapter 6 that interpretation by state courts of patients' rights to accept or refuse treatment is not the same as that of the Supreme Court. Further, where the *Cruzan* decision implies that all competent adults have the right to decline medical treatment, including artificial feeding, state living-will statutes impose restrictions on the right; that is, they limit living wills to people suffering from a terminal condition; some exclude artificial feeding from the life-sustaining procedures that may be refused; others hedge its refusal with limitations. In addition, five states have no living-will statutes, and there is considerable variance among the statutes of those that have, particularly with reference to artificial feeding and designation of proxies. The twofold result of the quoted provision of the act is that it: (1) presents health-care facilities with the immediate problem of ascertaining the laws of their particular state and of being sure that the information conforms to these laws; and (2) makes patients less rather than more aware that their rights may be greater than recognized by a state.

With its requirement that "all adult individuals receiving medical care" receive written information concerning advance directives, the act seems to require that even adult patients admitted to a hospital for routine services be supplied this information. Since all statutes authorizing living wills are limited to individuals who are terminally ill, supplying information about living wills to these patients seems absurd. Another difficulty with the act is its assumption that the information supplied will be understood by all adults. In many states—notably Arizona, California, Florida, New Mexico, New York, and Texas—Hispanics form an increasingly large proportion of the population. They do not necessarily understand written information not in Spanish. In many cities, other groups such as Asians in San Francisco or Haitians in Miami will not understand forms in English either. Even if these groups can read some English, it is improbable that they will be able to understand the contents of a form that is no more readable than an insurance policy.

The greatest defect of the act, however, lies in its provision that the written information it requires be provided "in the case of a hospital, at the time of the individual's admission as an inpatient." There is a similar provision applicable to nursing homes. The additional supposition of the act is that at this time patients who are furnished with information about advance directives will read it. Such an assumption is out of touch with reality. In a large hospital, such as the 750-bed county hospital on whose ethics committee I serve, a large proportion of patients come from the emergency room. An acutely ill patient cannot be expected to read the written material. Even for patients who are not acutely ill but are to be hospitalized, the time of admission to a hospital is one of stress and hardly the best for patients to be made aware of advance directives and to decide calmly whether they want life-sustaining treatment. The patient is caught in a web of questions and paperwork at the admissions desk. Questions must be answered about Medicare and supplemental insurance. A statement from Medicare concerning Medicare hospital patients and an announcement about billing from physicians who have different billing systems from the hospital must be read. Authorizations for treatment and the release of medical records must be signed. In these circumstances, the act virtually assures that yet another paper thrust at the patient about advance directives will be ignored or overlooked.

The legislation may have been intended as a "tremendous gain" to make people aware of their two rights to accept or decline treatment and to make advance directives, but its many difficulties—in particular, the manner, time, and place for doing so—stand in the way of accomplishing this goal.

To increase even more public awareness of the lesson of *Cruzan*, the legal and health communities should take active roles. Along with the federal government, they have the opportunity and responsibility to become spearheads in the educational campaign. There are at least four ways by which they can take the lead:

1. Bar associations should develop advance directives policies and distribute educational materials and advance directives to the public and without charge. Attorneys, as the stewards of the legal rights of their clients, also should encourage these directives. When clients are planning an estate or drawing a testamentary will, the attorney has an ideal opportunity as well as a responsibility to advise clients to draw up living wills as a means of protecting and asserting their fundamental rights to make and control health-care decisions while they still have the capacity to

do so. A client wishing to appoint an agent to perform acts on his or her behalf under a power of attorney similarly offers the attorney the opportunity to advise concerning the durable power of attorney for health care. These steps by the legal community would demonstrate its public commitment.

2. Medical societies should develop advance directive policies and distribute sample directives and educational information to their members as well as to the general public. This would show the medical profession's commitment to public service.

3. Health-care personnel, such as those supplying emergency medical services, visiting nurses, and home health-care workers, could disseminate advance directives and talk about them with patients and families.

4. Most important, we should recognize the grave shortcoming in the Patient Self-Determination Act and recognize that people need to make decisions about medical treatment before their admission to hospitals or before a critical illness and that their doctors should help them. These advance directives should be the concern and responsibility of physicians, not the admissions clerk in a hospital. As some observers have pointed out, "advance directives must be part of a clinical process, not an administrative one" (La Puma, Orentlicher, Moss, 1991:405).

Primary-care physicians have many opportunities to initiate discussions with their patients about advance directives and even help their patients complete a directive: during routine office visits, during a physical, when taking a history. Specialty physicians such as oncologists and nephrologists could also make their offices schools for advance directives. All these physicians can find out what a patient's values and treatment preferences are, and if and why a patient wishes to refuse or accept life-sustaining treatment. Emergency physicians may not be able to talk about these directives with critically ill patients, but they can distribute such directives to all coming to the emergency room: police, emergency medical services workers, and families of patients. Taking advantage of all these opportunities would be in line with what Justice Brennan said in the *Cruzan* case: "it might be wise social policy to encourage people to furnish such instructions" and what the American Medical Association said: "Physicians should encourage their patients to document their wishes regarding the use of life-prolonging medical treatments" (AMA, 1989).

But a survey of 405 patients of 30 primary-care physicians at Massachusetts General Hospital, as well as of 102 members of the general public, showed that one of the barriers cited most frequently by patients in planning and completing advance directives was their expectation that their physicians would take the initiative in discussing these documents and the failure of the physicians to do so (Emanuel et al., 1991). The unwillingness of doctors to initiate discussions of advance directives was also noted in another study (Bedell and Delbanco, 1984). These studies do not offer reasons for the failure to live up to the patient's expectations, but they look like the "horse on the dining room table syndrome." The whole subject of advance directives is disagreeable to health-care professionals and makes communication with patients difficult because these documents connote dying and death.

It would benefit both physicians and their patients if an educational program were established to lessen or remove this discomfort and allow physicians to communicate with patients about advance directives more effectively. Physicians might be helped to understand what questions patients are likely to have in the discussion, what vocabulary to use to talk in lay terms to patients about advance directives, how to elicit a patient's values and feelings about advance directives, how to reassure patients that the discussions do not signify a change in their health status and should not alarm them. It is encouraging to find that an interesting program of this kind is being carried out successfully in Oregon at the Oregon Health Sciences University and the Portland Veterans Affairs Medical Center (Gordon and Tolle, 1991).

It is strongly suggested that physicians consider voluntarily performing this needed public service even though it will require some time. The practice of medicine now is choked enough by government regulation and forms. Physicians don't need to invite more bureaucratic control. Yet the Patient Self-Determination Act, which requires health facilities receiving funds from Medicare and Medicaid to educate people about advance directives, suggests that, once it becomes apparent that the act's difficulties prevent it from accomplishing its goal, physicians also in receipt of these funds may be next in line and forced by law to educate their patients unless they do so freely and of their own will.

## Words of Caution

When a person makes a living will, what should be done with it? The statutes contain few directions. A friend told me that she had sent the document to herself by registered mail to show that it had been executed on a certain date. Apart from making the postal service happy, such an action is harmful because it defeats the purpose of the living will: to let others know how the declarant feels. It is, therefore, suggested that three things be done by declarants. They should keep the original with their important papers in an accessible place and not in a safe deposit box that no one can enter except the declarant. Then the declarant should provide copies of the documents to family, lawyer, clergyman, and friends—anyone who might want to protect the declarant's wishes. Above all, a copy should be given to the declarant's physician. Virtually all statutes have something to say on this point. They generally provide that the living will is inoperative unless the declarant has communicated it to the physician, and they require the physician to record it in the declarant's medical records. If the living will is written, it should be made part of the records, and if oral, the physician should note the fact of the declaration in the records.

Living wills are not the ideal solution—not as perfect as most people think and as the press makes out. A frequent complaint is that physicians neglect or refuse to comply with living wills. People can hope but never be sure that their wishes will be carried out.

The living will may not be the ideal solution for other reasons as well. A living will that is not drafted in precise and comprehensible language will present ambiguities and force surrogates and physicians into interpretations that may not be what the declarant wanted. It seems impossible, however, to avoid generalized language when we are trying to foresee the conditions of our dying. For unless a declarant is Nostradamus reincarnated, with extraordinary precognitive gifts, he or she cannot anticipate the specific medical condition from which he or she may suffer, the exact clinical situation that may confront him or her or the attending physician, or the new medical interventions that may be possible in the future. And if the living will is made a considerable time before it is needed, there even may be a question about how accurately it reflects the present wishes of the declarant. When adults have made living wills and continue to be competent, there is no problem in determining whether they have changed their minds about the instructions they have given to their physicians. But should they become unconscious or incompetent, a question may arise, especially in the case of an old living will. To avoid such doubts and to keep abreast of the constantly changing law, it is a good idea to review and update a living will periodically. It should be redated and reinitialed to keep it current. If kept current up to incompetency and loss of mental capacity, it can be inferred that the intentions of the declarant remain the same as when the individual was competent.

## Critique of Living-Will Statutes

A starting point for a critical examination of the living-will statutes is a study made of 175 competent nursing-home residents or the surrogates of incompetent ones to determine the effectiveness of living wills. Signed advance directives by patients expressing their preferences for future medical care were placed in their medical records and made accessible to physicians and nurses, as were directives signed by surrogates concerning care for incompetent patients. The study found that in 25 percent of the cases, the directives were not heeded and were ineffective (Danis et al., 1991). Although the study was limited to one nursing home, it seems to reflect a widespread grievance and is supported by one of the chief complaints families of incompetent patients have presented to the author: that care is not consistent with the wishes expressed in the living wills of family members and that these advance directives are ignored. The living will can be ignored because, although medical personnel may be ethically obliged to follow it and respect a patient's autonomy, the living-will statutes generally do not make it mandatory for physicians or health-care facilities to honor a patient's wishes expressed in it. This shortcoming also makes it possible to overcome case law laid down by such cases as *Bartling* v. *Superior Court*[10] that declare a patient's right of self-determination is paramount to the ethical or other concerns of health-care providers. The statutes impose no penalties on a physician who refuses to follow the declaration. The statutes do not even make noncompliance with the patient's wishes an instance of professional misconduct. All the great majority of living-will laws do is require that, if physicians are not willing to comply with a living will, they make reasonable efforts to transfer the patient to another physician. The only penalty imposed is that physicians pay the costs of the transfer. Even so, except in South Carolina,[11] there is no requirement that the transferee physician be one who will honor the patient's wishes either. Patients, therefore, may find themselves in the same position with the second doctor as they were with the first.

That physicans can ignore living wills points up how important it is for patients to be careful in the selection of physicians and to choose only those who are right for them and on whom, after an honest exchange of outlooks and values, they can count to respect their wishes. Otherwise no statute requires physicians to tell the patient that, for reasons of ethics, conscience, or religious beliefs, they are unwilling to comply with the provisions of a living will. A requirement of this kind would at least put patients on notice and allow them to get another physician willing to honor their wishes—but it does not exist in the living-will law of any state.

It is possible that the *Cruzan* decision will affect this situation and help aggrieved patients. By establishing a constitutional right for competent adults to refuse treatment, including artificial feeding, the case may supply patients with a remedy for imposing liability against recalcitrant doctors and health-care institutions who violate that right if they decline to honor its exercise in the living will.

Under the provisions of all statutes, the declaration may be made by a competent adult at any time but it is not effective until that person is terminally ill—generally defined as a condition which is hopeless and makes death imminent. This provision is a flaw because it excludes from participation in their medical decisions all people who are not diagnosed as terminally ill but are in a coma, persistent vegetative state, have Alzheimer's disease, or are in advanced age. People such as Karen Ann Quinlan, Nancy Cruzan, Elizabeth Bouvia, and Rosaria Candura, whose cases were cited in previous chapters, would not be protected. In some states, therefore, living-will legislation has been expanded to include a persistent vegetative state.

The statutes generally define a terminal condition as any "condition caused by injury, disease or illness from which, to a reasonable degree of medical certainty, there can be no recovery and which makes death imminent." What is an "imminent" death? Is it one that will take place even if all life-sustaining treatment is never withdrawn or withheld? Is an "imminent" death one that is a minute, hours, or a day away? If these are the meanings intended by *imminent*, then the living-will statute is useless. It will be a waste of time and money to ask a court for a ruling on whether treatment should be stopped or withheld, since death will probably take place before the court can make a ruling. *Imminent* so interpreted excludes from protection all people whose deaths are six months or a year away. To skirt these difficulties, it might be possible to define death instead in terms of a definite period of time, as "death within a year." But this phrase is not desirable either, since diseases and diagnoses are complicated. Such forecasts would be speculative and physicians do not like to attempt such definite assessments. The National Conference of Commissioners on Uniform State Laws (NCCUSL) in 1985 formulated the Uniform Rights of the Terminally Ill Act[12] in which a terminal condition was defined as resulting in death "within a relatively short time." In recommending its enactment by all states, the NCCUSL believed that the amended definition would eliminate the interpretation of *imminent* as immediate death; and while it still requires a doctor's assessment, it would also be more flexible than setting a definite span of time.

Some statutes make the living will of a pregnant woman ineffective. These provisions have not been challenged in any court, but their constitutionality may be questioned. They seem to strip the pregnant woman of her common-law and constitutional rights, including the right to refuse life-sustaining treatment, and to take these rights away in favor of a child not yet born. The whole subject of the rights of a fetus versus the rights of a mother is controversial. The ethical issues are whether a fetus has a moral status superior to that of the mother. Does the physician attending a pregnant woman have one patient or two? And if two, to which one does the physician owe allegiance? Does the physician or do we have any ethical duty to a fetus? The legal issue is: Whose rights should prevail when there is a conflict between the mother's and the fetus's interests? Apparently, state legislatures decided that the fetal interests should prevail, but others may disagree.

Many statutes exclude artificial feeding from the life-sustaining procedures that may be withdrawn or withheld. Others retain the prohibition but allow artificial feeding to be included as a life-sustaining procedure that can be withdrawn or withheld if requested in a living will. For people in states where this kind of statute exists and who do not want tubal feeding, a strong reason exists for drafting the living will: it is the sole means of stopping or preventing the procedure. Even so, this statutory authorization is hedged by severe limitations. For example, before it was substantially amended in 1992, a Florida statute[13] authorized the patient's family to overrule a declarant's wish in spite of the fact that it had been expressed in a living will. In other words, what had been given the declarant could hardly be called a right to refuse artificial feeding because it was subject to veto. It was a right only if it agreed with the family's wishes.

It should be noted again that artificial feeding is still not something many legislatures want to recognize as the same as any other medical procedure that can be refused. It is treated specially with restrictive provisions, reflective of the controversy over artificial feeding. As part of the *Cruzan* fallout, it is possible that the case will provide a basis for challenging the constitutionality of laws that either do not allow people to refuse artificial feeding by means of living wills or else hedge this refusal with limitations because they treat artificial feeding differently from other medical procedures. Since many justices affirmed in *Cruzan* that artificial feeding cannot be distinguished from other medical procedures, and there is a constitutional right to refuse it under the Constitution's due process clause, the type of statute under consideration may burden or restrain this right too much.

## HEALTH CARE SURROGATE

Advance directive statutes provide several alternative procedures for treatment decisions. The living will and the designation of a proxy in the will to make these decisions have both been mentioned. Another procedure permitted by many statutes allows treatment decisions for someone who has not make a living will to be made in accordance with a written agreement between the attending physician and guardian or other individuals in the following order of priority: guardian, person designated by the terminally ill patient, spouse, adult child or, if more than one, by the majority of adult children, parents or nearest living relative.

Besides these procedures, a principal can designate any competent adult as a surrogate to make health-care decisions and apply for public benefits for the principal if he or she is not able to do so. The designation generally must be made in writing, witnessed by at least two adults, and delivered to the surrogate. An alternate surrogate should be designated also in case the original surrogate is not able or willing to act. The most recent such laws were enacted in Florida, New York, and Massachusetts. Many of these laws, however, place restrictions on the health-care surrogates. For example, treating health-care providers and their employees and relatives are precluded from serving as such surrogates. Similarly, the operator or employee of a health-care facility in which a patient resides or the relative of the operator or employee cannot serve as a surrogate. Surrogates may not consent to abortion, sterilization, electroshock therapy, psychosurgery, or withholding or withdrawing life-sustaining procedures unless the person for whom the surrogate is acting has made a living will. In addition, under the provisions of some health-surrogate laws, the designation of the surrogate will terminate after the passage of a specified number of years following the designation.

## DURABLE POWER OF ATTORNEY

A further procedure that exists in all states is provided by their statutes on durable power of attorney. Both ordinary and durable powers of attorney permit a principal to designate a person as attorney-in-fact, on whom is conferred full and general powers to act for the principal with respect to the principal's real or personal property and business or private affairs. In addition to these general powers, it should have been possible to use the durable power of attorney to authorize an attorney-in-fact to perform any act not specifically prohibited by statutes, including consenting to or refusing medical treatment (Collin et al., 1984). To overcome any doubt concerning such authorization, however, a movement can be observed toward further legislation. Many states have passed or amended statutes specifically to provide procedures and forms for a durable power of attorney for health care that allows the appointment of an attorney-in-fact to make treatment decisions. Some forms confer both general powers and authority to make treatment decisions. But other forms are available for those who do not wish to confer broad powers and to appoint an attorney-in-fact with only the authority to perform health-care acts.

But there are differences among the provisions of the various statutes. By way of illustration, the statutes of California and Rhode Island provide that attorneys-in-fact may consent to or refuse medical treatment, including withdrawing or withholding life-sustaining treatment. On the other hand, while the statutes of Colorado, Florida, North Carolina, and Pennsylvania empower attorneys-in-fact to make decisions and consent to medical procedures, they do not expressly permit the attorney-in-fact to refuse them. These restrictive statutes, however, may create controversies over a principal's wishes concerning refusing, withdrawing, or withholding life-sustaining treatment. They seem to mandate that the durable power of attorney cannot be used to refuse such treatment and that the only authority for and means of doing so is the living will. It seems important, however, that an attorney-in-fact be permitted to make all treatment decisions—not merely to consent but as well to decline care and treatment if that is the principal's wish—and that the power of attorney expressly confers this authority.

Under the common law, an ordinary power of attorney remained effective until the principal died or revoked it. Similarly, under all statutes, the durable power of attorney remains valid until death or revocation; it does not terminate as does a health-care surrogate designation after the lapse of a certain number of years. What is the impact on these instruments of the incompetency of the principal? The common law rule is that ordinary powers of attorney cease on the later mental incapacity of the principal.[14] It is just at the crucial moment when principals are incapable of speaking for themselves and need someone who knows their wishes to speak for them that the authority of the attorney-in-fact to speak is revoked and the ordinary power of attorney becomes useless.

It is here that the durable power of attorney steps into the breach in one of two ways. Under some statutes, a "springing" durable power of attorney becomes effective upon the incapacity of the principal, while the provisions of other statutes permit an "immediate" durable power of attorney to become effective from the time of its execution by the principal and to remain so notwithstanding the subsequent incapacity of the principal.

Whichever alternative is permitted and used, the statutes generally require the durable power of attorney to include specific wording, such as "This durable power of attorney shall not be affected by the disability of the principal."

Whether the springing or immediate durable power of attorney is authorized and used, a provision should also be included to spell out just how the incapacity of the principal is determined, whether by a judge after a formal hearing regarding the competence of the principal or by written statements from two or more specified people, such as the principal's spouse, physician, and lawyer, that the principal is incapable of managing his or her own affairs and assets or of making health-care decisions.

One difficulty should the principal be adjudged legally incompetent is that a conflict may arise between the attorney-in-fact and the legal guardian appointed by a court for the incompetent principal. Again, one finds variations among the statutes on how to circumvent this conflict. Some statutes—Florida's, for example[15]—provide that, although the durable power of attorney shall not be affected by the subsequent incapacity of the principal, nevertheless it will be revoked automatically if the principal is adjudged incompetent. On the other hand, under the Uniform Durable Power of Attorney Act approved by the National Conference of Commissioners on Uniform State Laws in 1979 and since adopted by twenty-seven states, a durable power of attorney does not terminate in case a formal determination of incompetency is made by a court. The legal guardian, however, may revoke or amend the durable power of attorney. But these statutory solutions to the problem of conflict inadvertently may have spawned another problem. Since the Florida-type statute requires the durable power of attorney to be revoked automatically if the principal is adjudged incompetent, it may motivate the institution of incompetency proceedings by those people who want to get rid of an attorney-in-fact and frustrate the principal's wishes concerning the management of his or her property and affairs or health care. The other type of statute that permits revocation of the durable power of attorney at the will of a legal guardian may also encourage those interested in the property or affairs or health care of the principal to petition a court for an adjudication of incompetency in the hope of getting a guardian appointed who is sympathetic to them. Because durable power of attorney statutes vary from one state to the other and the durable power of attorney must conform to their provisions, readers are advised to consult the statutes and attorneys in their states.

The four advantages of appointing a health-care surrogate—or an attorney-in-fact under a durable power of attorney—should be obvious. The first is that such a person can make medical decisions on the spot in future medical situations that cannot be foreseen when an advance directive is executed or with respect to medical intervention tools that may not have existed at an earlier time. A second advantage is that a surrogate or attorney-in-fact can remove from health professionals the task of having to read and interpret a living will and can make available to them someone with whom medical treatment alternatives can be taken up and who is legally empowered to make decisions and tell professionals exactly what to do or not to do. There is a third advantage for the health professional: a surrogate or attorney-in-fact can eliminate the clash of desires that may arise and the physician's uncomfortable predicament when families cannot agree with the patient on the directions in a living will. The physician need deal only with the one individual designated by the patient to make treatment decisions on the patient's behalf. From the perspective of the patient, there is a fourth benefit to be derived from appointing a surrogate. Since living wills often do not seem to be effective and appear to be ignored by medical personnel whether or not present in the medical record and accessible, a health-care surrogate or attorney-in-fact is more effective as the means of preserving the autonomy of an incompetent patient. A flesh-and-blood representative speaking for a patient and discussing treatment choices with and giving instructions to medical personnel is much more difficult for a physician to ignore or refuse than the wishes of an incompetent patient expressed in a paper directive.

In comparison to the proxy appointed under the living-will statutes, the attorney-in-fact designated by a durable power of attorney seems to give the principal more protection. Under the living will statutes, a living will is not effective until the declarant is terminally ill. Many patients, therefore, such as Karen Ann Quinlan or Nancy Cruzan, are not covered by the statutes. A durable power of attorney would extend treatment decisions to all patients regardless of terminal illness.

The use of the durable power of attorney may be expected to increase because of its advantages and because of the concurring opinion of Justice Sandra Day O'Connor in *Cruzan*, in which she urged the appointment of someone authorized to make treatment decisions.

A problem with the durable power of attorney, however, is that there are people in hospitals who are alone and friendless and know of no person who will speak for them. Those in nursing homes and homes for the aged who have no one to whom to turn are included in this group. Other individuals who are not entirely alone may not be sure whom they can trust and who will respect their wishes. They may not know someone absolutely disinterested in their deaths and who will not benefit from them. They may not wish to designate as attorney-in-fact someone—say, a beneficiary under a will—who may wish them dead. Some of these friendless patients may request nurses to act as their attorneys-in-fact. But may nurses who are willing to act in such a capacity accede to the request? Nothing in the law prevents them from doing so. Under the durable power of attorney statutes and in contrast to the health-care proxy laws, which do not allow the employees of health-care providers or health-care facilities in which a patient resides to serve as health-care surrogates, there is no proscription against appointing a treating health-care provider or employee as attorney-in-fact. For other of these unfortunate classes of people, however, a living will may be preferable to a durable power of attorney. But there are other alternatives. One is to take advantage of the guardianship processes all states have and make a voluntary petition to a court for a limited guardian who will exercise the powers that are specified by a court to care for their rights and persons. A second alternative is available under the health-care surrogate legislation in many states. Under it, the health-care facility where they are patients designates a health-care surrogate to make health-care decisions for patients and provides informed consent if the patients are not capable of making these decisions or providing this consent.[16]

## DO-NOT-RESUSCITATE ORDERS

A do-not-resuscitate (DNR) order is a medical order written by a physician to deny the administration of cardiopulmonary resuscitation to a patient who has suffered cardiac or pulmonary arrest. It is often written by physicians unilaterally when they believe that CPR would be futile. While their action may be defended as reasonable medical practice and within the right of the physician to determine if treatment will or will not be beneficial to the patient (Blackhall, 1987), the deciding factor would seem to be the applicable state statute. For example, a statute[17] that defines a physician-prepared DNR order as one which documents instructions by the patient, the patient's designated health-care surrogate, or appointed proxy that CPR is to be withheld in the event of cardiac or pulmonary arrest seems to tie the order directly into a patient's autonomy and the right of a competent adult to make choices and advance directives regarding the refusal of life-sustaining treatment, including the administration of CPR. If, however, the patient is incompetent, the DNR order is tied to decisions by those acting on the patient's behalf. The ultimate justification for the DNR order is not medical judgment or prerogative but informed consent after discussions between physicians and the patient and family about cardiopulmonary arrest and CPR.

Advance directives come in different forms and offer different kinds of protection. The law does not preclude the execution of all forms—the living will, the health-care surrogate, the durable power of attorney for health care, and the do-not-resuscitate order—in order to be afforded maximum protection in all future medical situations.

## LEGAL CITATIONS

1. In re Guardianship of Estelle M. Browning, 543 S.2d 258, *aff'd* 568 S.2d 4 (Fla. Sup. Ct. 1990); In re Storar, 52 N.Y.2d 363, 420 N.E.2d 64, *cert. den.* 454 U.S. 858 (1981); In re O'Connor, 72 N.Y.2d 517, 531 N.E.2d 607 (N.Y. Ct. App. 1988); In re Estate of Longeway, 133 Ill.2d 33, 549 N.E.2d 292 (Ill. Sup. Ct. 1989); Leach v. Akron Medical Center, 68 Ohio Misc. 1, 426 N.E.2d 809 (Ohio Ct. C. P., Summit Co. 1980).

2. Cruzan v. Director, Missouri Department of Health, 497 U.S. 261, 111 L.Ed. 2d 224, 110 S.Ct. 841 (1990).

3. Brophy v. New England Sinai Hospital, Inc., 497 N.E.2d 626, 632, fn.22 (Mass. Sup. Jud. Ct. 1986).

4. Alabama, Alaska, Arizona, Arkansas, California, Colorado, Connecticut, Delaware, Florida, Georgia, Hawaii, Idaho, Illinois, Indiana, Iowa, Kansas, Kentucky, Louisiana, Maine, Maryland, Minnesota, Mississippi, Missouri, Montana, Nevada, New Hampshire, New Jersey, New Mexico, North Carolina, North Dakota, Ohio, Oklahoma, Oregon, Rhode Island, South Carolina, South Dakota, Tennessee, Texas, Utah, Vermont, Virginia, Washington, West Virginia, Wisconsin, Wyoming.

5. John F. Kennedy Memorial Hospital v. Bludworth, 452 S.2d 921 (Fla. Sup. Ct. 1984).

6. In re Storar, see *supra*, note 1.

7. Saunders v. State, 129 Misc.2d 45, 492 N.Y.S.2d 510 (N.Y. Sup. Ct. 1985)

8. Omnibus Budget Reconciliation Act 1990. Title IV. Public Law 101-508. Section 4206. Amends several sections of 42 U.S. Code, in particular section 1395 cc(a)1.

9. 384 U.S. 436 (U.S. Sup. Ct. 1966).

10. 163 Cal. App.3rd 186, 209 Cal. Rptr. 220 (Ct. App. 1984).

11. Death with Dignity Act, Sec. 44–77–100 (1986).

12. Secs. 1–18, 9A U.L.A. 456 (Supp.1986).

13. Florida "Right to Decline Life-Prolonging Procedures," Sec. 765.075(b2). In 1992, this was retitled "Health Care Advance Directives" and significantly amended.

14. Millman v. First Federal Savings and Loan Assn., 198 S.2d 338 (Fla. Dist. Ct. App. 1967).

15. Florida Statutes, Sec. 709.08.

16. See, for example, Florida Statutes, Sec. 641.61 et seq.

17. Florida Statutes Sec. 765.101(5), 765.307(2).

## REFERENCES

American Medical Association Board of Trustees. 1989. Report OO, A–89:135–37.

Bedell, S. E., and Delbanco, T. L. 1984. "Choices About Cardiopulmonary Resuscitation in the Hospital: When Do Physicians Talk with Patients?" *New England Journal of Medicine* 310: 1089–93.

Blackhall, L. J. 1987. "Must We Always Use CPR?" *New England Journal of Medicine* 317:1281–85.

Cassel, C. K., and Zweibel, N. R. 1987. "Attitudes Regarding Life-Extending Medical Care Among the Elderly and Their Children." *Gerentologist* 27:229A.

Collin, F. F., Lombard, J. L., Moses, A. L, and Spitler, H. 1984. *Drafting the Durable Power of Attorney—A Systems Approach.* Lexington, SC: R.P.W. Publishing Co.

Concern for Dying/Society for the Right to Die. 1991. *Newsletter*, Spring.

———. News release, December 14, 1990.

Danis, M., Southerland, L. I., Garrett, J. M., Smith, J. L, Hielma F., Pickard, C. G., Egner, D. M., Patrick, D. L. 1991. "A Prospective Study of Advance Directives for Life-Sustaining Care." *New England Journal of Medicine* 324: 882–88.

Emanuel, L. L., Barry, M. J., Stoeckle, J. D., Ettelson, L. M., Emanuel, E. J. 1991. "Advance Directives for Medical Care—A Case for Greater Use." *New England Journal of Medicine* 324:889–95.

Emanuel, L. L., and Emanuel, E. J. 1989. "The Medical Directive: A New Comprehensive Advance Care Directive." *Journal of the American Medical Association* 261:3288–93.

Feifel, H. 1977. "Death in Contemporary America" quoting Woody Allen. In H. Feifel, ed. *New Meanings of Death.* New York: McGraw-Hill.

Gordon, H. G., and Tolle, S. W. 1991. "Discussing Life-Sustaining Treatment." *Archives of Internal Medicine* 151: 567–70.

Kutner, L. 1969. "Due Process of Euthanasia: The Living Will, a Proposal." *Indiana Law Journal* 44:539–54.

La Puma, J., Orentlicher, D., and Moss, R. J. 1991. "Advance Directives on Admission: Clinical Implications and Analysis of the Patient Self-Determination Act of 1990." *Journal of the American Medical Association* 266:402–05.

Orentlicher, D. 1990. "Advance Medical Directives." *Journal of the American Medical Association* 263:2365–67.

# V

## Determination of Death

# 9

## Defining Death

The law of dying and death deals with three categories of patients. In earlier chapters involving dying patients, we looked at the first two categories: living people who are competent and those who are incompetent. Now we examine a final category: those considered legally dead.

### IMPORTANCE OF DETERMINING DEATH

There are several public-policy reasons that give the determination of death real and practical importance.

#### Legal and Social Importance

To know when someone is dead:

1. Abates some actions at law.
2. Allows the inheritance of real property under the laws of descent and of personal property under the laws of distribution if the dead person dies without a will.
3. Transfers ownership and control of jointly held property to the survivor.
4. Matures a life insurance policy.
5. Vests in the next of kin a quasi-property right in a corpse.
6. Allows a judicial decision to be made concerning which of joint tenants died first in simultaneous death situations, as in the case of *Smith* v. *Smith*.[1]

7. Starts the time for grieving.

8. Makes a deathbed gift effective.

9. Begins the payment of Worker's Compensation benefits and those from Social Security and the Veterans Administration.

10. Ends a marriage.

11. Ends a partnership.

12. Allows the disposition of property under a will to become effective.

13. Allows actions to be brought by survivors if death was caused by a wrongful act.

14. Starts tolling the period within which some actions can be brought, such as wrongful death actions (two years in some states).

## Medical Importance

To know when death has occurred:

1. Ends all duties of health-care personnel to provide medical treatment. The consent of the family to the stoppage of treatment is not necessary, either. The normal procedure on brain death is to declare the patient dead, record the determination and time of death on the patient's chart, and withdraw all life support, except when a patient is pregnant or is a potential organ donor.

2. Causes nurses to wash the corpse and to place it in a condition in which it can be seen. The next of kin are advised by the hospital in which the patient died so that the body can be turned over to them.

3. Ends all moral and medical issues raised by the patient's refusal of treatment. Legal issues raised by a case also generally become moot and are not decided by a court if a patient dies during litigation. In some cases, however, medicolegal issues are not ended even if a patient has died while litigation is pending. In spite of death, a court may decide to resolve any right-to-die or other issues that it considers of significant public importance and the case is of the kind that is bound to be repeated.[2] In *Satz* v. *Perlmutter*,[3] Abe Perlmutter, the patient, was suffering from amyotrophic lateral sclerosis (Lou Gehrig's disease) and had a

mechanical respirator attached to his trachea. He petitioned a court to have it disconnected. The trial judge came to his bedside and granted the patient's request. Perlmutter died forty hours after the respirator was disconnected. But because of the importance of the issues raised by his case, they continued to run through the judicial machinery for fifteen more months after Perlmutter's death until finally decided by the Supreme Court of Florida.

4. Allows hospital beds, equipment, and personnel to be used for patients who have some hope of recovery.

5. Begins an autopsy by the coroner or medical examiner who will investigate the cause of any death that is suspicious.

6. Starts the harvesting of organs to be transplanted. Whereas prior to the twentieth century physicians were concerned with the importance of a correct determination of death in order to forestall premature burial, with the development of organ transplantation, today medical practitioners are more concerned with the determination of death as the signal for beginning the surgical removal of organs. Cadaveric donors are the primary source for organs and are central to the transplant program.

## MEDICAL DEFINITION OF DEATH: MEDICAL HISTORY

When is a person dead? It never used to be hard to determine when a person was dead. The onset of putrefaction has always been accepted as the clearest equivalent of death. But, in addition, since everyone has always known what the normal indicia of life are—breathing and a beating heart—it also seemed easy enough to decide when these vital signs stopped. Tests of death, such as placing a mirror in front of the nostrils or a feather before the lips, were not difficult to apply and required no special training. In Shakespeare's *Henry IV*, for example, the Prince of Wales, using the feather test, takes the crown from his father's head, and in *King Lear* a looking-glass is placed in front of Cordelia's nostrils. But in reality, these tests sometimes led to horrendous mistakes. In Shakespeare again we find one of them immortalized: Romeo mistaking Juliet for dead poisons himself after he finds her in a crypt pale and apparently not breathing because of a potion Friar Laurence gave her. Mistakes in certifying people dead also either resulted in their premature burial or, in one case reported from France, in pregnancy and birth. In this case, a girl believed dead had been placed in a coffin preparatory to burial. A monk, spending the night in the room with the coffin, removed the clothes from the body and engaged in sexual intercourse with it. Following his departure the next day, the girl was found to be alive. After nine months had passed, a child was born to her (Mant, 1968).

The fallibility of the tests and the resulting gruesome mistakes in determining death led a committee of the English House of Commons to take note of "the carelessness and ignorance of the people" (Abbott, 1901) in making these determinations and to recommend an amendment to the Births and Deaths Registration Act of 1836 and 1874 to the effect that medical practitioners inspect the body and give a prescribed certificate of death. In 1903, the United States likewise adopted legislation making the registration of death and its certification by physicians compulsory. So to the question of when a person is dead, the operational and legal answer seems to be when a physician examines the body, certifies death, and completes the death certificate. Among the criteria used by the physician for defining death were not only the standard used by laymen as the permanent and complete cessation of respiration and circulation but as well other guidelines such as pallor, eye changes, and rigor mortis.

But this was going to change. In the 1950s, cardiopulmonary resuscitation was common practice in hospitals and was carried out by trained teams of doctors and nurses. With this practice, they were able to reduce mortality rates if patients at risk of cardiac or pulmonary arrest were reached early enough and resuscitation procedures carried out. But soon the teams found out that it was useless to resuscitate patients if respiration or circulation had been stopped for a considerable time and had caused great brain damage. If there was no recovery of the brain possible, the patient was declared dead. The 1960s marked the beginning of a new standard: the criterion of brain death.

In the 1960s, developments in medical technology, such as the respirator or ventilatory support and cardiopulmonary resuscitation, produced a problem of "respirator brain"—that is, loss of brain function while other biologic functions of the body were maintained by respirators or cardiogenic drugs. Because of these developments, biologic functions such as respiration or circulation could be maintained for days, weeks, or longer, yet without any hope of bringing back life; at the same time, the electroencephalogram showed brain death. This problem produced the need to use a further definition of death besides the centuries-old general and medical one and brain death became the standard for recognizing that a person was dead.

In 1967, a committee of scholars and scientists from Harvard University was convened to work out specific criteria for determining when a person was dead. In 1968, the Ad Hoc Committee of Harvard Medical School to Examine the Definition of Death issued its report. It made the absence of all brain function or brain death the definition of death—the same definition that had been recognized by the medical community for many years. The committee listed the six necessary criteria as: (1) unreceptivity and unresponsitivity to externally applied stimuli; (2) no movement of breathing; (3) no reflexes; (4) a flat encephalogram—that is, when the use of an EEG machine in continuous monitoring shows a flat or isoelectric pattern indicative of the cessation of cerebral activity; (5) repetition of the tests in twenty-five hours; (6) no evidence of hypothermia (a subnormal temperature of the body) or central nervous system depressants.

Besides the developments in medical technology that permitted biologic functions to be maintained artificially and led to the brain-death definition, there has been one that more than any other development mandated the adoption of this definition: organ transplantation. This development in biomedical technology has made it necessary to declare a person dead as soon as it is clear that the brain is irreversibly damaged and cerebral functions have stopped. The idea is to be able to declare life over at brain death in order to be able to harvest organs from donors while their hearts are still beating and the organs are fresh in order to increase the chances of a successful transplant. The wide gap between the need for organs and the supply of them also made the brain-death definition inevitable. Since an estimated 20,000 people are brain dead annually while their biologic functions are artificially maintained by apparatus, they are potential donors of organs and a source of supply that cannot be ignored.

## LEGAL DEFINITION OF DEATH

The legal and medical professions hold different conceptions of death. The former looks on death as a specific event that occurs at an exact moment in time (Friloux, 1975). But the medical profession sees death as a gradual and continuing process. Death occurs in stages. With the stoppage of respiration and circulation there is death at the clinical level. The brain now goes. With the deprivation of oxygen, the adult cerebral cortex survives for about four minutes while the cortices of infants and fetuses may survive longer. But there is no whole brain or biological death until the functioning of the brain stem ceases. In the adult, it may survive for about twenty minutes without oxygen. Finally, there is death at the cellular level, but again gradually, since the ability of all cells to survive without oxygen varies.

There is another interesting comparison between the two professions. Medicine always is called on to decide what death is and when it has occurred. Although courts are called on constantly to apply the many laws applicable to dying and death enacted by legislatures, judges and lawmakers rarely are troubled by these questions. Determining questions of fact as to when death occurred are issues that arise principally in a small class of cases where the transfer of property depends on the priority of death. This kind of case generally involves joint tenants of property. In the eyes of the law, joint tenants take and hold property as if they were a single person. If one dies, the interest of that individual passes to the surviving joint tenant or the heirs of the latter. This result does not follow when people own property as tenants in common because no survivorship rule applies to them. To deal with joint tenants who die in a common disaster, such as an auto, airplane, or train accident, under legislation passed in every state the presumption is that they died simultaneously unless the evidence suggests otherwise. In cases such as *Smith* v. *Smith*,[4] the question was which joint tenant predeceased the other. Hugh Smith and Lucy Smith, husband and wife, were in an automobile accident on April 19, 1957. The husband was dead at the scene and the wife was taken to the hospital still breathing but in a coma because of a brain injury. She died there on May 6, 1957. The petitioner claimed title to the property they had owned claiming that both had died simultaneously and that the wife did not survive the husband.

The court relied on the historic traditionalist definition of death used by the law. For centuries, judicial decisions had always used the common law definition of death given in *Black's Law Dictionary*:[5] "The cessation of life; defined by physicians as the total stoppage of the circulation of the blood and a cessation of the animal and vital functions consequent thereon such as respiration, pulsation, etc." The court applied the common law definition of death and, since Lucy Smith's breathing had not stopped, dismissed the petition.

But the advent of new medical technologies of life-supporting techniques and organ transplantation created a responsibility for the law and legal profession to arrive at a definition of death not given in *Black's Law Dictionary*. When courts in cases such as *Smith* v. *Smith* and *Thomas* v. *Anderson*[6] relied on the traditional common-law definition of death, they failed to recognize its impracticability in the light of modern means of sustaining heartbeat and respiration.

Also the legislatures of the states had not defined death. The anatomical gifts acts they passed, which authorized the gift of all or part of a human body effective at death, provided that physicians attending donors could determine the time of death but failed to define death for them or set forth criteria to use to determine death. In view of the advances in transplantation surgery coupled with the scarcity of organs to be transplanted, this omission was a great oversight because it afforded no or very little protection against the pressures for finding organs to meet the need for them and the premature removal of an organ. Controversies were bound to occur over the question of whether patients were actually dead before organs were removed from their bodies.

## BRUCE TUCKER CASE

Thus we arrive at the Bruce Tucker case.[7] Bruce Tucker, a black laborer, age fifty-four, fell in May 1968 and suffered a massive brain injury with a lateral basilar skull fracture on the right side and brain stem contusion and subdural hematoma on the left side. He was taken to the Medical College of Virginia Hospital, the hospital of the (late) Paul M. Hume, a prominent heart-transplant specialist, where a patient named Joseph Klett needed a heart transplant. A temperopatietal craniotomy was performed on Tucker and he was fed intravenously and attached to a mechanical respirator. The next morning, the treating physician gave his prognosis as "nil and death imminent." An EEG was reported by a neurologist at 1 P.M. that afternoon as showing "flat lines with occasional artifact . . . no clinical evidence of viability and no evidence of cortical activity." At 2:45 P.M., Tucker was taken to the operating room to be prepared for the removal of his heart. At this time, however, with the respirator he maintained vital signs of life, normal body temperature, normal blood pressure, and normal rate of respiration. At 3:30 P.M., his respirator was disconnected. At 3:33 P.M., Tucker was certified as dead. At 4:32 P.M., his heart was removed and a moment later his kidney. The heart was transplanted into Joseph Klett. William E. Tucker, Bruce's brother, sued the transplant team for $100,000 damages on the ground that they were part of a "systematic and nefarious scheme to use Bruce Tucker's heart and had hastened his death by shutting off the mechanical means of support." The brother said that he was not notified by the team, although the team had his name and address, and his consent was never given to the removal of the heart. The transplant team defended on the ground that this was a case of brain death and that Tucker was dead at 1 P.M. before his heart was removed.

If you were the jury, would you find:

- For William Tucker because the transplant team had wrongfully let Bruce Tucker die and hurried Tucker to his death?
- For the transplant team because Tucker was already brain dead when they removed his heart?

In this case, after a seven-day trial, the jury in the court of law and equity rendered a not-guilty verdict in favor of the defendants. The case made headlines. "Virginia Jury Rules That Death Occurs When Brain Dies" was the one run in the *New York Times* (1972). Its story said that the suit focused on the issue of when death occurs and that medical opinion that death occurs when the brain died was reinforced by a jury. Medical periodicals also reported it as a brain-death case. Dr. Paul Hume, one of the defendants and the heart specialist at the Medical College of Virginia Hospital, said that the law merely confirmed something known by the medical profession: that brain death is the death of the individual. So this case became famous because the press, public, and medical profession treated it as the first time a court was asked to apply the brain-death test to determine death and confirmed that test. Although the plaintiff's attorney, State Senator L. Douglas Wilder, said the case would be appealed to the Virginia Supreme Court, it never was.

An analysis of this case, however (see Veatch, 1976), shows it to have a number of strange features. The first is a certain confusion on the part of the trial judge, A. Christian Compton. Under the common-law definition of death, Tucker was not dead because with a supporting respirator he still had all vital signs: he breathed and had a heartbeat. The defendants argued and offered neurological evidence that Tucker had no registered brain waves when the heart was removed and that he was brain dead at the time the heart was removed. The court rejected this argument as an effort to redefine death on the basis of loss of brain functions and held that the common-law definition of death should be used. This was a correct legal ruling and surely would have won the case for the plaintiff. But later in the trial in his instructions to the jury, Judge Compton permitted them to consider lack of brain function as an alternative definition. The jury returned a verdict for the defendant; they accepted brain death as a criterion for determining the time of death. So the judge, after first ruling that the law did not recognize brain death, reversed himself by allowing the jury to consider it.

The *Tucker* case is also worth examining both from an ethical point of view and to see what really happened. While generally regarded as a case involving the brain-death standard, the facts suggest otherwise. It appears that the transplant team did not really apply this standard although at the trial they made this claim. It appears that they applied the old common-law definition of death. The facts show that at 1:00 P.M., the neurologist said that Tucker showed no evidence of cortical activity. If the transplant team were following the brain-death test, Tucker was then dead. But instead we find that the respirator was disconnected at 3:30 P.M. and that five minutes later, at 3:35 P.M., he was officially declared dead. From this, it seems possible to infer that the transplant team did not think that Tucker was dead while he still had a heartbeat and still breathed and that the intention was to produce a stoppage of Tucker's heart and lungs. He would then really be dead and they could proceed with removing his heart. The case would then not be a brain-death case but a case of withdrawing life-sustaining treatment. If the case, as it looks to be, is one of the surgeons simply letting Tucker die by withholding treatment from him, it raises a serious ethical question as well as a legal one. It suggests that Tucker's brother may have been right in alleging a wrongful death and that the jury was wrong in finding in favor of the transplant team.

Two events made the legal profession and the public aware of the need for a realistic definition of death within which both the legal and medical professions could operate. One was the supposition that the Tucker case had been a brain-death case. The other was the case of Karen Ann Quinlan, which we examined in Chapter 7. One of the questions in the *Quinlan* case was whether this young woman in a coma was dead. She showed no evidence of cortex function but she did show evidence of brain stem activity. Under the brain-death criteria of the Ad Hoc Committee, she was alive.

## STATUTORY DEFINITION OF DEATH

With the Harvard Medical School report, the question was how to have the law recognize the brain-death criterion. One way was to have the courts adopt the standard in their case-by-case decisions. But this method would have been slow and not sure because all courts might not agree on the standard. The other way was to have states enact a statutory definition of death.

Between 1970 and 1978, with Kansas the first state to do so, nineteen states passed brain-death legislation. In 1978, the National Conference of Commissioners on Uniform State Laws approved the Uniform Brain Death Act. In 1980, the NCCUSL drafted the Uniform Determination of Death Act to supersede the Brain Death Act and recommended its adoption by the states. The majority of states responded by passing brain-death legislation.[8]

In these states, uncertainty about the standard has been eliminated as well as differences between one court decision and another. But these statutes are not uniform. Some provide for an alternate definition of death—one based on brain death, one based on the absence of spontaneous respiration and cardiac function. Some states recognize brain death only when the heart and lungs are artificially maintained. Other statutes provide that only brain death shall be the standard for determining death with no other standard recognized.

In states such as New York, which have not adopted the Uniform Determination of Death Act, interesting scenarios and issues of civil and criminal liability may arise, especially where patients are being maintained by artificial life supports. A civil suit may be started and a wrongful-death issue presented as it was in the *Tucker* case, where the question was whether a patient whose life support is terminated and from whom organs were removed was dead or was hastened to his death by the transplant team. Or a criminal case with a murder scenario may develop as it did in New York in *People* v. *Bonilla*.[9] A defendant shot a drug dealer once in the right shoulder and once in the head, the bullet entering the brain but not destroying the brain stem. The victim was rushed to a hospital. He was comatose, totally unresponsive, and placed on a respirator. His respiration and blood pressure were artificially supported. Two encephalograms were flat and he was pronounced brain dead. Subsequently his kidney and spleen were removed for transplantation. The defendant, charged with first degree murder, maintained that he could not be convicted because New York had no legal definition of death and without it the case could not be resolved. He also argued that the patient's death could not be attributed to him but to the physicians who shut off life support mistakenly or hastily. Although the court upheld the conviction because the defendant's action was the proximate cause of the victim's death and the court believed that a statutory definition of death was unnecessary, the case demonstrates the kind of difficulties that may be produced by the absence of a statutory definition of death.

A brain-death statute adopted by Florida in 1980[10] is fairly typical of statutes providing for alternate standards of death. Several key points should be noticed.

It provides that where respiratory and circulatory functions are maintained by artificial means of support so that we cannot tell whether those functions have stopped, "irreversible cessation of the functioning of the entire brain, including the brain stem" is the definition of death. In other words, the statute adopts the brain-death definition and medical concept of death. This definition covers both cortical and brain-stem activity, thus excluding anyone with some brain-stem activity. This definition, therefore, would exclude all incompetent patients in comas and those, such as Karen Ann Quinlan and Nancy Cruzan, who are in a persistent vegetative state.

The statute also contains this language: "Except for a diagnosis of brain death, the standard set forth in this section is not the exclusive standard for determining death." Thus while states with statutes similar to this one recognize brain death, they also provide an alternate definition and standard of death. They maintain the traditional common law standard given in *Black's Law Dictionary* quoted before, under which a person is considered dead if there is a medical determination of a cessation of respiratory and circulatory functions—that is, absence of all vital signs. This is one clinical situation, and if it exists there is no need to evaluate brain function. For example, where a patient not on a life-support system has died of respiratory failure and the attending physician makes that determination, this criterion for determining death is satisfied and there is no need to assess the patient's brain function. But if a life support system maintained cardiopulmonary functions artificially so that its use precluded a determination that these functions have stopped, brain functions then would be assessed and neurological criteria used to determine whether brain functions have irreversibly ceased.

The *Quinlan* and *Cruzan* cases were instances in which the alternative criteria for determining death were not satisfied. Karen Ann Quinlan was in a vegetative state and respiratory functions were maintained by a respirator. But since the functions of her entire brain had not ceased, she was not brain dead and not legally dead according to the statutory definition of death. Nancy Cruzan was being maintained artificially with food and water, but her respiration and circulation had not ceased and were not being maintained artificially. She was therefore not dead according to the common-law definition requiring cessation of respiratory and circulatory functions.

The statute also provides that the determination of death must be made by two physicians, one the treating physician, the other a neurologist, neurosurgeon, internist, pediatrician, surgeon, or anesthesiologist. The statute goes on to provide that the next of kin of a patient be notified of the procedures used to determine death.

The next of kin are to have the death-evaluation process explained to them by the attending physician and their understanding of the process documented in the medical records.

## CRITIQUE OF BRAIN-DEATH STATUTES AND CONCEPT

One of the practical matters mentioned in connection with the importance of determining death is the maturation of a life insurance policy. But the brain death concept may present a difficulty unless the policy is clarified to prevent disputes arising under it about the obligation to make payment. The typical life insurance policy provides that a beneficiary will be paid on "due proof" that the insured has died. Many policies also provide for doubling the benefits if there is accidental death and death takes place within ninety days of the accident. If an insured is determined brain dead and maintained artificially for a prolonged period, so that circulation and respiration are not stopped for ninety days, a strict interpretation of the policy under the common-law definition of death might allow the insurance company to refuse payment either on the ground that the insured had not been proved dead or that death had not taken place within ninety days of an accident. But if life insurance policies were to use the brain-death standard so that "brain death" and "insured death" were the same, this would allow an insured to be determined brain dead before the expiration of ninety days and the difficulty with the brain death concept avoided. Absent such a clarification, it remains.

There is, however, a more serious difficulty: Is a brain-dead individual really dead? Brain death is a concept grieving and shocked families find hard to accept when their loved ones whose pulses, nutrition, blood pressures, and body temperatures are being maintained artificially do not appear dead in any conventional sense. Their hearts are beating, their bodies are warm, and they urinate. It is incumbent on health-care providers, especially those who may be involved with the organ donation process and must approach families about donations of their dead relatives' organs, to counsel these families to make them aware of the extensive examinations that have been made and of the indisputable clinical findings supporting the brain-death diagnosis. Continued denial of it can only produce emotional turmoil.

But this counseling is obstructed by a fundamental barrier. An important study reveals that many health professionals responsible for talking with families of brain-dead patients about organ donations are themselves confused about the clinical and legal applications of the brain-death standard (Youngner et al., 1989). The study of 195 physicians and nurses in four university-affiliated hospitals with active organ-transplant programs showed that only sixty-eight respondents, or 35 percent, correctly identified the legal and medical criteria for determining death. It suggests that the brain-death standard is as difficult for the health-care provider to think about, understand, and accept as the families they are to approach.

The vertebrate brain has evolved over millions of years and in the human being is in its most complex form. So the brain-death standard is not easy to understand. Nor is it free from doubt and many continue to deny it. Among their criticisms are the following:

First, cases have been reported that may cast doubt on the validity of the brain-death standard. One dramatic case was that of a Cuban man who, in July 1990, became comatose after drinking a soft drink known as Pony Malta de Bavaria that had been contaminated with lethal doses of cocaine. He was maintained for a month in a Miami hospital by a respirator. A neurologist declared him brain dead in August. Four days later and on the day the respirator was to be disconnected, his mother, Margarita Rabaza, came to the hospital to bid him goodbye. Suddenly he began to take some shallow breaths after the respirator had been removed for about a minute for some routine procedure. He also moved his arms and legs. His mother, who had decided to have the respirator disconnected, now refused. She had given her son life; she would not allow it to be taken away. But after four encephalograms, a cerebral angiogram, and several expert medical opinions that her son was really brain dead and that his respiration and muscle movements were only muscle spasms, the mother finally accepted his death, agreed to have the respirator disconnected, and her son died thirteen minutes later (*Miami Herald*, 1990).

Critics reject arguments based on spasms and spinal cord reflexes. They cite another type of case reported in which, after a determination of brain death and as the transplant team is making the initial incision, the "corpse" reacts. Its arms, legs, and abdominal muscles became tense or its blood pressure or heart rate rise in the absence of an anaesthetic. In one case of this kind a "corpse" was saved from having his organs removed by a transplant team only because his Adam's apple moved at the last minute (Paris and Cranford, 1982).

Second, it is possible in such cases that the diagnostic neurological criteria used to make a diagnosis of brain death were faulty. This brings up a further objection to the brain-death statutes. Although they adopt the brain-death definition, none of them specify any clinical diagnostic criteria to avoid mistakes in declaring a person dead. Nor do they insist on confirmatory tests such as a cerebral blood flow or an electroencephalogram. Nor are there any requirements that tests be conducted for all sedatives, tranquilizers, or narcotics or for hypothermia, all of which can produce a flat EEG and give an appearance of brain death. Statutory provisions along all these lines might provide some assurance of the validity of a determination of death. Instead, the legislatures failed to specify the criteria for brain death and left it to the medical profession to determine brain death "in accordance with currently accepted medical standards." But these standards are bound to change as new developments take place in medical technology or there are advances in our understanding of brain physiology, and as they change so will the determination of brain death. Nor is there any assurance that the tests used or to be used for assessing brain functions will be reliable enough to allow a person to be declared dead. Even a test such as a flat EEG may not always be correct since either the machine or the operator may make mistakes. A finding based on them that there is no evidence of brain or brain stem functions may be erroneous.

Third, assuming that medical standards and the clinical diagnostic criteria now or to be applied in the future are valid, a deeper problem is that death is a conceptual problem, not one to be resolved by technical criteria or data, such as the brain-death test.

Death raises many interesting questions. One is, what happens at death? There seem to be three commonly held views that color our lives and affect our thoughts (Berger, 1987). A second question directly implicated in the brain-death criterion, or any test for determining death, is, what is death? The answer would be simple if, like the ghosts who reportedly have appeared to people since ancient times, human beings just dematerialized and vanished all at once and without warning at the moment of death. But as we have noted, death is a gradual sequence of stages with different kinds of deaths taking place at different levels.

Any data or criterion for determining death must depend on and flow from how we conceive of these stages and define death and what it means (Pallis, 1984). Brain death—the irreversible cessation of the functions of the whole brain—is a strictly medicolegal and technical criterion for determining death that is related to and derived from an understanding of death as the hopelessly irretrievable loss of the attributes of the cortex, consciousness, cognition, and personhood, and the capacity to interact with the outside environment. It is a concept that treats death as the cessation of the meaningful and interacting individual as a whole and is one that seems to have gained the acceptance of lawyers, physicians, and the general public. But it should not be forgotten that there are also other competing and alternate concepts and definitions of death from which the brain-death criterion does not follow and for which it is immaterial.

One is based on another kind of death: the cessation not of the whole human being but of each of the parts of which the individual is composed—organs and cells. Human life is the product of their interaction and interdependence. Although there may be brain death, there may still be cell life as oxygen and metabolism continue in them. While they live the individual is not dead. Many brain-dead "corpses" with life support have continued to breathe, be warm, dispose of wastes, have blood pressure, and other evidence for several days—conditions found generally in people who are alive, not dead. They are not dead, only dying. Any sign or form of life in the individual, no matter how small or apparently meaningless, has an absolute value and cannot be ignored regardless of how hopeless recovery may seem. To elevate brain function as the only or primary sign of life is purely arbitrary because organs and cells are also vital indicia of life.

The development of sophisticated life-sustaining technology has added another concept of death based on an assessment of the quality of life. It also rejects the brain-death criterion because it considers brain-dead patients alive but it considers them dead enough to warrant pulling the plug if this technology has merely placed them in a twilight zone, a hopeless form of existence in which the real person no longer exists and appears to have no interest in going on.

Fourth, to leave the determination of brain death in the hands of physicians may be dangerous because of the pressure for organ transplantation. The brain concept and definition was the direct outcome of the development of organ transplantation and the scarcity of organs. Serious ethical and legal issues are created because, except for kidneys and segments of livers, organs cannot be harvested from living donors. There may be a temptation to fail to make all efforts to save the lives of patients who have agreed to be donors and to declare them brain dead in order to allow their organs to be harvested. Indeed, one reason why people shy away from carrying organ-donor cards is that they are afraid that they may be inviting hospitals and physicians to hasten their deaths (Dept. of Health and Human Services, 1986:38). They see the specter of Bruce Tucker hovering over all hospitals that are also transplant centers and where the situation of wrongful death can arise. Potential donors are given some assurance that it will not arise by a present law that prohibits determination of brain death by physicians involved in the retrieval or transplantation of organs. But to avoid even further any suggestion of conflict of interest or that all life-saving efforts have not been made in the cases of potential donors, a hospital might adopt a policy that any pronouncement that a potential donor is brain dead should not be made by physicians on the hospital staff nor by any who have privileges at such hospitals. Such a policy would strengthen the hospital's image in the eyes of potential donors, society, and the courts.

The position of the proponents of the brain-death standard has not been weakened by such criticisms. On the contrary, it has been strengthened by the benefits that are reaped from organ transplantation and strengthened also by the adoption of brain-death statutes by twenty-eight states and by the approval of the Uniform Determination of Death Act by the American Medical Association and American Bar Association. These statutes in effect admit that the common-law concept and definition of death is obsolete. They bring the law abreast of the advances in medical technology and with medical opinion that death is brain death. They recognize that medical technology has made it possible for a dead human being to be maintained artificially and to be given spurious and mechanically contrived signs of life. This technology replaces the natural mechanisms of breathing and heartbeat with factitious ones and, as if with a magic wand, make it appear that a dead body is really alive. The brain statutes say that spurious signs of life shall not be mistaken for true ones and that a person will be considered dead if two physicians determine that the individual has suffered total and irreversible brain function.

Nevertheless, criticisms still continue to be voiced by the National Conference of Catholic Bishops, some Jewish leaders, and nonreligious critics who have grave misgivings about brain death, such as Veatch (1976). Misgivings must be greatest and most painful among those Catholic and Jewish physicians who reject the brain-death standard as a legal fiction because of their religious and intellectual beliefs that their patients are still alive, yet who are willing to go along with their medical colleagues and use it anyway in their practices as ending their medical duties and thus allow the stoppage of life support and permitting the harvesting of organs.

## THE CORPSE

With death, the human body is deprived of life and transformed into a corpse, as Justice Lumpkin said in 1905, "the strangest thing on earth."[11] What was warm and aware has become cold and unresponsive, stillness and silence have taken the place of movement and speech. The corpse is an even stranger phenomenon today. In 1905 and in the author's early childhood, the body of a loved one was always in the American home where family and friends could look at it for the last time. But today it has vanished from the home and reappeared in hospitals and nursing homes where 80 percent of the deaths in the United States each year take place (President's Commission, 1983).

Under the common law of England, a corpse had no rights to take or hold property. It also was not the subject of property or considered by the courts as an object of any value. For this reason, a grave robber did not commit the crime of larceny for stealing a corpse. The robber, however, would have been guilty of larceny of the coffin, graveclothes, or objects buried with the corpse.[12] The law of the United States was generally in accord with the English view in holding that there were no property rights in a corpse except in cases relating to the burial of a dead body and the interests of the next of kin in it. In an early case,[13] a tort action was brought by a widow against a railroad company to which she had delivered the body of her deceased husband to take from the place of death to a place of burial. The court sustained her complaint that because of the company's negligence her husband's body was mutilated, the coffin and shroud were damaged, and she was subjected to humiliation and mental suffering. The corpse was considered quasi-property in which the next of kin has rights a court will protect.

When a patient dies, the hospital becomes the custodian of the body. Unless the patient has given different directions, such as donating his or her body to some facility or person, the hospital has the duty to the next of kin not only to notify them about the patient's death but also to release the body to the proper person in the condition it was at the time of death. The proper person would be, first, the surviving spouse or, if no spouse or the spouse waives his or her right, then to the adult child, the parent, or adult sibling, in that order of priority. Release of the corpse to the wrong person or delay in releasing it can subject a hospital to liability.

Most dead-body statutes provide that, if no one claims a patient's corpse after reasonable efforts are made to locate the next of kin, hospitals must notify public authorities of the unclaimed body so that public officials can arrange to dispose of it. These authorities include the division of universities of a state's education department. The division then takes fingerprints of the body and sends them to the FBI in an attempt to identify the body. The body is retained by the division for at least forty-eight hours before giving it to medical science for research. Statutes generally allow an unclaimed body to be donated to medical or dental schools or teaching hospitals, or loaned for study to licensed funeral directors.

## DEATH CERTIFICATE

One of the immediate consequences of death is a special document "that must, without exception, be completed (in due time) for each reader, and which, under no possible circumstances in this world, can any reader ever see completed for himself" (Shneidman, 1973:121). It is the death certificate a physician or medical examiner signs. The funeral director then completes the certificate and it is filed in the vital statistics section of the health department of every state. The first part of the death certificate identifies the dead person, the middle portion describes the cause and manner of death, and the last part gives information about such matters as the place of burial and the name of the funeral director.

The quotation from Shneidman, while generally correct, does not take into account one circumstance in which readers may see their own death certificates completed. If they are willing to fill one in for themselves and, as part of the exercise, to think about where, when, and how they will die and their funerals, such an experiential approach will force them to examine their deepest feelings about death and to appreciate Jung's well-known observation that "life is a disease with a bad prognosis because its outcome is always fatal" (Jung, 1960: xlii).

The importance of the death certificate extends in several directions. It settles questions about property rights. It is needed in the administration of estates. It is required for life insurance claims and pension payments. It is of great value to mortality statisticians because it furnishes them with mortality rates for males and females, life expectancies, and where and when people die. Since the typical death certificate provides for showing the four modes of death—accident, suicide, homicide, or natural—one can see how over the years, the suicide and homicide rates have increased. It is equally valuable for the medical profession because it gives the causes of death. Through the death certificate, it has been possible to tabulate the leading causes of death and to note that those that were leaders in 1900, such as influenza and pneumonia, tuberculosis and diphtheria, have dropped dramatically as killers. At the same time, heart disease and cancer, the fourth and eighth leading causes of death in 1900, became in 1989, respectively, the first and second with respiratory diseases and infectious and parasitic diseases, including AIDS, occupying third and fourth positions. Such mortality data are of immense help in the guidance of medical education and research.

## AUTOPSY

An inevitable effect of any death whose cause physicians cannot certify—accidents, suicides, homicides, drug overdoses, and deaths in hospitals that may be due to negligence, or the result of a contagious disease that is a public danger—is that it must be reported to a coroner or medical examiner. Criminal penalties and civil liability in damages may be imposed on health professionals or hospitals for failing to make these reports. The coroner or medical examiner are the public officers who have the duty to investigate such deaths. But the two offices are not the same. The coroner's is a political office held by someone who is elected and usually not trained in law or medicine. In Great Britain and some parts of the United States, coroners hold inquests and choose juries to render verdicts and identify suspects in cases of deaths that may involve murder or manslaughter. A medical examiner, on the other hand, is appointed and required to be a physician and probably is a forensic pathologist.

The investigation of sudden or suspicious death includes toxicological and bacteriological tests, chemical analyses, and the autopsy—an examination of a cadaver and its vital organs and tissues, generally by dissection, in order to establish the cause of death. The ancient Egyptians did not conduct autopsies although they took out organs to preserve them, nor did the early Greeks and Indians, who preferred to cremate rather than examine their dead. The autopsy began during the Renaissance and continues today reinforced by modern medical technology. The autopsy is a consequence of death of the highest value for medicine.

The anatomical-gift acts give people the right to donate their bodies to hospitals, surgeons, or physicians as well as to medical or dental schools for medical or dental research. Under this provision and in keeping with the purpose of the acts—that is, to promote medical research—individuals may donate their bodies for autopsies. The same principle of free choice behind organ donations is also behind a donation for autopsy. Even if it disapproves, the family cannot override the person's consent. Absent this consent, the autopsy generally is done at the request of a family. The statutes of a majority of states provide that the next of kin have the right to consent to it, the first priority going to the surviving spouse, then to the adult child, followed by the parent, an adult sibling, and legal guardian. Again, we see the same principle of voluntary consent at work in the procedure for organ donation present for the autopsy, and should a health-care facility perform an autopsy without the consent of the next of kin, it becomes subject to liability to them for damages for mutilating or disturbing the corpse and for their mental suffering.[14] But the analogy between organ donation and autopsy breaks down because, the contrary wishes of the decedent or the next of kin notwithstanding, the trained coroner or medical examiner is empowered by statute to perform an autopsy when required for investigation. The state again plays god and decrees that its interests will override the wishes of individuals.

It was mentioned that, under U.S. law, a corpse is quasi-property in which the next of kin have a right. This right includes the right to possess the corpse in the condition it was in at death and to bury it. The only public officer who has a right greater than theirs is the coroner or medical examiner.

The autopsy plays a significant role. It can be very important to the family to know how a relative died. Death by natural causes is always easier to accept than death by suicide, homicide, or negligence. But whether performed by a coroner, medical examiner, or in a hospital, it has a special, multidimensional significance for the medical field.

In the area of medical jurisprudence, where there is a connection between law and medicine, the autopsy achieves great importance. The testimony of the forensic pathologist who has examined and dissected the organs of a corpse and can give an opinion may be vital in criminal cases where poisoning is suspected. In cases of rape or murder, this testimony, given on the basis of trace samples of the genetic material known as DNA taken from the blood or tissue of a victim, can convict or even acquit a person charged. Findings based on the autopsy are valuable as well in miscellaneous civil suits, such as those where the issue is when a person died, what the alcoholic content of the blood level of a driver was, or whether death benefits under insurance policies or Worker's Compensation laws are payable.

But it is in the area of medical education that the autopsy is an invaluable tool. It becomes the instrument by which medical students learn the fundamental sciences of physiology and anatomy and the physiological impact of drugs and surgery. Indeed cadavers and autopsies seem an indispensable part of the training of young physicians-to-be. Autopsies are an important part of a teaching hospital's program. Hospitals that want to establish a reputation as teaching hospitals recognize that it is necessary to perform a large number of autopsies to train physicians and conduct research.

The autopsy is also the tool for confirming or disconfirming clinical diagnoses, and for revealing medical mistakes or disclosing communicable diseases that threaten the public or new ones not suspected.

## LEGAL CITATIONS

1. 299 Ark. 579, 517 S.W.2d 275 (Ark. Sup. Ct. 1958).

2. Matter of Claire Conroy, 98 N.J. 321, 486 A.2d 1209 (N.J. Sup. Ct. 1985); Rasmussen v. Fleming, 154 Ariz. 207, 741 P.2d 674 (Ariz. Sup. Ct. 1987).

3. 362 S.2d 160, *aff'd* 379 S.2d 359 (Fla. Sup. Ct. 1980).

4. See *supra*, note 1.

5. 4th ed. 1968.

6. 96 Cal. App.2d 372, 215 P.2d 478 ( Dist. Ct. App., 4th Dist. 1950).

7. Tucker v. Lower, Docket N. 2831 (Richmond, Virginia, Court of Law and Equity, May 23, 1972)—no appeal taken.

8. Alabama (1979), Alaska (1974), Arkansas (1977), California ( 1974), Connecticut (1979), Florida (1980), Georgia (1975), Hawaii (1978), Idaho (1977), Illinois (1975), Iowa (1976), Kansas (1978), Louisiana (1976), Maryland (1972), Michigan (1975), Montana (1977), Nevada (1979), New Mexico (1977), North Carolina (1977), Ohio (1982), Oklahoma (1975), Oregon (1975), Pennsylvania (1982), Tennessee (1976), Texas (1979), Vermont (1981), Virginia (1973), West Virginia (1973), Wyoming (1979).

9. 95 A.D.2d 396, 467 N.Y.S.2d 599, *aff'd* 63 N.Y.2d 341, 472 N.E.2d 286 (N.Y. Ct. App. 1984). Cases with similar factual situations are in accord with *People* v. *Bonilla*: State v. Watson, 191 N.J. 464, 467 A.2d 590 (N.J. Sup. Ct., App. Div. 1983); People v.

Eulo, 97 A.2d 682, 467 N.Y.S.2d 464, *aff'd* 63 N.Y. S.2d 341, 472 N.E.2d 286 (N.Y. Ct. App. 1984).

    10. Florida Statutes Sec. 382.085.

    11. Louisville & N.R. Co. v. Wilson, 123 Ga. 62, 51 S.E. 24, 25 (Ga. Sup. Ct. 1905).

    12. Blackstone, *Commentaries*, 429.

    13. See *supra*, note 11.

    14. Torres v. State, 228 N.Y.S.2d 1005 (N.Y. Ct. of Claims 1962); Gould v. State, 46 N.Y.S.2d 313 (N.Y. Ct. of Claims 1944); French v. Ochsner Clinic, 200 S.2d 371 (La. Ct. App. 1967).

## REFERENCES

Abbott, S. 1901. "Death Certification." In Albert H. Buck, ed., *Reference Handbook of the Medical Sciences*. New York: William Wood.

Berger, A. S. 1987. "Three Views of Death and Their Implications for Life." Paper presented at the Sixteeenth International Conference on the Unity of Sciences. Atlanta, Georgia, November 26–29, 1987.

Department of Health and Human Services. April 1986. "Report of the Task Force on Organ Transplantation." In *Organ Transplantation: Issues and Recommendations*. Washington, DC: Human Resources and Services Administration, Office of Organ Transplantation.

Friloux, C. A., Jr. 1975. "Death, When Does it Occur?" *Baylor Law Review* 27:10–19.

Jung, C. J. 1960. "Psychological Commentary." In W. Y. Evans-Wentz, ed., *The Tibetan Book of the Dead*. London: Oxford University Press, xxxv–lii.

Mant, A. K. 1968. "The Medical Definition of Death." In A. Toynbee et al., eds., *Man's Concern with Death*. New York: McGraw-Hill, 13–24.

*Miami Herald*, "Drug-Spiked Soft Drink Victim Dies." August 21, 1990, 1A.

*New York Times*, "Virginia Jury Rules That Death Occurs When Brain Dies." May 27, 1972, 15.

Pallis, C. 1984. "Brainstem Death: The Evolution of a Concept." In P. J. Morris, ed., *Kidney Transplantation: Principles and Practice*. New York: Grune and Stratton, 101–27.

Paris, J. J., and Cranford, R. E. 1982. "Brain Death, Prolife and Catholic Confusion." *America*, December 4.

President's Commission for the Study of Ethical Problems in Medicine and Biomedical and Behavioral Research. 1983. "Deciding to Forgo Life-Sustaining Treatment." Washington, DC: Government Printing Office.

Shneidman, E. S. 1973. *Deaths of Man*. New York: Quadrangle/New York Times Book Co.

Veatch, R. M. 1976. "Brain Death." In Edwin S. Shneidman, ed., *Death: Current Perspectives*. Palo Alto: Mayfield, 232–40.

Youngner, S. J., Landefeld, S., Coulton, C. J., Juknialis, B. W., Leary, M. 1989. " 'Brain Death' and Organ Retrieval: A Cross-Sectional Survey of Knowledge and Concepts Among Health Professionals." *Journal of the American Medical Association* 261:2205–10.

# VI

## Anatomical Gifts

# 10

## The Gift of Life: Law and Ethics

The law of dying and death also relates to the donation of organs, a subject inseparably linked to death since donation becomes effective at death and organs generally but not always are supplied by donors declared brain dead. Through the donation and transplantation process, a precious gift of life is offered to thousands. The lives of people threatened or disrupted by organs or tissues that do not function may be saved or restored; the immobile can walk again with a bone; the blind can see again with a cornea; the badly burned can be helped with skin; the incapacitated can be benefited with a heart, liver, or kidney.

### ORGAN DONATION AND TRANSPLANTATION—DEVELOPMENT AND CENTERS

The first reference to the use of a part of the body of one human being to give life to another appears in the Old Testament: In order to make a helpmate for the first man, Yahweh fashioned the first woman out of Adam's rib (Genesis 2:21–22). But the modern transplant procedure, in which a healthy tissue or organ from one individual is surgically implanted in another individual to ameliorate or save the life of the latter, began to be developed in the twentieth century. Five years mark its progress: 1905—the first corneal transplant; 1918—the first blood transfusion; 1954—the first kidney transplant; 1967—the first heart transplant.

The greatest problem in the way of the early transplants was the immune system of the human body. Because a transplanted organ is as alien to the body as an infection virus, the immune system responds by attacking and rejecting a transplanted organ as a foreign substance. Beginning in the

1960s, the discovery and development of effective immunosuppressive drugs such as cyclosporine, Imuran, and prednisone slowed down the immune system and reduced the possibility of rejection. In the 1990s, the goal of some research programs is to eliminate the use of immunosuppressive drugs that can have side effects and to encourage the body's own mechanisms to accept transplants. There also have been improvements in surgical techniques and anesthesiology that make transplants a realistic option for many people.

These developments opened the door to transplanting a great number and variety of organs and tissues, such as kidneys, hearts, lungs, livers, bone, bone marrow, skin, corneas, and pancreases.

These improvements also produced enormous growth in the number of transplant centers and their procedures. In 1981 there were 157 kidney transplant centers that transplanted 4,855 kidneys. In 1986, there were 201 centers that performed 8,976 kidney transplants. Where there were eight heart transplant centers in 1981, there were 117 in 1986, and heart transplants went from 62 in 1981 to 1,368 in 1986. Similarly, the number of liver transplants rose 58 times between 1981 and 1986 with liver transplants increasing from 26 in 1981 to 924 in 1986.

The transplant centers report improving survival rates: 60 percent among patients receiving kidneys, 50 percent among those receiving hearts, 95 percent among those receiving corneas. As of 1990, the longest period of survival for recipients of transplants were twenty-five years (kidney), twenty years (heart), twenty years (liver), twelve years (pancreas), nine years (heart-lung), and two years (lung).

Transplant candidates waiting for organs are listed and registered with transplant centers in the states where they reside. But to increase their chances of receiving the organ they need, they also may be listed with the transplant programs in other states. A resident of Florida who requires a heart may be listed at one of the nine Florida hospitals performing solid organ transplants— the Shands Teaching Hospital in Gainesville, for example—while at the same time this individual may be listed with the programs at the Texas Heart Institute or Rush Presbyterian–St. Luke's Hospital.

## UNITED NETWORK FOR ORGAN SHARING

The United Network for Organ Sharing (UNOS), located in Richmond, Virginia, under an arrangement with the Health Resources and Services Administration of the Public Health Service in the U.S. Department of Health, operates the nation's Organ Procurement and Transplantation Network. Pursuant to the National Organ Transplant Act of 1984, UNOS also operates a scientific registry or computer system that contains data on organ donations and heart, liver, kidney, pancreas, and bone marrow transplantation procedures since 1987. Data also are included on immunosuppressive therapies, tissue typing and matching, surgical techniques, and problems resulting from transplants. Among the most significant data collected by the registry are those relating to recipients of transplants. Beginning with their identification and registration as transplant candidates, when their ABO blood group and other data are collected, followup checks after the transplant are made by the registry on their health status and other matters until their deaths. The entire national database is available to the medical sector. The registry is supervised by a Scientific Advisory Council composed of the UNOS staff, the staff of the Health Resources and Services Administration, and those representing the transplant sector (Harmon, 1990).

In addition to this registry, the National Organ Transplant Program Extension Act of 1990 mandated the creation of a registry of voluntary bone marrow donors. As of 1990, the National Marrow Donor Program had registered 140,000 potential donors. The aim is to register 250,000 donors and create a donor pool large enough to increase the chances of matching for those requiring marrow transplants.

All transplant centers are required by the Consolidated Omnibus Reconciliation Act of 1986 to become members of UNOS. Those unable to meet UNOS's membership criteria are threatened with loss of revenues from Medicare and Medicaid for all procedures, not merely transplants. The transplant centers list people waiting for transplants and the national waiting list maintained by UNOS is made up of these lists. Under the national system, organs are implanted in those candidates who, as shown by the national computer registry, match the donor's characteristics, such as blood type, and have the greatest and most urgent medical needs. An organ is to be used to meet local needs first, however. If no suitable recipient is in the same area as the donor, other candidates in the country will be shown on the national registry. Time is of the essence in transplant procedures. UNOS also maintains a twenty-four-hour telephone service to help to match donor organs with people on the waiting list and to coordinate placement efforts with transplant centers.

## ANATOMICAL GIFT ACT: PURPOSE AND DONATION

The progress in developing new drugs and techniques, the improvement in survival rates, and the demand for organs raised the public consciousness. There were several legislative responses to the great public pressure and three kinds of legislation were enacted. One was brain-death legislation in order to make it legal for organs to be obtained from brain-dead donors while their hearts were still beating and their organs were fresh. A second was the passage by Congress of the National Organ Transplant Act of 1984 that: (1) set up a task force to study organ procurement and transplantation; (2) authorized grants to organ procurement agencies; (3) established a national organ sharing network and scientific registry; and (4) prohibited the sale and purchase of organs.

A third kind of law encouraged and stimulated people to donate organs. In July 1968, the American Bar Association and the National Conference of Commissioners on Uniform State Laws promulgated a type of legislation that fell into this category: the Uniform Anatomical Gift Act. All fifty states and the District of Columbia have now adopted anatomical-gift acts.

There was still another reason for the passage of anatomical-gift acts. A number of states had statutes relating to the disposition of dead bodies but they were not uniform. Other states had no statutes and the common law was confusing concerning the rights to a dead body and its parts. Legal rules relating to these matters were unclear and differed one from another. Legislation was needed to clarify and make them uniform.

The purpose of the anatomical-gift acts is to promote medical research by implementing the donation of organs and by defining by whom and how a gift of parts of the body can be made, to whom it may be made, and other matters. Under the acts, any individual who can make a will can donate all or part of his or her body. To have testamentary capacity, one must be at least eighteen years of age. This gift, to take effect upon death, can be made in several ways. First, it can be by will or by a document other than a will, such as a Uniform Donor Card. If made by the latter document, it must be signed by the donor and two witnesses. It can also be made by a telegraphic or recorded message or by a donor registration card issued by a state department of motor vehicles as part of the process of issuing or renewing drivers' licenses. If the donation is made by will, it is still a valid gift even if the will is not probated or is invalid. The procurement and transplantation of an organ, therefore, will not be delayed by probate proceedings or will contests. The gift may be made to hospitals, physicians, surgeons, medical schools, dental schools, licensed or accredited banks or storage facilities, or to any specified individual who requires a transplant. If no person is specified, the physician attending the donor may accept the gift. If the gift is of a part of the body, the donee must have the part removed without unnecessary mutilation of the body and, after the part is removed, must return the body to the surviving spouse or next of kin for disposition. The donor, however, can amend or revoke the gift at any time by a signed statement or oral statement before two witnesses and communication of the amendment or revocation to the donee.

There are also provisions in the anatomical-gift acts regarding the family. In order of priority, spouse, adult child, parent, sibling, or guardian can donate all or part of a decedent's body. But if an adult son or daughter objects, a spouse cannot make the gift, and if anyone in a higher priority or in the same class objects or if there is evidence that the decedent expressed opposition to donation on religious or other grounds, the gift cannot be made. The family cannot stop the gift of the donor even if they don't like the idea of donation.

The anatomical-gift legislation also protects from civil or criminal liability medical personnel who act in good faith in a transplant situation.

## REQUIRED REQUEST AND ROUTINE INQUIRY LAWS

Besides their anatomical-gift acts, states enacted other types of legislation generally to implement the organ donation and transplant program. Legislation was passed to authorize medical examiners to remove corneas, funeral directors to enucleate eyes, and state residents wishing to be donors to register with departments of motor vehicles.

Legislatures under their anatomical-gift acts have also authorized their departments of health and motor vehicles to develop continuing programs to educate and inform medical professionals and the general public concerning state laws relevant to anatomical gifts and the general need for them.

In an attempt to bring home to families the need and opportunity for a donation, forty-four states and the District of Columbia have passed one of two kinds of laws. The "required request" law obliges hospital administrators or people designated by them to make it a routine procedure at the time a patient has died or is near death to make an explicit request of the patient's family or guardian to agree to donate all or part of the patient's body unless the patient has given actual notice to the contrary. The "routine inquiry" kind of legislation requires hospitals to let the family know, as distinguished from asking outright for a donation, that they have the opportunity to make a gift and to allow them to opt for a donation or to refuse one. In 1987, as part of the Consolidated Omnibus Budget Recommendation Act, Congress required all hospitals in Medicare or Medicaid programs to make a "routine inquiry."

## IMPLEMENTATION OF REQUIRED REQUEST AND ROUTINE INQUIRY STATUTES

But a survey indicates that, in practice, "required request" and "routine inquiry" laws are implemented similarly (Maximus, 1988). Departments have been established in all states to develop rules, standards, and guidelines for health programs and the internal procedures in hospitals, including the implementation of the "routine inquiry" and "required request" laws. Some of the typical rules are: (1) that the hospital administration or its designees making an inquiry or request of the next of kin be trained in the procedures to be used; (2) that a formal written policy and procedure be established for the identification and referral of organ and tissue donors and the identification and designation of trained personnel who will approach the next of kin and who will be available on a twenty-four-hour "on call" basis; (3) that medical examiners be notified in all medical examiner cases and that they release organs and tissues for transplantation; (4) that all identified donors be referred to an organ procurement agency whose function is to coordinate cadaver organ and tissue retrieval and distribution; (5) that the family be approached at or near the time of death in connection with the donation of organs and tissues; (6) that the inquiry or request be documented and a form be completed and made part of the patient's medical record.

The hypothetical case of *patient A* illustrates how the anatomical gift, "required request," "routine inquiry" laws, and departmental rules should be carried into effect in the donation process. After *A* has been pronounced brain dead and evaluated by an organ procurement agency as a potential vital organ and tissue donor, the family is approached with the terrible news of *A*'s death. The news is conveyed with compassion, a rapport is established with the family, an explanation is given of brain death and why loss of brain function makes *A* dead; and a request is made for organ and tissue donation. *A*'s family elects to donate *A*'s organs because doing so makes it easier to cope with *A*'s death—a belief that motivates most of the families who decide on organ donation. The family's wishes are documented and noted in the medical record. Should *A*'s death be of the kind that needs to be investigated by the medical examiner, the next step is to notify the medical examiner of the affirmative wishes of the family and obtain authorization from the medical examiner to allow the donation process to continue. (The data indicate that authorization in medical examiner cases is refused in only about 4 percent of the cases.) If authorization is needed and given, *A* is maintained on a ventilator to provide oxygen in order to maintain a heartbeat and supply oxygen to the organs.

*A* also is stabilized with drugs and fluids. *A*'s age, blood type, and weight is compared with those of transplant candidates on the national waiting list maintained by the United Network for Organ Sharing, although preference is given to candidates in *A*'s local area. The recipient matching *A* most closely, in most critical need and longest on the waiting list, is identified. Surgical teams are alerted and organized at the local hospital where *A* was a patient, in preparation for retrieval of organs and tissues. Still on the ventilator, *A* is brought to the operating room. Once the surgical team has removed the organs, the ventilator is disconnected and the organs preserved with cold packaging and in special solutions. Following the retrieval of organs, tissues are retrieved. On completion of the retrieval process, *A*'s body is treated with respect, reconstructed, and surgically closed. Then it is released to *A*'s family, who proceeds with normal funeral and burial arrangements.

## WORKING OF THE VOLUNTARY SYSTEM

"That transplantation exists today is a tribute to the humanness of mankind. It derives from the compelling desire to help fellow human beings, nothing more" (Bailey, 1990:25). Almost all religious and ethical systems support the humanitarian wish to reduce human suffering and death through organ and tissue donation. Altruism is also one of the bases of the anatomical-gift acts.

Other bases of the acts are volunteerism and informed consent. Donors and their next of kin are free to consent to making a donation. These principles underlying the anatomical-gift legislation are in contrast to the laws in other countries, such as France, Austria, and Israel, where consent is presumed and organ retrieval is automatic unless donors have expressly repudiated donation—by, for example, carrying a nondonor card.

Under the principles of the U.S. legislation, organs cannot be retrieved without appropriate permissions. In the chapter on defining death, we examined the case of Bruce Tucker, in which the surgeons removed Tucker's heart and kidney either after considering him brain dead as they claimed at the trial or by letting him die by shutting off the respirator. But Tucker never donated his heart to the hospital nor was anyone in his family, in this case, Tucker's brother, notified or asked to consent to the removal. The surgeons may have been under pressure to find a heart for the patient who was waiting in the hospital and apparently yielded to this pressure. If a Tucker-type factual situation were to arise today, the actions of the surgeons in retrieving Tucker's organs without permission would probably subject them to medical malpractice. They would not be protected from civil or criminal liability by the anatomical-gift legislation because we cannot say that they acted in good faith. In defense of the surgeons in the actual *Tucker* case, however, it needs to be pointed out that this legislation had not been passed when they acted in May 1968. The Uniform Anatomical Gift Act was not drafted until two months later. It may be that under the laws of Virginia at the time or because of the confused state of the common law, the surgeons did not act wrongfully.

But American free choice, a voluntary system, is not working well. A survey made by Gallup in 1985 showed that, while 75 percent of those polled approved of the idea of organ donation, only 27 percent said that they were willing to make a donation of their organs and 17 percent said that they had completed donor cards (Gallup, 1985). Apparently the pollsters did not ask why 73 percent of the respondents were unwilling to donate their organs and why 83 percent had not completed donor cards. If they had, they might have discovered "the horse on the dining room table syndrome" in addition to the belief that if donor cards were carried, what happened to Bruce Tucker might also happen to them. Organ transplantation is inevitably associated with death, the event that triggers organ removal and that is feared. Completing a donor card, like making one's living will or last will or pre-arranging one's funeral, forces people to cope with a subject they would rather avoid and deny.

Another reason for the sluggishness of the voluntary system may be the prevalence of the "horse on the dining room table syndrome" among medical professionals as well. Developing rules and guidelines for the implementation of the "required request" and "routine inquiry" laws is not enough to ensure the achievement of these laws: increasing the supply of organs. Indeed, the laws seem to be falling short of their aims (Caplan, 1988). Government standards and guidelines do not approach families; hospital personnel do. Although, under the "required request" and "routine inquiry" legislation, they are to approach families of dying or brain-dead patients, they are reluctant to question grieving relatives about organ donation at this anguished time. Even if they finally do approach the family, they are unable to explain to the family why a brain-dead patient is truly dead. Most hospital personnel find death painful and, if they have thought about the subject at all, have only unclear ideas about it and are unable even to identify the legal and medical criteria for determining brain death. Expecting them to speak to families about death or why a brain-dead family member patient is really dead is like expecting a miracle something Ambrose Bierce once described as beating a normal hand of four kings and an ace with four aces and a king (Bierce, 1967).

## LIFEBOAT SITUATION

In 1985, a twenty-two-year-old victim of a robbery died after being shot in the head. His heart, kidneys, and liver were removed and transplanted in four different recipients. Removed as well were his corneas and fifty-two tissue grafts, including bone, bone marrow, and a hip joint. The recipient of his liver died in 1985 of complications following transplant surgery, but the three recipients of his other organs all died of AIDS—the heart transplant patient in 1986 and the two kidney patients in 1988 and 1990, respectively. The recipient of the hip joint was found to have AIDS and dozens of others in sixteen states who received his tissues may have been infected similarly (*Miami Herald*, 1991). The case—the first involving one donor infected with AIDS who may have infected a large number of recipients—demonstrates one of the risks presented by a transplant. But the AIDS risk has not been enough to prevent the buildup of a great demand for transplants of organs and tissues. The national registry of potential organ recipients grows at an average annual rate of about 2 percent over the number of transplants performed. In the last two years, the number of those awaiting organs and tissues has risen about 40 percent. As of 1992, UNOS reported 19,851 adult patients in the United States awaiting kidneys, 2,337 awaiting hearts, 1,825 awaiting livers, 652 awaiting pancreases, 708 awaiting lungs, and 161 awaiting heart and lung combinations. Over 1,400 pediatric patients await transplants of vital organs. But the demand far exceeds the supply of organs and tissues and the gap between supply and demand keeps growing. Few of those awaiting transplants will receive them and their chances of living are slight.

We are in a lifeboat situation with more passengers than the supply of organs and tissues can keep alive. The first and most urgent problem is how to overcome the shortage. To address this problem the anatomical-gift acts were passed by all fifty states. A second legislative approach consisted of the "routine inquiry" and "required request" laws that require hospital staff to ask the next of kin of dead or dying patients to consider or approve organ and tissue donations. But merely passing legislation to make voluntary donation legal has failed to produce a continuing and adequate supply of organs and tissues (Caplan, 1983; Overcast et al., 1984).

Because the shortage of human organs prevented allografts (between members of the same species), researchers, looking for a new source of supply, began to think of xenografts or heterografts (between members of different species), although the notion of combining the parts of different species was not a novel one. Homer's *Iliad* describes a fire-breathing monster with the body of a goat, the head of a lion, and the tail of a dragon that terrorized Lycia and Caria until killed by Bellerophon. Beginning in the 1960s, researchers attempted to create their own twentieth-century chimeras—animal livers being transplanted in children (Starzl et al., 1974; Starzl, 1969) and human subjects receiving animal hearts (Hardy and Chavez, 1968; Barnard, Wolpowitz, Losman, 1977).

One of the latest instances of a human-animal chimera occurred in 1984, at Loma Linda University Hospital in California, when Dr. Leonard L. Bailey and his group of surgeons transplanted the heart of a seven-month-old baboon into a newborn child who suffered from a fatal heart abnormality (Bailey, Nehlsen-Cannarella, Concepcion, Jolley, 1985). The Baby Fae attempt, however, produced such controversy over the ethics of killing animals for organs to be transplanted in human beings that it threatened the use of primates as organ donors. Without challenging or minimizing the seriousness of the ethical issues raised, the legitimacy and logic of the controversy is open to doubt in view of the prevailing general attitude toward animals. If we are willing to sanction killing them for food, for sport, and for medical research and drug testing, why do we suddenly oppose killing them to save the lives of the terminally ill? The inconsistency is difficult to explain and can be justified only in terms of our highly sensitive and unique perception of organ transplantation. In addition, the controversy only succeeded in blinding many of us to two important facts: Baby Fae, who lived for twenty days, lived longer with her baboon's heart than Dr. Christiaan Barnard's patient who received the first human heart transplant; and the infant did not die because her immune system rejected the animal heart but because of an ABO blood group incompatibility (Bailey, 1990), an outcome that would be preventable in the future with perfected donor-patient selection.

While the ethical problems caused by xenotransplantation for the moment may have menaced chimps and baboons as a source of organs, they have not destroyed scientific interest in animal-to-human transplants and in chimeras. Is it a sign of the future that the American Society of Transplant Surgeons adopted as its symbol the monster described by Homer? In any case, research efforts in xenotransplantation and experiments in this field continue, including one in 1992 in which a human being received a baboon liver and those in which animal cells producing insulin are transplanted into human diabetics.

There are other alternatives less controversial than xenotransplantation for overcoming the shortage of organs. Two possibilities increasingly are suggested as the organ shortage worsens. To afford pediatric patients with fatal illnesses the chance to live, the first possibility is to use anencephalic infants, in whom the brain has never developed, as sources of organs. There are approximately 2,000 anencephalic fetuses born each year—enough to give children awaiting transplants the gift of life. But, under existing brain-death statutes, anencephalic infants cannot be used as organ donors because they are not brain dead. Although their brains are absent and they have no upper brains, they have brain stem activity. In order to create the anencephalic as another source of organs, either the brain-death statutes might be amended to except brain-absent individuals from their provisions or to redefine death as cortical brain death instead of whole brain death, or amendments might be made to the anatomical-gift acts to allow the anencephalic infants' parents to donate the infants' organs.

To help adult patients, a second possibility is to pay potential donors for their agreement, effective at death, to donate organs or to make a payment to families asked to donate the organs of dead donors. Such attempts to commercialize organ donation would seem to fall under the heading of free business enterprise. Moreover, if transplants can be big business for hospitals and physicians, why shouldn't donors profit from them as well? But offering money for body parts generates ethical fears that the poor, anxious to sell their bodies for needed money, would be exploited by the rich, although exploitation of someone willing and able to perform a service for money is difficult to see. The idea also flies in the face of federal and state law. The National Organ Transplant Act and the state anatomical-gift acts prohibit the sale or purchase of organs. Less obvious commercializing attempts to increase the supply of organs might consist of holding out inducements to potential donors or the families of dead ones, such as entitlement to a discount on health insurance premiums, federal benefits in the form of funeral or cemetery allowances, or a reduction in estate taxes. But these attempts also might fall within the prohibitions of federal and state laws unless they were amended to make exceptions in such cases.

To a thanatologist, however, it seems clear that, because organ donation is generally linked to the death of a donor, all legislative and other steps as those just mentioned are not directed at the real problem: the unwillingness of people to face their mortality and how to get them to face it. The thanatologist proposes a new approach to the organ donation process. Its thrust is fundamentally attitudinal: to change negative attitudes and encourage positive ones. It is to get people to stop avoiding and to square off to face their mortality. The primary objective is to increase organ donations. To accomplish it and to lead people to this point, the program encourages people to anticipate difficult situations the future may bring, including physical or mental incapacity and death, and to become willing to make advance financial and legal plans for themselves and those who survive them. Besides such advance plans in the form of life insurance,

wills, living wills, durable powers of attorney for health care, and funeral
pre-arrangements, plans for organ donation are another positive action that
people can take? I have initiated a program of this kind and have proposed
it to the Health Resources and Services Administration, Division of Organ
Transplantation.

## ETHICAL QUESTIONS AND IMPORTANCE

Because we are in a lifeboat situation, we have to be concerned with
whether the rationing of organs is done ethically. In recent years, there has
been much controversy over ethical issues during the stage of the donation
process when transplant candidates for a particular organ are selected from
waiting lists. Many people have raised questions of the rightness and
wrongness in the allocation of organs at transplant centers. Charges have
been made of bias in the transplant process when it comes to selecting
patients who will receive transplants.

There are allegations that income, race, and sex are factors now affecting
access to transplantation, especially kidney transplantation. The claim is
that, based on studies, the poor, blacks, and women are not chosen as
potential kidney recipients because white, male, young, high-income
patients are preferred (Held et al., 1988).

Some people are disturbed because rich foreign nationals are receiving
organs ahead of U.S. citizens waiting in the pool or bumped off waiting
lists because of financial considerations. One reason for this disturbance
is the feeling that organs and tissues donated by U.S. citizens or their
families are inherently and impliedly intended to give life to their fellow
Americans, who may be medically suitable candidates and qualified
recipients, and not to foreigners first. We may be inclined to shrug off this
"Americans first" argument as mere flag waving or misplaced chauvinism.
But in its defense, there are three evils of transplanting organs or tissues
into foreign nationals ahead of Americans:

1. *Medicare Costs*. Transplanting into foreign nationals raises the
   costs of Medicare we all pay eventually. The transplantation of a
   kidney into an American on dialysis and on Medicare instead of
   a foreign national, for instance, saves Medicare large amounts of
   money because kidney transplants cost less than dialysis. It is
   estimated that there would be a saving of about $6,000 over a
   five-year period for each Medicare recipient. In addition to the
   cost factor, recipients receiving a kidney transplant would be
   spared dialysis and enjoy a better quality of life.

2. *Scientific Registry and U.S. Research.* Among the data collected by the scientific registry operated by the United Network for Sharing Organs are information related to organ transplant recipients. After transplantation, the registry follows up their health status, immunosuppressive medications, graft status, serology and other factors. But when foreign nationals receive transplants and afterwards return to their own countries, they cannot be followed up and the registry, all U.S. transplant centers, and the entire medical community are deprived of important followup data that might be used for future education and research. The purpose of the anatomical-gift acts under which Americans donate organs is to aid in the development of research. This purpose is frustrated when these donations cannot do so because they are diverted to foreign nationals.

3. *Organ Sharing.* When transplant centers use organs locally to perform transplants into foreign nationals, they do not participate in the UNOS program, the organs are not shared with other transplant centers, and are denied to Americans who may be matched with a donor, have urgent medical needs, and have been on the waiting list long before the foreign national.

Even before allocation decisions are made at the selection stage, when a candidate is chosen from a waiting list at a particular medical center, there is a preliminary problem. What people will be considered eligible to receive a transplant, be admitted into the pool of candidates, and placed on a waiting list? This decision does not depend strictly on medical factors, such as blood type, size of organ, need, and who will best survive a complex and invasive transplant procedure, or on medical judgments. There are also factors having to do with our code of ethics, fair play, and social and political values. Because of these values many are concerned when the test applied in determining who will be eligible to get a donor heart, kidney, or bone marrow is the ability to pay. Transplants are big business for hospitals, which turn away people in need of transplants because they cannot pay in advance the large amounts asked by hospitals, horrendous for most of us: liver transplants—$135,000–$238,000; heart transplants—$57,000–$110,000; kidney transplants—$25,000–$30,000. These figures represent only the costs of the procedures and do not include costs both before a procedure and after, such as the costs of transporting an organ or of immunosuppressive drugs, which may double the expense of a procedure.

The question of transplanting organs into foreign nationals is obviously important to every American citizen who is a suitable recipient and who has been bumped off a waiting list because preference was given to a foreign national able to pay more money for a transplant than is allotted by Medicare. That UNOS policies have tried to place a ceiling on the number of transplants a given facility may perform on foreign nationals, and that a comparatively small number of these nationals receive transplants, brings no solace and is not acceptable to those Americans who have been bumped. The question of ability to pay is important to all individuals who have been refused admission to a hospital and placement on a waiting list because they could not prepay the bill and have been forced to beg for money to pay for the transplant through the newspapers, television, or even local bake sales.

From a broader and deeper perspective, the ethical issues are critically important because of the adverse impact they may have on the already short supply of organs and tissues and on all efforts to increase it. It was pointed out that, unlike some countries which presume consent to the retrieval of organs, organ procurement in the United States is based entirely on free choice, altruism, and the willingness of donors and their families to give voluntary and informed consent before organs can be removed. But volunteerism and altruism go only so far. The belief or perception by U.S. citizens that those in charge of distributing organs and tissues are being unfair must arouse strong feelings. They have the potential and probable effect of undermining or at least slowing down volunteerism and altruism and of widening the gap between supply and demand. A case in point is the Parent Child Development Council, a statewide group in Oregon. In 1988, so aroused by the fact that the poor are denied access to transplantation, it mounted a campaign across the state to have poor people delete from their drivers' licenses their consent to be organ donors and to encourage them to deny all requests by hospitals that families donate the organs of dead relatives ("Organ Transplant Backlash Feared in Oregon," 1988).

## MEDICAL AND ETHICAL SOLUTIONS

It can be said rightly that medicine and medical ethics are not concerned with race or nationality. Physicians should be concerned with medical needs only and not with which American or foreigner receives care and which not. In theory at least, medical ethics should not be concerned with who has the ability to pay for care either, although that theory has a hollow ring in the real world. While these issues may not involve medical ethics, they are ethical problems in that area of health care involved with transplants. These problems encompass personal, social, and political values and should be resolved by the public, ethicists, philosophers, lawyers, and legislators. They are problems that need political solutions.

Historically, health care and medicine in the United States have been free of control. But because transplantation raises deep emotions, and the gift of an organ from one individual to give life to another involves profound questions of human fellowship and personal identity and, as in the case of patient *A*'s family, may also involve the grieving process, it is different from any other kind of health care and it needs regulation to ensure equitable distribution of organs and tissues.

To protect the integrity of the voluntary system, public leaders should take steps to remove the inequities in determining who will be admitted to a pool of waiting candidates and in the allocation to those candidates of organs and tissues for transplantation. Among these steps are: (1) addressing the problem of affordable health care in this area so that all individuals who are suitable recipients and in need of organ and tissue transplants can get them; and (2) addressing the problem of U.S. citizens versus foreign nationals. In this connection and in line with a bill I prepared for the Florida legislature, I have recommended that access to organ transplantation be given first to U.S. citizens who are otherwise suitable recipients identified by a matching program or regional transplant program. If a U.S. citizen cannot be identified as a suitable recipient for the transplantation of a specific organ, a patient who is a foreign national may be given access to such organ.

## REFERENCES

Bailey, L. L. 1990. "Organ Transplantation: A Paradigm of Medical Progress." *The Hastings Center Report*, January-February:24–28.

Bailey, L. L., Nehlsen-Cannarella, S. L., Concepcion, W., Jolley, W. B. 1985. "Baboon-to-Human Cardiac Xenotransplantation in a Neonate." *Journal of the American Medical Association* 254:3321–29.

Barnard, C. N., Wolpowitz, A., and Losman, J. G. 1977. "Heterotopic Cardiac Transplantation with a Xenograft for Assistance of the Left Heart in Cardiogenic Shock After Cardiopulmonary Bypass." *South African Medical Journal* 52:1035–38.

Bierce, A. 1967. *The Devil's Dictionary.* New York: Castle Books.

Caplan, A. L. 1988. "Professional Arrogance and Public Misunderstanding." *Hastings Center Report* 18:34–37.

———. 1983. "Organ Transplants: The Cost of Success." *Hastings Center Report* 13 (6):23–32.

Gallup Organization. June 1985. *Attitudes and Opinions of the American Public Toward Organ Donation and Transplants.*

Hardy, J. D., and Chavez, C. M. 1968. "The First Heart Transplant in Man." *American Journal of Cardiology* 22:772–81.

Harmon, R. G. 1990. "The National Organ Scientific Registry." *Journal of the American Medical Association* 264:436.

Held, P. J., Pauly, M. V., Bovbjerg, J. D., Newman, J., and Salvatierra, O., Jr. 1988. "Access to Kidney Transplantation: Has the United States Eliminated Income and Racial Differences?" *Archives of Internal Medicine* 148:2594–600.

Maximus. April 1988. *Evaluation of Methods Used by States to Expand the Number of Organ and Tissue Donors.* HSRA Contract Fund Report, Falls Church, Va.

*Miami Herald*, May 18, 1991, p.11A.

"Organ Transplant Backlash Feared in Oregon." 1988. *Hospital Ethics* March–April:6.

Overcast, T. D., et al. 1984. "Problems in the Identification of Potential Donors: Misconceptions and Fallacies Associated with Donor Cards." *Journal of the American Medical Association* 251 (12):1559–62.

Starzl, T. E. 1969. "Orthotopic Heterotransplantation." In T. E. Starzl, ed., *Hepatic Transplantation.* Philadelphia: W. B. Saunders Co., 408–21.

Starzl, T. E., Ishikawa, M., Putnam, C. W., Porter, K. A., Picache, R., Husberg, B. S., Halgrimson, C. G., Schroter, G. 1974. "Progress in and Deterrents to Orthotopic Liver Transplantation, with Special Reference to Survival, Resistance to Hyperacute Rejection, and Biliary Duct Reconstruction." *Transplant Proceedings* 6 (4 Suppl):129–39.

# VII

## Law: Forms and Sources

# 11

## Law: Forms, Systems, and Procedures

When people in the health-care professions talk about the issues addressed and problems raised by the law of dying and death, they inevitably ask, "What does the law say?" In prior chapters we have tried to answer that question.

Now we need to go further. Because of the ubiquitous presence of the law in our professions, relations with others, and daily lives, writers such as Herman Melville, Anton Chekhov, Mark Twain, John Galsworthy, Charles Dickens, Sir Walter Scott, Arthur Koestler, and William Shakespeare have been drawn to the dramatic issues or comedic situations it often presents. Perhaps the most successful of these was Erle Stanley Gardner, whose eighty novels about his lawyer character Perry Mason were among the best selling of all time. Television also has been quick to seize on the possibilities offered by the constant interaction of law with life. To Americans who, according to audience-measurement services, watch television seven hours a day, it offers gripping courtroom scenes, brilliant cross-examination, and shrewd lawyer tricks in such shows as the dramatic series "L.A. Law." But apart from their entertainment value, neither literature nor television has helped us understand the nature of the law itself—its structure, sources, and the anatomy of a lawsuit—or answered another question health professionals ask: "Where do we find what the law says?" About these matters we remain confused or ignorant. In this and the final chapter, we hope to turn some of this darkness into light.

## FORMS

Law comes in as many forms as Proteus. In contrast to the natural state where might and right are identical and natural law is the equivalent of lawlessness, there is the state of civilized society where "law" takes on different forms. To scholars, political scientists, and commentators, it assumes a social form that organizes and controls a civilized society. Without control, the millions of people who make up society could not exist. A society is civilized precisely because its members adjust to one another and the individual to the group. The traffic-congested streets of New York are examples of regulation by which this adjustment is brought about. There is no control when drivers make Broadway into an Indianapolis speedway and pass and smash into one another's cars with reckless abandon. But with speed limits, stop signs, and traffic-control signals at Times Square and other busy intersections, accidents are reduced and traffic moves in a more or less orderly fashion. The same principle of control is the basis of civilized society. It is orderly, generally speaking, because people are controlled and conduct themselves according to the rules that minimize their interfering with or hurting one another.

There are four ways society may be controlled: custom, force, religion, and law. In one of its forms, then, *law* can be defined as a system of order and rules of social conduct decreed by the state. The system is administered by courts that enforce the system according to legal principles of justice and that, for violations of the rules, imprison violators, award monetary damages to individuals whose rights have been violated, and issue injunctions against or orders for the specific performance of acts.

But the scholar's theoretical model of "law" takes on a totally different split personality character in its everyday operation. In the citizen's daily life, when it is written up in law journals and books or medicolegal books such as this one, when it is practiced by the legal profession, and when it is used by the courts in deciding controversies, the other sides of "law" are revealed.

In one of its personalities, it consists of legislation—namely, federal and state constitutions, statutes of Congress and state legislatures; formal enactments of the subdivisions of a state, such as county, city, town or village; and the rules made by the administrative agencies of federal, state, or local governments. A second personality consists of decisions made by courts of all levels to resolve issues. Law in the sense used by scholars as a control or adjustment of relations is made possible only by law in the sense of legislative acts and judicial decisions.

To permit relations to be adjusted, the multiple personality becomes even more complex. It now divides into branches. To deal with rights and duties among citizens toward their contracts, property, and conduct and to afford them remedies for wrongs such as breach of contract or injuries caused by a tortious act, it becomes *substantive* law. *Adjective* law relates to rules of procedure. *Administrative* law governs the organization of federal, state, or local administrative agencies and their powers, duties, functions, and transactions with citizens. *Public* law affects the relations between citizens and government or between states or nations.

Law becomes further differentiated. More branches deal with specific areas and virtually all problems that may arise among citizens or between them and government. Some of the many branches into which it is split include: comparative law, criminal law, domestic relations law, health law, insurance law, international law, landlord and tenant law, maritime law, military law, negotiable instruments law, patent law, real property law, tax law, tort law, and the law of wills. To these older branches we have now added the "law of dying and death" to embrace issues in new areas carved out by developments in medical technology.

## LEGISLATION

Legislation is one of the principal sources of law in its several forms. The Constitution of the United States and the separate constitutions of the fifty states give us the rules and principles that create and define the powers and functions of the federal and state governments and establish the rights of the individual vis-à-vis government. Of particular importance are the First, Fourth, Fifth, Ninth, and Fourteenth Amendments to the Constitution, in which courts have found guarantees that figure so strongly in the protection of rights to refuse life-sustaining treatment.

Legislation in the form of statutes enacted by Congress or state legislatures are important as well because they express public policy and try to address changing conditions and the new needs and problems they create for a variety of classes, sectors, and segments of society. The living-will statutes are prime examples of attempts, however imperfect, to speak to fresh developments in medical technology that allow the dying process to be prolonged artificially, to establish a policy that gives terminally ill people the choice of accepting or declining life-sustaining procedures, and relieves the medical profession of fear and uncertainty concerning civil or criminal proceedings or penalties if life-sustaining treatment is withdrawn or withheld in conformity with a living will. We have also mentioned brain-death and anatomical-gift legislation prompted by changing conditions in other dying and death areas.

## JUDICIAL DECISIONS AND SYSTEMS

When some of us refer to the law, we generally think in terms of the Constitution (the "supreme law of the land") or legislation that has been enacted. Legislation is the written law, but judicial decisions make up the equally powerful unwritten law. Courts do not enact legislation, but they interpret constitutions and statutes or, when the factual situation in a case presents a novel issue not covered by existing legislation, a court's holding establishes new law. The holdings in *Quinlan* and *Cruzan* exemplify this law-making process. Judicial decisions over the centuries have developed the common law, a highly significant source of law in all its classifications.

While constitutions and statutes have an undeniable importance, judicial decisions may be even more important. Legislation generally follows in the wake of social developments and medical advances and issues, whereas courts usually grapple with current issues and problems that develop into the controversies the judiciary is called on to decide. Indeed, state courts frequently bring to the attention of legislatures the need for new laws and public policies that will help resolve controversies in regard to life-sustaining treatment in private rather than judicial forums or will guide court decisions pertaining to such matters.[1] Courts also have a special importance for health-care professionals. Over the years courts have been the principal forum in which their tort and criminal liabilities have been decided and, with respect to dying and death issues, have provided virtually all the law in the United States relating to the disposition of property, withdrawing and withholding life-sustaining treatment, competence and incompetence and surrogate decision making.

Mention "courts" and the average person usually thinks of the highest tribunal in the United States. While the U.S. Supreme Court has no rival for importance, other courts in the United States make significant decisions as well. A description of them will help us understand the legal system and process though which a case passes.

The American judicial system consists of state and federal courts. Although there may be differences in their titles and matters of jurisdiction, there is little difference in the system of all courts in the fifty states.

At the top is the court of final appeal that, at its discretion, reviews cases appealed from lower courts. In each state, it is the court of last resort except that some decisions may be appealed to the U.S. Supreme Court. These courts of last resort are called variously "Supreme Court" (as in New Jersey, Illinois, Michigan, or Florida) or "Court of Appeals" (as in New York and Maryland). The next level of court is the intermediate tribunal that generally must review questions of law raised in trial courts, such as interpreting a statute or any errors of law made by the trial court in reaching a decision. As was pointed out in Chapter 5, this tribunal cannot consider evidence not introduced in the trial. Its title may be "Appellate Division" (as in New York), or "Court of Appeal" (as in Michigan, Oregon, or California). The next lower level is occupied by trial courts of general jurisdiction over criminal and civil cases. The titles of these may vary from "Supreme Court" and "County Court" (as in New York), "Circuit Court" (as in Florida), and "District Court" (Idaho) to "Superior Court" (in Maine and the District of Columbia). At still a lower level are courts with jurisdiction limited to matters involving juveniles, domestic relations, family, probate, traffic, small claims, felonies, and misdemeanors.

The federal judicial system, like that of the states, is tiered. From the highest court in the nation, the Supreme Court, composed of a Chief Justice and eight associate justices, there is no appeal. At its discretion, it reviews the decisions of the U.S. Courts of Appeal, those of the state courts of last resort, and of U.S. District Courts. The Court also has original jurisdiction in some matters, such as cases in which a state or foreign ambassadors or ministers are parties. The next tier consists of eleven U.S. Courts of Appeal that review decisions of federal trial courts on the level below known as U.S. District Courts. They hear civil cases as well as federal crimes. There are also courts with limited jurisdiction called U.S. Magistrate's Courts where minor violations of federal criminal law are heard.

Although trial courts in the state and federal systems are far from the top in the hierarchies of these systems, generally they have a greater immediate significance for litigants than appellate courts because from the trial level most cases decided are never appealed. Thus, these cases are resolved once and for all. But from three other perspectives, the appellate tribunals are more important. Unlike the majority of decisions made by trial courts, the decisions of appellate courts are usually reported. Lawyers, judges, and the public can read and be guided by their opinions. While an appellate decision settles the one case being reviewed, it may also exert influence on many others and in many ways. *Cruzan*, for example, stopped Nancy Cruzan's parents from discontinuing her tubal feeding but it also produced an enormous public demand for living wills; provoked reactions by patient's rights and pro-life advocates; required ethicists and the legal and medical professions to reconsider their ways of thinking and practicing; sparked legislative action in Congress; and, by holding that the U.S. Constitution did not prevent Missouri from requiring "clear and convincing" evidence of a person's wishes expressed when competent to stop life supports, it may have encouraged the imposition of similar procedural standards by other states. And beyond and before *Cruzan*, all the legal principles and decisions in the dying and death areas that have concerned us were the results of cases appealed to and adjudicated by appellate courts that made judicial policy and precedent.

## STAGES OF A CASE

The rules of procedure vary according to the kind of case. If it is a criminal case—involving the trial of a person accused of an offense against the public—a criminal procedure is followed including charges, jury, and a public trial. If it is a civil lawsuit to enforce private rights, a civil procedure is followed. Because the risk of criminal prosecution for stopping or not starting life support is negligible and since few health providers will ever be involved with criminal cases while most are constantly faced with potential involvement in civil ones, the focus here is on the stages of a civil case in court. What follows is a summary of these seven stages.

### Stage One

People have offered different reasons for seeking out a lawyer. In one of his plays, George Bernard Shaw—the Irish dramatist, wit, and critic—advised: "Whenever you want to do anything against the law, Cicely, always consult a good lawyer" (Shaw, 1966). But for the vast majority of litigants, the reason is that they do not or cannot represent themselves in court either as plaintiffs (individuals who start a civil lawsuit against someone else) or defendants (individuals forced to respond to a civil lawsuit started against them and also those accused of a crime in a criminal prosecution). At this initial stage, the case must be analyzed and prepared by the lawyer. This legal expert's function is to evaluate and develop a client's case, interview witnesses identified by the client or uncovered by further investigation, and discover and examine all pertinent documents.

A word about what to expect from a lawyer. When we ask, "What does the law say?" the question implies a conception of the law as a settled body of rules that all the legal expert needs to do is consult to be given the correct answer to a question or solution for a case. Again the example of *Cruzan*—where the U.S. Supreme Court split five to four—tells us that this is not so. *Cruzan* confirms the words of William O. Douglas, an associate justice on the Supreme Court from 1939 to 1975: "The law is not a series of calculating machines where definitions and answers come tumbling out when the right levers are pushed" (Douglas 1948:104,105). Anyone who has seen how frequently lawyers are in doubt or how judges cannot agree and write opposing opinions in the same case knows that no legal expert can always be sure of what the law is or how others may interpret it. It is here that another comparison to medicine is enlightening. Attending physicians making a diagnosis may consult with other physicians, but in the end the attending physician is the decision maker and the decision is final. The decision made by lawyers, on the other hand, can never be final because a lawyer's understanding of and arguments concerning the applicable law will always be challenged by other lawyers with equally convincing arguments and may be overruled by trial or appellate courts.

### Stage Two

The second stage is the commencement of an action on behalf of the plaintiff by the service of a summons or by the issuance by the court of a writ or summons served by the sheriff commanding the defendant to appear in court.

### Stage Three

The next stage involves the preparation and service of pleadings. One pleading is the plaintiff's complaint that alleges the facts concerning what took place and the defendant's conduct that breached a contract or caused injury to the plaintiff's person or damages to the plaintiff's property, and sets forth the amount of money the plaintiff asks as compensation. For instance, the complaint in a battery case brought by the estate of a dead patient against a physician and hospital might allege that life-sustaining treatment, such as a ventilator or nasogastric tube, was given to a patient without authorization, when no emergency existed and in the face of the patient's express refusal. The claim in such a case might be for damages for pain and suffering and for medical expenses incurred while the unauthorized treatment continued.

The complaint is then served on the defendant to apprise the defendant of the claim. The defendant may make a motion for dismissal if the complaint fails to state a cause of action a court will entertain or if the jurisdiction of the court is challenged. If none is made—or if made, it is dismissed by the court—the defendant prepares a pleading in the form of an answer that may admit but generally denies the plaintiff's allegations. The answer may also present a counterclaim against the plaintiff. In the battery case mentioned, the hospital might counterclaim for its unpaid bill for hospital services and the physician for unpaid professional fees. The answer might also present affirmative defenses, such as the statute of limitations that, if it has run, will bar the plaintiff's claim. The purpose of the pleadings is to crystallize just what the issues of liability and damages are in the case. At this stage, there may be efforts by the litigants to settle out of court.

### Stage Four

If these efforts fail, the next step is the pretrial stage during which both sides begin trial preparations. They may use discovery proceedings to get information and documents from the other side and to see just what kind of case the opponent has. Interrogatories or questions put to a party must be answered. One side will take depositions of the other. Also as part of the pretrial steps, a pretrial conference is held with a judge to sharpen the issues and to see if a last-minute compromise is possible. During this pretrial stage, one party or the other may make a motion for summary judgment that, based on the pleadings, affidavits, depositions, or documents gotten through discovery proceedings, there are no material factual issues to be tried.

### Stage Five

Assuming that such an issue does exist, the trial stage in a case tried before a jury is reached in which witnesses are called and cross-examined and evidence produced before the jury as the trier of fact. During the trial, the judge will rule on objections to evidence made by one side or the other and, applying the rules of evidence, will determine whether evidence is admissible. Following the presentation to the jury of the plaintiff's case, a defendant may ask the judge both to rule as a matter of law that the plaintiff has not offered evidence strong enough to sustain the plaintiff's burden of proof and also for a directed verdict. Such a verdict will end the trial in favor of the defendant. If the case is tried before a judge alone, the trial proceeds similarly except that the judge will decide the facts and the law and will render a decision.

### Stage Six

The after-trial stage in a case heard by a jury will consist of closing arguments by counsel made to the jury, the judge's instructions to the jury on the applicable law, and the jury's verdict in favor of one party or the other. The losing party may then make a motion for the judge to direct a verdict notwithstanding the jury's verdict on the ground that no material issue existed for the jury. If not granted, judgment will be entered and from it the losing party may appeal to a higher court that will review the case.

### Stage Seven

If judgment has been entered, not appealed, or appealed and sustained, and it is not paid voluntarily by the losing party, steps may now be taken to collect it. They may consist of a writ of execution under which a sheriff will take possession of the losing party's property and sell it at a public auction to satisfy the judgment. Or an order of garnishment may be obtained that requires a third party to pay the winning party money owed by the third party to the loser. Typically, a losing party's salary will be garnished and the employer required to pay a percentage of the salary to the winner.

## NONJUDICIAL BODIES

Besides the courts, there are various nonjudicial mechanisms for the settlement of disputes that have the advantage of doing so faster, less expensively, and with more privacy than is possible in the courts.

Arbitration is such a mechanism. Commercial agreements by individuals to submit existing or future disputes to a specified third person or persons for resolution are common. In these agreements, the parties agree to accept as final and to perform the decisions of the third party. State statutes generally validate arbitration agreements and provide for the enforcement of any award made if the arbitration hearing has been conducted fairly and impartially.

By the 1970s, the number of medical malpractice suits had reached staggering numbers and the problem became critical as physicians and hospitals were faced with being bankrupted by large verdicts against them. Malpractice insurance premiums soared from 100 to 400 percent, and some insurance companies refused to issue malpractice insurance policies. The insurance problems created a crisis for hospitals and physicians. But it also created one for patients who, in the form of increased hospital and professional fees, ended up paying the increased premiums. There were boycotts by neurosurgeons and obstetricians who would not deliver babies and physicians began to leave some states. But in the years after the 1970s, the crisis seemed to be over as states enacted legislation, some statutes to prevent frivolous suits and some to require malpractice claims to be submitted first to arbitration panels of laymen, lawyers, and physicians. While awards made by the panels might be appealed to the courts and trials requested, the arbitration proceeding and its decision could be admitted in evidence at the trial. Arbitration of claims or suits against physicians and hospitals may also be offered to patients as one of the conditions of admission to a hospital.

Federal and state administrative agencies, which exist as authorities for carrying out the laws of the federal and state government, are another nonjudicial mechanism. State boards of nursing that issue licenses and take disciplinary action to control the profession are an example. Administrative agencies such as these have quasi-judicial powers and serve as administrative tribunals to adjudicate disputes between individuals and the executive power. To protect people affected by the rules or actions of these agencies, however, the courts will review and reverse their decisions if arbitrary. But before judicial review can be obtained, all administrative remedies, including appeals to the next higher agency in the administrative hierarchy, must be exhausted.

In the medical field, the ethics committee in a hospital is a nonjudicial body for dealing with significant medical and ethical problems confronting the medical profession. The notion of an ethics committee—also known as a Human Values Committee or Medical-Moral Committee—was born in 1976 when the New Jersey Supreme Court in *In re Quinlan*[2] suggested that treatment decisions to discontinue life support be made by the patient and a hospital ethics committee. Many took a "dim view"[3] of this approach as an attempt to shift decision making away from the courts and it did not receive much support. However, great interest in these committees started in 1982, when the Department of Health and Human Services issued its Baby Doe regulations based on recommendations of the American Academy of Pediatricians. The regulations provided that hospitals set up infant care review committees to create guidelines for the withholding or withdrawing of life-sustaining treatment from infants. A year later, a report from the President's Commission (1983) provoked more interest in ethics committees when it recommended that health-care institutions set them up as part of their procedures for addressing patient's rights and reviewing medical problems.

Today many hospitals have created these committees. Usually such committees try to plan educational programs on biomedical and ethical issues for their hospital staffs and, as the result of ethical problems presented during the care of an individual patient, formulate or amend general policies and procedures for the care of other patients and the resolution of ethical issues. Since these committees are generally multidisciplinary and include physicians, attorneys, nurses, social workers, ethicists, philosophers, and clergy, they provide a forum in which diverse ideas and perspectives are allowed to flow into the making of policies. These policies and procedures have a positive effect on medical and nursing practice at hospitals since they offer guidance on the ethics of treatment decision making and help the hospital staff assist patients and families with such decisions.

When the ethics committee on which I serve was created a few years ago, its mission, like the functions and purposes of most committees, was limited to education and policy making. It was prevented from being an ultimate solution for many ethical, legal, and medical dilemmas. It did not make case-by-case decisions or act as an ethics review board. Now, however, it has become apparent that its mission needs to be expanded to allow it to act as an ethics review board and, by promoting dialogue, objectively analyzing facts, and encouraging reflection, to assist physicians, medical staff, patients, and families involved to arrive at decisions. Assistance can be extended either by the committee or by designated consultants. Which alternative is used will depend on the circumstances of a case (Swenson and Miller, 1992). The committee may be preferred if the ethical problem raised may affect hospital policy; consultants may be preferred if close personal contact and dialogue with a patient seems desirable. Whichever model is used, if the claims, grievances, or lawsuits of patients were to be brought before the full committee and debated openly and fully or were to be handled by consultants in an informal atmosphere and dialogue, an enlightened and acceptable resolution of problems might be arrived at which would make resort to the courts improbable. Thus, if an ethics committee has case review as one of its goals, it can serve as an alternate method for the out-of-court settlement of disputes.

Several other nonjudicial entities also function to deal with legal, medical, and ethical issues and to help in their resolution. Examples are the President's Commission for the Study of Ethical Problems, the American Medical Association, the American Hospital Association, the Hastings Center, the Kennedy Institute of Ethics at Georgetown University, and cross-professional groups such as the American Society of Law and Medicine, and the Ad Hoc Committee on Biomedical Ethics of the Los Angeles Medical Association and the Los Angeles Bar Association.

## LEGAL CITATIONS

1. Severns v. Wilmington Medical Center, Inc., 421 A.2d 1334 (Del. Sup. Ct. 1980), the Delaware Supreme Court saying: "we earnestly invite the prompt attention of the General Assembly ... with the hope that it will enact a comprehensive State policy governing these matters which are, in the words of Quinlan, of 'transcendent importance' "; In re Guardianship of Estelle M. Browning, 543 S.2d 258, *aff'd* 568 S.2d 4 (Fla. Sup. Ct. 1990), where the District Court of Florida stated: "The legislature could clearly enact a more sophisticated remedy or create procedures based on interests in addition to the patient's consitutional right of privacy"; also Satz v. Perlmutter, 362 S.2d 160, *aff'd* 379 S.2d 359 (Fla. Sup. Ct. 1980) where the Florida Supreme Court said that the question

raised by the refusal of life support by a competent, terminally ill patient "is not one which is well suited for resolution in an adversary judicial proceeding. It is the type which is more suitably addressed in the legislative forum."

2. 70 N.J. 10, 355 A.2d 647 (N.J. Sup. Ct.) *cert. den. sub.nom.* In re Garger v. New Jersey, 429 U.S. 922 (1976).

3. Superintendent of Belchertown State School v. Saikewicz, 373 Mass. 728, 370 N.E.2d 417 (Mass. Sup. Jud. Ct. 1977).

## REFERENCES

Douglas, W. O. 1948. "The Dissent: A Safeguard of Democracy." *American Judicature Society* 32: 104, 105.

President's Commission for the Study of Ethical Problems: Medicine and Biomedicine and Behavioral Research. 1983. *Deciding to Forgo Life-Sustaining Treatment.* Washington, DC: Government Printing Office.

Shaw, G. B. 1966. *Captain Brassbound's Conversion.* In *Four Plays by George Bernard Shaw.* New York: Dell.

Swenson, M. D., and Miller, R. B. 1992. "Ethics Case Review in Health Care Institutions." *Archives of Internal Medicine* 152: 694–97.

# 12

## Sources of Law:
## How to Look Them Up

### RESEARCH

Research is the endeavor to investigate and solve problems. Since it is undertaken in virtually every area of human interest, the problems are as specialized as the tools used. They may require researchers to resort to personal interviews, questionnaires, or computers, and may take researchers to the laboratory or require them to make field investigations in faraway places.

Research in law leads lawyers in Western nations in one direction and to one nearby place. While their counterparts in Islam find the law in the *Shari' ah*, the sum of the teachings of the prophet Muhammad, for lawyers operating within the Anglo-American system of jurisprudence the law is found in the law library. U.S. legal researchers will discover there bibliographical material relating to federal laws, the statutes and common law of each of the fifty states, and all the main subjects of law treated in treatises, encyclopedias, and periodicals. Comprehensive law libraries are maintained in law schools and bar associations and are found in law offices where, depending on space and budget limitations, they vary from several thousand volumes in large law firms to a few basic tools, such as local statutes and case reports in the offices of sole practitioners. Many city and county public libraries provide not only for general reading but also have reference libraries with limited collections for legal research.

Before describing the procedures and sources of legal research, it is well to point out that there is nothing scientific about legal research and that its methodology cannot be presented as a mathematical formula. Method is purely the objectifying of subjective processes. Behind and dominating method are the creative and intellectual faculties and the individual goals of the researcher.

Thought processes come into play at the very outset, for the first step in looking up the law, even in the most cursory way, must be to examine and evaluate the factual situation confronting a researcher and to try to distill from it a legal question or set of questions. Most people prefer to go to professional counsel whose training prepares them for this task, and this chapter is not intended to suggest or recommend that health-care professionals avoid seeking legal advice that may be needed. But it is not beyond the ability of the intelligent man or woman who is not a lawyer and may not wish to consult one to draw from the facts a concrete issue that requires clarification or an answer. If, for example, we are confronted by an organ donor who has stipulated on his donor card that his heart can be transplanted only into a certain named person, the question for us is whether a donor may lay down this condition and designate a particular donee for transplantation. The affirmative answer is found in the anatomical-gift statute enacted by our state. Or, in another factual situation, a husband warns his wife's doctor that he does not want her to have a hysterectomy because he wants his wife to bear children. But the physician performs one anyway. Does the husband have a cause of action against the physician for going ahead with the procedure without the husband's consent? Each problem facing a health-care provider as well as every court case and legal issue is produced by some set of facts. These facts and this issue were before one court in the case of *Murray* v. *VanDevander*[1] where it was decided that the husband's consent was not required.

## STATUTORY LAW

Statutes are a primary source of law, and researchers will generally want to know if any apply to and govern the issue raised by the factual situation. Federal and state statutes are published in bound volumes either in the form of official codes that contain the text of the laws or as codes published by commercial publishers. The unofficial volumes are annotated—that is, besides the text of the statutes are notes containing abstracts of and citations to court decisions in which the text was applied or interpreted.

The codes are arranged under subject titles and contain an index to facilitate locating the statutory provisions applicable to the subject being investigated. A numbering system is used and each statute is numbered. If researchers know that the nursing practice statute in New York is Section 690 of the New York Education Law, they can locate that section number in the Education volume of *McKinney's Consolidated Laws of New York*

*Annotated.* If researchers want to know the provisions of the Florida statute relating to durable powers of attorney but do not know the section, a statutory researcher will attempt to break down the subject into key words or ideas and then check them in the subject index provided by the unofficial codes. Probably the index would be checked first under the obvious words "durable power of attorney" and, when this entry is not found (because it was not so obvious to the preparer of the index), "power of attorney" would be checked and found to refer to the section number of the durable power of attorney statute—namely, Section 709.08 of *West's Florida Statutes Annotated.*

The unofficial publications also contain supplements called "pocket parts" that update the statutes annually and show new ones passed or those which have been repealed or amended. Annotated codes that may be consulted for federal laws and all the states are shown under "Statutes" in Appendix B: Guide to the Law Library.

## CASE REPORTS

The famed eighteenth-century English jurist, Sir William Blackstone said that the chief source of the laws of England was general and immemorial custom. But even before Blackstone's time, the decisions of judges were authoritative and became precedents that later judges could not ignore. In England as well as in the United States, which derived its legal system from England, reported court decisions were another primary source of law. Case reports were cited by judges and lawyers and were systematically recognized as authority. Judicial decisions not only disposed of the particular case being heard; the rule of *stare decisis* ("let the decision stand") required courts to abide by case precedent and, unless the case were overruled or changed by statute, to follow it and to make the same decision in a similar case as was made by a court in the same jurisdiction and on the same or higher tier in the judicial system. The rule of *stare decisis* allows principles and propositions of law to be settled by a series of consistent judicial decisions and gives rise to stability and certainty in the law. It is undoubtedly a salutary rule and it remains a foundation of the common law. However, it must be realized that life and times change and occasions may arise when, rather than invoke the doctrine and insist that old cases and old law be followed, departure from the doctrine to make new law consonant with the new times may be necessary.

Each legal question challenging the researcher has been produced by a set of facts. If these facts have been addressed by a statute or by a court, some principle of law has been applied to resolve the question. If a statute is applicable and controls, the researcher should examine judicial decisions that have been made under the statute to determine how it has been construed. If no statute applies, the researcher will try to locate the case in the researcher's jurisdiction or, if there is none, in another jurisdiction, that has rendered an opinion with respect to the set of facts resembling the ones confronting the researcher. A judicial opinion provides authority and furnishes the researcher with the point of law and clarification wanted on the issue raised by the factual situation.

Decisions of courts of final appeal are published in case reports. Some decisions of courts of intermediate appeal are published also, but virtually none of those rendered by trial courts are published. At this level there may be transcripts of a trial, but these are not published nor is the trial court's opinion, if one even was written.

The decisions of courts of final appeal (and some intermediate courts) are published in bound volumes of case reports numbered consecutively. The reports may be official or unofficial. If unofficial, they are published by a commercial publisher as part of a national reporter system that covers every region of the country. These are shown under Case Reports in Appendix B. Many reports are published in a second or third series after the preceding series has stopped at some point. When a new series is started, the numbering of the reports begins again. *California Reports*, for example, began its third series in 1969 with volume 1.

Among the thousands of judicial decisions rendered, many will interest us because they are pertinent to and significant for patient care. For example, *Nishi* v. *Hartwell*, 473 P.2d 116 (Sup. Ct. Hawaii 1970) involved the therapeutic privilege of physicians. Cases affecting the rights of patients to refuse life-sustaining treatment, such as *In re Quinlan*, 70 N.J. 10, 355 A.2d 647, 669, *cert. den. sub. nom. In re Garger* v. *New Jersey*, 429 U.S. 922 (1976), provided a constitutional basis for the right to decline such treatment. *Lane* v. *Candura*, 376 N.E. 2d 1232,[2] involved an amputation where the issue of competence was raised. The captions of these cases are typical and if we wish to look up these cases, or any others whose facts or legal issues are similar to the ones of immediate interest to us, we ought to understand their captions and the elements they incorporate: names, letters, and numbers.

The names are those of the parties. The first name, "Nishi," for instance, is the plaintiff's—the individual who begins a lawsuit at the trial court level. If the case is appealed to the next level of appellate courts, the first name would represent the appellant—the person appealing. The second name ("Hartwell") is the defendant's, the person who responds to a plaintiff's civil suit for damages. In an appellate court, the name would represent that of the appellee. The cited cases were all civil cases. But if a case were criminal, as was *People* v. *Pierson*,[3] the defendant would be the person charged with a crime.

The letter designations in the captions—"P." in *Nishi*, "N.J.," "A.," and "U.S." in *Quinlan*; and "N.E." in *Lane* —refer to the official or unofficial case reports in which the cases were published. "P." is the unofficial Pacific reporter group that includes California and fourteen other states;[4] "N.J." represents the official New Jersey state report; "U.S.," the official report of U.S. Supreme Court decisions; and "N.E.," the unofficial North East reporter group comprising New York, Massachusetts, Ohio, Illinois, and Indiana.

The numbers in the captions preceding the letters—"473" in *Nishi*; "70," "355," and "429" in *Quinlan*; and "376" in *Lane*—are the numbers of the volumes of case reports in which the cases were published; the numbers immediately following the letters tell us in which series a case was reported. In all three cases, the number "2d" represents the second series of an unofficial reporter. The numbers appearing next—"116" in the *Nishi* caption; "10," "647," and "922" in *Quinlan*; and "1232" in *Lane*—all give us the numbers of the pages in the case reports on which the case starts.

So the *Nishi* case would be found in Volume 473 of the Pacific second series unofficial reporter system at page 116. The *Quinlan* case is located in the volume numbered 70 in the New Jersey reports at page 10. If the New Jersey reports were not on the library shelf, the case would be found on page 647 in the 355th volume of the Atlantic second series unofficial reporter system. Volume 376 of the North East second series unofficial reporter would show the *Lane* case at page 1,232.

The *Quinlan* caption is further instructive. The words "In re" are used to indicate matters in which a question has been raised about a person, property, or estate. It also advises us that the case was appealed under the name (*sub. nom.*) of *Garger* v. *New Jersey* to the U.S. Supreme Court which (*cert. den.*) refused to issue a writ of certiorari to review questions of law in the case. Also the page number "669" after the initial page number "647" in the unofficial reporter tells us the page on which the court made a statement considered significant by the person who referred to or wrote up the case.

The designation in parentheses after the *Nishi* case advises us that the case was decided by the highest state court and gives us the date when it was decided.

When we look for and finally find a case in the unofficial reporter, we will discover more than merely a report of the case. Besides the caption giving the names of the parties, the level of the court in which the case was decided, and the date of the decision, the following seven additional elements of great value to researchers appear on the first page of the case even before the opinion of the court is given: (1) a synopsis of the case, (2) a digest of the topic or point of law involved in the case and a key number whose function will be described below, (3) a reference to any statutes interpreted, (4) a reference to any words or phrases interpreted, (5) a syllabus by which the court summarizes its holding in the case, (6) the names of the attorneys appearing in the case, and (7) the name or names of the judges by whom the case was decided.

For centuries and up to the 1970s, access to court decisions was limited to the case reports published in musty volumes. Today cases are accessible through computers. Most large law libraries have computers that can supply access to databases containing judicial decisions. WESTLAW is one research service furnished by one of the largest commercial publishing companies.

## KEY NUMBERS AND DIGESTS

When the researcher finds in an unofficial reporter a decision of a case whose factual situation is similar to the one with which we are confronted, he or she may wish to find more cases in point. When a case is published in an unofficial reporter, it is accompanied by a headnote or paragraph that summarizes the set of facts in the case and the specific point of law decided by it. Each headnote begins with a topic description and key number—for instance, "Physicians and Surgeons 43." The key number is an important research tool. If the case dealt with a set of facts like that facing us, the key number can guide the researcher to other cases in point that have been decided at any time and that are classified under the same topic and key number. These key numbers will be located in the *Key Number Digests* published in federal digests and for each state (See Digests in Appendix B).

If at the outset of research the researcher knows of no case in point or key number, another research method is to analyze the factual situation as described earlier under Statutory Law and try to break it down into descriptive key words or ideas that sum up the principal facts. The researcher then checks the words selected in the indices provided by the digests. Those chosen probably match some of the thousands of words in the indices. These, in turn, will describe rules and points of law and lead the researcher to a topic and key number and eventually to a case or cases in point.

## ENCYCLOPEDIAS

Another method of research is to use a secondary source: the legal encyclopedia. Hundreds of legal topics are given in alphabetical order. Established principles covering the whole range of law are described in a sweeping way with references to judicial decisions from every jurisdiction. Indices are provided to locate topics of interest. But the sweep of the encyclopedia is too general to be of any real value in specific cases. For this reason, legal encyclopedias are used only rarely in court decisions or lawyers' briefs as authority for the law. Nevertheless, they remain excellent sources for finding a comprehensive treatment of a subject and for finding case law and reports for further research. The titles of legal encyclopedias are set forth under Encyclopedias in Appendix B.

## DICTIONARIES

Research requires an understanding of terms. For the lay person to whom legal jargon may be mystifying, law dictionaries are very useful because they define thousands of unfamiliar legal terms. Some dictionaries are useful as well because they list words and phrases and refer to judicial decisions in which they have been defined. An example is "Abortion. People v. Nixon, 210 N.W. 2d 635, 638, 42 Mich. App. 332." Appendix B supplies the names of dictionaries.

## PERIODICALS

An excellent secondary source are legal periodicals. Containing articles on various subjects, they are valuable contributions to the legal literature because they offer researchers explanations and analyses of these subjects and references to cases, statutes, and other literature. Periodicals include law reviews published by law schools and journals from organizations oriented toward virtually every field, including health care. Indices in the periodicals can be consulted under topical headings for articles of interest. (See Legal Periodicals Index in Appendix B). Periodicals may also be located by using computer research programs, such as WESTLAW and LEXIS.

## LEGAL CITATIONS

1. 522 P.2d 302 (Okla. Ct. App. Div. 1 1974).
2. Massachusetts Court of Appeals 1978.
3. 176 N.Y. 201, 68 N.E. 243 (N.Y. Ct. of App. 1903).

4. Alaska, Arizona, Colorado, Hawaii, Idaho, Kansas, Montana, Nevada, New Mexico, Oklahoma, Oregon, Utah, Washington, Wyoming.

# Appendices

# Appendix A:
# Death-Related Statutes
# and Common-Law Doctrines

## ABATEMENT

Under the common-law doctrine of *actio personalis moritur cum persona*, actions and proceedings at law terminated with the death of a party. While all actions arising out of contract or property rights were allowed to survive the party's death, those for tort actions expired with the expiration of a plaintiff or defendant. These actions were considered personal and included libel, slander, malicious prosecution, false imprisonment, and assault and battery. Some courts considered this rule intolerable. In an action for libel where the plaintiff died, one said "there is no just reason why [the action] should not survive his death. To say that a man's defamed reputation dies with him is to ignore the realities of life and the bleak legacy it leaves behind.... Why should a claim for a damaged leg survive death, where a claim for a damaged name does not. After death, the leg cannot be healed, but the reputation can."[1] Today ten states have enacted "survival statutes" to allow defamation and other actions to survive the death of a wrongdoer. The actions are allowed to continue against the executor or administrator of the deceased party. Exceptions are divorce actions and paternity suits that do not survive.

## AGENCY

In the law of agency, death is regarded as the revocation of any power given by a principal to another person whereby the latter acts as an agent to perform specific acts or take steps of a general nature. A power of attorney, for example, which is a written instrument appointing an attorney in fact and specifying powers and duties, expires with the death of the principal.

## CEMETERIES

Burial of the dead is a right and burial places are indispensable. While it is not within the police power of the state to destroy or prevent that right, municipalities acting under the police power may and do regulate where cemeteries are located, whether further burials may be made in a particular cemetery, and whether interred bodies may be removed.

## CIVIL DEATH

State statutes recognize a type of death that is not identical with physical death or *mors naturalis*. "Civil death" or *mors civilis*, is the status of one who has lost all civil rights and is considered dead under the law—*civiliter mortuus*—generally because of a sentence of life imprisonment or death. The property of one who is civilly dead is transferred to the heirs as if actual death had taken place. Under the common law, civil death and forfeiture of rights followed a conviction for treason or felony.

## DEATH PENALTY

The statutes of thirty-six states impose capital punishment. The federal government also authorizes it. Congress enacted legislation allowing the death penalty for various crimes, including espionage, treason, air piracy, and murder. Execution may be by electrocution, the gas chamber, lethal injection, the gallows, or the firing squad. Executions on death row were stayed temporarily after the U.S. Supreme Court decision in *Furman* v. *Georgia*[2] which struck down a death-penalty statute that failed to set standards for playing god and decided who should live or die, as cruel and unusual punishment in violation of the Eighth Amendment of the U.S. Constitution. In 1976, however, new death-penalty statutes were not ruled unconstitutional by the High Court[3] and executions began again in the following year. By 1991 more than 150 prisoners convicted of crimes had been executed while over 2,000 others waited their turns on death row.

## DISQUALIFICATION AS WITNESS

Under the statutes of most jurisdictions, parties to a civil action who have some interest in the outcome of the suit are absolutely disqualified from testifying against the estate of a dead person with regard to any personal transactions with the deceased. The law mutes the one where death has muted the other.

## ESCHEAT

All states have laws of escheat by which the state takes the real or personal property of an intestate if there are no heirs.

## ESTATE TAXES

Federal and state estate tax laws levy taxes, usually according to graduated tax schedules, on the right to transfer property on death. Generally, the value of the property must exceed a specified amount. These transfers include all dispositions of property that are effective at death as well as all dispositions motivated by death. For example, Section 2035 of the Internal Revenue Code imposes an estate tax on all property transfers made "in contemplation of death," the value of which must be included in the gross estate. The assets of an estate are applied to the payment of estate taxes.

## JOINT TENANCY

In a joint tenancy with right of survivorship, whether in real property, personal property, bank accounts or safe deposit boxes, two or more people are the joint owners of the property with equal rights of possession. Under common law principles, on the death of the other joint tenant(s), the sole ownership and control is transferred to the survivor.

## LIFE INSURANCE

The insuring of a life means that only one contingency will cause the policy to mature: death. Questions of fact for a court to decide may arise, however, if the insurance policy contains exceptions to the risk, such as clauses excepting some causes of death from the policy (for example, exposing oneself to dangerous activities or committing suicide).

## MARRIAGE

The common law recognizes the legal termination of a marriage by the physical death of a spouse. Under the common-law principle the marriage relationship ended also when a spouse was civilly dead. On death, any obligation to pay alimony ends; under some marriage and divorce acts, however, the parties to a marriage may agree in writing or a court may decree that death does not terminate the obligation to pay future maintenance.

## PARTNERSHIP

Similarly, both under the common law and the Uniform Partnership Act, the death of a partner will dissolve a partnership.

## PRESUMPTION

Under the common law, and under many statutes as well, a presumption of death arises from the unexplained absence of a person from his or her last residence for seven years if no word from that person has been received by those most likely to have heard, if the person has not been seen alive, and if inquiries have been made. The Uniform Probate Code adopted by the National Conference of Commissioners on Uniform State Laws has reduced the period of unexplained absence from seven to five years at which time the presumption arises.

## SEAT BELTS

Statutes enacted in many jurisdiction that make the wearing of seat belts in automobiles or the wearing of helmets on motorcycles mandatory can be considered dying and death laws since they seem aimed at the prevention of taking high and unnecessary risks.

## SURVIVING SPOUSE

Even before the Norman Conquest, the English common law gave every widow a right to dower or right to the real estate of her husband. The right was recognized if there was a valid marriage and the property was owned by the husband. But the right was not perfected and was an expectancy only so that it would not support any claim by the wife during the life of the husband. It was only on her survival of his death that the wife's dower became vested and consummated. Today, statutes have abolished dower (as well as an analogous right of the husband's called curtesy). This right has been replaced with a surviving spouse's right, in the absence of a testamentary provision for the spouse in a will, to elect to take an absolute share of the husband's (or wife's) estate as in intestacy.

## WORKER'S COMPENSATION

Worker's Compensation laws, for which there are no precedents in the common law, were enacted to provide benefits to workers or their dependents for losses caused by injury, disability, or death that occurred during their employment. Besides compensation based on percentages of the employee's wages, employers are generally obliged to pay funeral expenses.

## WRONGFUL DEATH

While in common law there was no action for damages recoverable for the death of a human being—perhaps on the theory that revenge, allowed during life, would not be allowed beyond the grave—statutes everywhere have been enacted that recognize that dual claims may be made for a wrongful act or neglect that caused the death of a person: one for the wrong and loss suffered by the dead person, another for the wrong and pecuniary loss suffered by the person's survivors. Wrongful death damages are determined by several methods, including calculating damages in terms of the decedent's normal longevity and lost earnings.

## LEGAL CITATIONS

1. MacDonald v. Time, Inc., 554 F. Supp. 1053, 1054 (U.S. Dist. Ct. D. N.J. 1983).
2. 408 U.S. 238 (1972).
3. Gregg v. Georgia, 428 U.S. 153 (1976).

# Appendix B:
# Guide to the Law Library

**STATUTES**

U.S. Code Annotated

Code of Alabama (Michie)

Alaska Statutes (Michie)

Arizona Revised Statutes Annotated (West)

Arkansas Code of 1987 Annotated (Michie)

Deerings California Code Annotated

Colorado Revised Statutes (Bradford)

Connecticut General Statutes Annotated (West)

Delaware Code Annotated (Michie)

District of Columbia Code Annotated (Michie)

West's Florida Statutes Annotated

Georgia Code Annotated (Harrison)

Hawaii Revised Statutes Annotated (Michie)

Idaho Code (Michie)

Smith-Hurd Illinois Annotated Statutes (West)

West's Annotated Indiana Statutes

Iowa Code Annotated (West)

Vernon's Kansas Statutes Annotated (West)

Kentucky Revised Statutes Annotated (Michie)

West's Louisiana Statutes Annotated

Maine Revised Statutes Annotated (West)

Annotated Code of Maryland (Michie)

Massachusetts General Laws Annotated (West)

Michigan Compiled Laws (West)

Minnesota Statutes Annotated (West)

Mississippi Code 1972 Annotated (Harrison/Lawyers Coop)

Vernon's Annotated Missouri Statutes (West)

Montana Code Annotated

Revised Statutes of Nebraska

Nevada Revised Statutes Annotated (Michie)

New Hampshire Revised Statutes Annotated (Equity)

New Jersey Statutes Annotated (West)

New Mexico Statutes Annotated (Michie)

McKinney's Consolidated Laws of New York Annotated

General Statutes of North Carolina (Michie)

North Dakota Century Code (Michie)

Baldwin's Ohio Revised Code Annotated (Banks-Baldwin)

Oklahoma Statutes Annotated (West)

Oregon Revised Statutes Annotated (Butterworth)

Purdon's Pennsylvania Statutes and Pennsylvania Consolidated Statutes Annotated (Bisel/West)

General Laws of Rhode Island 1956 (Michie)

Code of Laws of South Carolina 1976 Annotated (Lawyers Coop)

South Dakota Codified Laws (Michie)

Tennessee Code Annotated (Michie)

Vernon's Texas Statutes and Codes Annotated (West)

Utah Code Annotated (Michie)

Vermont Statutes Annotated (Equity)

Code of Virginia 1950 Annotated (Michie)

West's Revised Code of Washington Annotated

West's Virginia Code (Michie)

West's Wisconsin Statutes Annotated

Wyoming Statutes Annotated (Michie)

## CASE REPORTS

United States Reports:

United States Supreme Court Reports, Lawyers' Edition

Supreme Court Reporter

Federal Reporter

Federal Supplement

There are many official state reports. But since most law libraries, even large ones, do not shelve them, researchers will do best to locate the volumes of seven unofficial national reporters which give state appellate court decisions in all jurisdictions. These include:

Pacific (covering Washington, Montana, Oregon, Idaho, Wyoming, Nevada, Utah, Colorado, Kansas, California, Arizona, New Mexico, Oklahoma, Alaska, Hawaii)

Northwestern (covering North Dakota, South Dakota, Minnesota, Wisconsin, Michigan, Iowa, Nebraska)

Southwestern (covering Missouri, Kentucky, Tennessee, Arkansas, Texas)

Northeastern (covering Illinois, Indiana, Ohio, New York, Massachusetts)

Atlantic (covering Pennsylvania, Maryland, New Jersey, Delaware, Connecticut, Vermont, Maine, New Hampshire)

Southeastern (covering Georgia, South Carolina, North Carolina, Virginia, West Virginia)

Southern (covering Louisiana, Mississippi, Alabama, Florida)

## DIGESTS

In addition to a separate digest of judicial decisions for each state, there is the U.S. Supreme Court Digest, West's Federal Practice Digest, 2d and 3rd series, and an American Digest (Century Digest, Decennial Digest, and General Digest) for all court decisions throughout the nation.

## ENCYCLOPEDIAS

Corpus Juris (outdated but still valuable for older citations)

Corpus Juris Secundum (101 volumes)

Ruling Case Law (outdated but good for early citations)

American Jurisprudence (outdated but valuable for early citations)

American Jurisprudence 2d series (82 volumes)

## DICTIONARIES

Black's Law Dictionary

Ballantine's Law Dictionary

Words and Phrases

## LEGAL PERIODICAL INDICES

Index to Legal Periodicals

Current Law Index

# Selected Bibliography

The chapter references are to writings on the topics covered by this book. The following list is a further selection of titles pertinent to these topics.

## DEATH: ISSUES AND LAW

Aries, P. 1974. *Western Attitudes Toward Death.* Baltimore: Johns Hopkins University Press.

Choron, J. 1964. *Death and Western Thought.* New York: Collier Books.

Fulton, R., ed. 1976. *Death and Identity.* Rev. ed. Bowie, MD: Charles Press.

Hamner, J. E., and Jacobs, B. J. Sax, eds. 1986. *Life and Death Issues.* Memphis: University of Tennessee.

Kastenbaum, R., and Aisenberg, R. 1972. *The Psychology of Death.* New York: Springer.

Weir, R. F. 1977. *Ethical Issues in Death and Dying.* New York: Columbia University Press.


## THE DYING PATIENT

Armstrong, D. 1987. "Silence and Truth in Death and Dying." *Social Science and Medicine* 24(8):651–57.

Cantor, N. L. 1987. *Legal Frontiers of Death and Dying.* Bloomington: Indiana University Press.

Eggerman, S., and Dustin, D. 1985–1986. "Death, Orientation and Communication with the Terminally Ill." *Omega* 16(3):255–65.

Gadow, S. 1980. "Caring for the Dying: Advocacy or Paternalism." *Death Education* 3(4):387–98.

Graham, H., and Livesley, B. 1983. "Dying as a Diagnosis: Difficulties of Communication and Management in Elderly Patients." *Lancet* 2(8351):670–72.

Krant, M. 1974. *Dying and Dignity.* Springfield, IL: Charles C. Thomas.

Kübler-Ross, E. 1975. *Death: the Final Stage of Growth.* Englewood Cliffs, NJ: Prentice-Hall/Spectrum.

Hastings Center. 1987. "Guidelines on the Termination of Life-Sustaining Treatment and Care of the Dying."

Langone, J. 1974. *Vital Signs.* Boston: Little, Brown.

Pearson, L., ed. 1969. *Death and Dying.* Cleveland: Press of Case Western Reserve University.

Robertson, J. A. 1983. *The Rights of the Critically Ill.* Cambridge, MA: Ballinger.

Verwoerdt, A. 1966. *Communication with the Fatally Ill.* Springfield, IL: Charles C. Thomas.

White, L. P., ed. 1969. "Care of Patients with Fatal Disease." *Annals of the New York Academy of Sciences,* Vol. 164.

## RIGHT TO DIE

Angell, M. 1990. "Prisoners of Technology: The Case of Nancy Cruzan." *New England Journal of Medicine* 322(17):1226–28.

Barnard, C. 1980. *Good Life/Good Death.* Englewood Cliffs, NJ: Prentice-Hall.

Beloff, J. 1988. "Do We Have the Right to Die?" In A. S. Berger, P. Badham, A. H. Kutscher, J. Berger, M. Perry, and J. Beloff, eds. *Perspectives on Death and Dying: Cross-Cultural and Multi-Disciplinary Views.* Philadelphia: Charles Press.

Callahan, D. "On Feeding the Dying." *Hastings Center Report* 13:22.

Capron, A. M. "Ironies and Tensions in Feeding the Dying." *Hastings Center Report* 14:32.

Carson, R. A. 1979. "Euthanasia or the Right to Die." In H. Wass, ed. *Dying, Facing the Facts.* Washington, DC: Hemisphere, 336–404.

Hirsch, H. L., and Donovan, R. E. 1977. "The Right to Die: Medico-Legal Implications of *In re Quinlan." Rutgers Law Review* 30:267.

Horan, D. J. 1980. *Death, Dying and Euthanasia.* Frederick, MD: Alethia Books, University Publications of America.

Landau, R., and Gustafson, J. M. 1984. "Death is not the Enemy." *Journal of the American Medical Association* 252(17):2458.

Lo, B., Rouse, F., and Dornbrand, L. 1990. "Family Decision-Making on Trial." *New England Journal of Medicine* 322(17):1228–32.

Meisel, A. 1990. *The Right to Die.* New York: Wiley Law Publications.

Misbin, R. 1991. "Physicians' Aid in Dying." *New England Journal of Medicine* 355:1307–11.

Nelson, L. J., ed. 1983. *The Death Decision.* Ann Arbor, MI: Servant Publications.

Snyder, L. 1990. "Life, Death and the American College of Surgeons: The Cruzan Case." *Annals of Internal Medicine* 112(11):802–804.

*The Physician and the Hopelessly Ill Patient: Legal, Medical and Ethical Guidelines.* 1985. New York: Society for the Right to Die.

Tribe, L. H. 1978. *American Constitutional Law.* New York: Foundation Press.

Williams, G. 1957. *The Sanctity of Life and the Criminal Law.* New York: Knopf.

Wolf, S. M. 1990. "Nancy Beth Cruzan: In No Voice At All." *Hastings Center Report* January-February 38–41.

## ADVANCE DIRECTIVES

Annas, G. J. 1991. "The Health Care Proxy and the Living Will." *New England Journal of Medicine* 324:1210–13.

Cotler, M., Ouslander, J., Osteweil, D., and Fried, A. 1988. "Evaluation of the Durable Power of Attorney for Health Care." *Gerentologist* 28:186A.

Davidson, K. W., Hackler, C., Carradine, D. R., and McCord, R. S. 1989. "Physicians' Attitudes on Advance Directives." *Journal of the Americal Medical Association* 262:2415–19.

Emanuel, E. J., and Emanuel, L. L. 1990. "Living Wills: Past, Present and Future." *Journal of Clinical Ethics* 1(1):9–19.

Hackler, C., Mosely, R., and Vawter, D. E. 1989. *Advance Directives in Medicine: Studies in Health and Human Value*. New York: Praeger.

*Handbook of Living Will Laws*. 1987. New York: Society for the Right to Die.

*Handbook of Living Will Laws: 1981–1984*. 1986. New York: Society for the Right to Die.

## DETERMINATION OF DEATH

"A Definition of Irreversible Coma: Report of the 'Ad Hoc' Committee of the Harvard Medical School, Under the Chairmanship of Henry K. Beecher, M.D., to Examine the Definition of Brain Death." 1968. *Journal of the American Medical Association* 205: 85–88.

Lamb. D. 1985. *Death, Brain Death and Ethics*. Albany: State University of New York Press.

Moraczewski, A. S. 1982. *Determination of Death: Theological, Medical, Ethical and Legal Issues*. St. Louis, MO: Catholic Health Association of the United States.

Morley, T. P. 1981. *Moral, Ethical and Legal Issues in the Neurosciences*. Springfield, IL: Charles C. Thomas.

President's Commission for the Study of Ethical Problems in Medicine and Biomedical and Behavioral Research. 1981. *Defining Death: Medical, Legal and Ethical Issues in the Determination of Death*. Washington, DC: U.S. Government Printing Office.

Veatch, R. W. 1975. "The Whole-Brain Oriented Concept of Death: An Outmoded Philosophical Formulation." *Journal of Thanatology* 3:13.

## ANATOMICAL GIFTS

Annas, G. J., Law, S. A., Rosenblatt, R. E., and Wing, K. R. 1990. *American Health Law*. Chap. IX. Boston: Little, Brown.

Caplan, A. L. 1983. "Organ Transplants: The Costs of Success." *Hastings Center Report* 13:23.

Caplan, A. L., and Bayer, R. 1985. *Ethical, Legal and Policy Issues Pertaining to Solid Organ Procurement*. Hastings-on-Hudson, NY: Hastings Center.

Committee on Science and Technology, U.S. House of Representatives. 1984. Hearing on Procurement and Allocation of Human Organs for Transplantation. Washington, DC: U.S. Government Printing Office.

Hessing, D. J., and Elffers, H. 1986–1987. "Attitude Toward Death, Fear of Being Declared Dead Too Soon, and Donation of Organs After Death." *Omega* 17(2):115–26.

May, W. F. 1985. "Religious Justifications for Donating Body Parts." *Hastings Center Report* 15(1):38–42.

Sadler, A. M., Sadler, B. L., and Stason, E. B. 1968. "The Uniform Anatomical Gift Act." *Journal of the American Medical Association* 206:2501.

Task Force on Organ Transplantation. 1986. *Organ Transplantation: Issues and Recommendations*. Washington, DC: Office of Organ Transplantation, Department of Health and Human Services.

Youngner, S. J., et al. 1985. "Psychosocial and Ethical Implications of Organ Retrieval." *New England Journal of Medicine* 313(5):321–24.

## LAW: FORMS AND SOURCES

Ball, M. S. 1981. *The Promise of American Law: A Theological, Humanistic View of the Legal Process*. Athens: University of Georgia Press.

Brody, D. E. 1978. *The American Legal System: Concepts and Principles*. Lexington, MA: D.C. Heath.

Cataldo, B. F., et al. 1973. *Introduction to Law and the Legal Process*. New York: Wiley.

D'Amato, A. A. 1988. *How to Understand the Law*. Ardsley-on-Hudson, NY: Transnational Publishers.

Friedman, L. M. 1975. *The Legal System: A Social Science Perspective*. New York: Russell Sage Foundation.

Rombauer, M. D. 1973. *Legal Problem Solving: Analysis, Research, and Writing*. 2d ed. St. Paul, MN: West.

Soule, C. C. 1953. *The Lawyer's Reference Manual of Law Books and Citations*. Buffalo, NY: Dennis.

Statsky, W. P. 1974. *Legal Research, Writing and Analysis: Some Starting Points*. St. Paul, MN: West.

Stromme, G., ed. 1979. *Basic Legal Research*. rev. 4th ed. San Mateo, CA: Research Group/American Law Publishing Service.

# Table of Cases

# Index

## ABOUT THE AUTHOR

ARTHUR S. BERGER is Director of the International Institute for the Study of Death, President of the Survival Research Foundation, member of the Broward General Medical Center Bioethics Committee, and Vice-President of Cross-Cultural Affairs of the Foundation of Thanatology at Columbia-Presbyterian Medical Center in New York City. He is the co-editor of *To Die or Not to Die? Cross-Disciplinary Cultural, and Legal Perspectives on the Right to Choose Death* (Praeger, 1990), and *Perspectives on Death and Dying* (1989). He is also the author of several books including the critically acclaimed *Lives and Letters in American Parapsychology* and the co-author of the *Encyclopedia of Parapsychology and Psychical Research* (1991).